Alpha to Omega

Journey to the End of Time

DEDICATION

To my beloved son, Darren. Love with all of your being; accept, forgive and understand. Happiness coincides with the discovery of the reason for our existence. Yearn to find it and you will recognize all experience as God's guidance on the road to discovery. Peace, abundance and happiness await you

GRATITUDE

My sincere thanks and adulation to Jessica Rowell, publisher and editor of Giuseppina Magazine and founder of J-Chans Designs. You are surely one of the most talented and creative artists of our times.

A heartfelt thanks to Peggy Sealfon who took the time to read my finished work and offer her genuine words of encouragement.

Thanks also to Kimberly Martin at Jera Publishing, for your professional assistance.

Alpha to Omega

Journey to the End of Time

Awaken to the Inherited
Assumptions that Shape our Destiny

Matthew A. Petti

TWO SENSE PUBLICATIONS

New Jersey, USA

Copyright © 2012 by Matthew A. Petti

Published by Two Sense Publications; PO Box 564, Brigantine, New Jersey 08203 USA. Special quantity discounts are available for bulk purchases, premiums, and sales promotions, educational and institutional use. Please submit all inquiries by email: sales@twosensepro.com, Fax: 888-776-9557. Public comments are welcome and can be posted at http://matthewpetti.com or visit any online bookstore.

All rights reserved. No part of this book, except for brief quotations defined as "fair use", may be reproduced by any means including, but not limited to, mechanical, photographic, digital or phonographic (audio); nor may it be stored in any retrieval system for transmission, or otherwise copied for public or private use without the express written permission of Two Sense Pro, LLC or Matthew A. Petti.

All Scriptural quotes are taken from the Holy Bible Revised Standard Version – Catholic Edition Copyright 1946, 1952, 1965, 1966 by Division of Christian Education of the National Council of Churches of Christ in the USA. Printed and published by Thomas Nelson and Sons for the Liturgical Press, Collegeville, MN.

Library of Congress Cataloging-in-Publication Data

Petti, Matthew A.

Alpha to Omega – Journey to the End of Time / Matthew A. Petti. First edition

ISBN 9780985685522 (Ltd. ed. hardcover); ISBN 9780985685539 (hardcover); 9780985685508 (pbk.); 9780985685515 (e-book); p. cm.

LCCN: 2012940907

Catalogue Suggestions

1. Civilization, Ancient. 2. Civilization, Philosophy. 3. Philosophical anthropology. 4. Metaphysics. 5. Spirituality. 6. Eschatology. 7. Christianity.

Ltd. ed. Hardcover ISBN: 978-0-9856855-2-2

"Our job now, our opportunity, is to place before the world a set of ideas from which a brand new discussion may begin."
– Neale Donald Walsch

CONTENTS

Introduction   1

PART I
Land of Demigods

CHAPTER 1   Days of Future Past   13

           Alpha and Omega   13
           Somewhere in Time   22
           The History of History   32

CHAPTER 2   Heart of the Matter   47

           Origins   47
           Supreme Being   51
           God   54
           The Big Mistake   64
           Angels, Demons and Aliens   71

CHAPTER 3   Bridge over Troubled Waters   83

           Supreme Mandate   83
           The Great Pyramid   91
           Noah's Arc   109

PART II
Lost in Translation

CHAPTER 4	His-story and My-story	119
	Wisdom of the Ages	119
	Of Gods and Men	134
	Gods of the Ignorant	142

CHAPTER 5	Figure of Speech	165
	Bliss of an Infant	165
	Ball of Confusion	171
	Metaphysics of Faith	185

PART III
Back to the Future

CHAPTER 6	Welcome the Judge	201
	The Christ Principle	201
	No Wasted Time	205
	Take me to Higher Love	210
	Gnostic Wisdom	219

CHAPTER 7	Runaway Train	233
	Roman Siege	233
	Hereafter Forever	244
	Collective Reflection	250
	The Harbinger of Doom, Fear and Hope	257

CHAPTER 8   Rise and fall of the Hegemon   265

           War of Wars   265
           New Demigods, Old Mistake   270
           Dual Torment   280
           Omega   284

Epilogue   291

References   295

About the Author   303

ONLY THE SIXTH SENSE CAN EXPOSE
WHAT THE OTHER FIVE HAVE HIDDEN

INTRODUCTION

Imagine if we were to be awakened one morning only to find ourselves in a state of total amnesia—unaware that we had lost our memory because our memory would not exist in an empty mind. Everything around us would be completely foreign and indefinable because our mind would be void of thought, imagination and emotions. Objects would appear, but without a shape or texture because our associative memory wouldn't exist. Concepts of time, love, hate, fear, hope, anxiousness and guilt, worry, vengeance, empathy and sympathy, happiness, sadness, judgment and scores of other emotional feelings would be nonexistent. Think about this for a moment.

Our friends and family would immediately rush to our aide in an attempt to communicate with us, but we would not understand the garbled sounds of their speech. They would constantly help us to associate our sensory information with meaningful concepts, which would slowly help us to define our environment. Our ideas about our world and our place in it would depend on what we were taught and how we assimilated the enormous flood of information impressed upon our senses. Eventually we'd begin to recognize ourselves as one similar to those around us and develop comparable habits and concepts.

All of us experience this exact scenario during our infancy. Our deep seated perspectives are determined by the earliest subconscious impressions of our environment. The primary foundations to our concepts of the world and reality are nurtured by inherited patterns of thought and behavior. These archetypes, as Carl G. Jung explained, reside in the subconscious of every individual and are passed to succeeding generations. Unfortunately, some of the most common patterns of thought and behavior can be demonstrated as an obstacle to human progress and the cause to our calamities.

How many times have we heard that we create our own destiny? The principle is being taught today by countless speakers and coaches, and we know it's true. Our individual and collective future is determined by both our individual and collective decisions and actions.

Our world is a reflection of everything we do and everything we *believe* as a collective species because our beliefs govern the actions that determine our fate. The most deeply embedded beliefs of human awareness are the historical and religious models of thought, which govern our perspectives about the world and our place in it.

Beliefs about our origins, God and history, which have been inherited by age-old habits and teachings, encompass every aspect of our lives and decisions. The confusion is continually expressed in our behavior allowing centuries of ingrained habits to become infused into the collective mindset and reflected in the world we live in. We need only to look at our current world to acknowledge the critical effects caused by obvious flaws in the foundations of human thought and the behavior promoted by them.

The fate and destiny of mankind rests upon the collective beliefs of humanity. Gregg Braden hits it on the nose:

INTRODUCTION

New discoveries regarding our origin, our past, and the most deeply held ideas about our existence give us reasons to rethink the traditional beliefs that define our world and our lives—beliefs that stem from the false assumptions of an incomplete and outdated science. When we do, the solutions to life's challenges become obvious, and the choices become clear. [1]

If we begin with inaccurate beliefs, then the false conclusions of our reasoning will affect both individual and collective progress. Humanity's cumulative miscalculations have inundated the entire world-system and the effects are easily observed in today's fragile world.

As long as our beliefs are misaligned, we will continue to suffer the consequences of our mistakes. Our goal may be Paradise but our destiny is determined by the errors in our beliefs. The inseparable junction between past and future is seen as the cause and effect of our beliefs, which lead to the actions and behaviors shaping our world and destiny.

Where are we headed? If a major catastrophe is on our doorstep, what must we learn to move forward? What have we done or failed to do to create this for ourselves? What are we missing? These questions are inching closer to the forefront of the human psyche. Many people are beginning to believe we live in a time of looming upheaval and major historical changes. Could this be a collective awakening to the observable vulnerabilities of our volatile world?

Globally, there is an increasing awareness that swift and marked changes must occur in order to avert drastic consequences from pollution, global warming, mass starvation, war and many other impending disasters. People the world over are paying closer attention to the prophecies of the Maya, Nostradamus and the book of Revelation because of the noticeable increase in worldwide calamities and confusion. There seems to be a sense of urgency.

If we closely examine the inescapable metaphysical bond between past and future, we can find answers to things we have long believed to be unanswerable. By recognizing our confusing beliefs as obstacles to our progress, we see the future as an effect of our misconceptions and resultant decisions. This implies that clarity of vision makes for a perfect world and future. How do we expose the errors?

First, we must define the human purpose—our goal. Without having a definite purpose would be like getting into our car without knowing where we are going or why. How can we expect to find the obstacles to our progress if we cannot accurately define our ultimate goal?

Identifying the purpose for human existence has been one of the most nagging questions of humanity, but it can easily be answered. We are here to discover All Truth—God—the answers to everything. When we do, all of our errors will disappear in the clarity of truth.

I'm sure many readers will agree with me, but there is much more to this than we have previously pondered and it is evidenced by the maladies we see in the world today. Who or rather, what is God? We can ask ten people to define God and we will get ten different answers. Ironically, the vast majority of the world believes in a blurred concept of God, which serves as the foundation to our dilemmas.

INTRODUCTION

Our world is saturated with vague notions impressed upon us by religious dogma, incomplete science and embellished history. Indistinct notions foster a complacent attitude that pervades humanity and steers us away from actively seeking answers to things deemed unanswerable. By believing our lives to be brief and unexplainable, we are automatically more concerned with the temporal nature of the physical world while placing little attention upon the hereafter and our eternal souls, God, human purpose and destiny. The habit is deeply woven into the fabric of human behavior, which prevents us from observing the subtle truths and nature of our existence and contributes to the ongoing dilemma.

So, the second thing we must do is clarify the vague beliefs about our history, origins and God, which prove to be fundamental obstacles in the foundation of human thought, and clarify them with agreeable hypotheses. Without a clearer view of our origins, we cannot see the road to our destiny.

For centuries we have relied on the portrayals of religion and secular history to answer these questions for us. Their endeavors have produced seemingly clarified depictions of a very dim past, many of which are responsible for the presumptions we believe to be unquestionable fact. But, there is a slow awakening to the increasing discoveries of unexplained phenomena in our past—mysteries that conflict with our concepts of human history and religion.

New research is exposing glaring errors in the evidence used to support the standing historic portrayals of ancient times, while uncovering new proof that contradicts the long accepted chronology of human history. The Sphinx of Egypt is only one of countless examples, where uncovered evidence indicates it was constructed over 12,000 years ago—a major challenge to the accepted beliefs imposed upon us by established history.[2]

Increasing emergence of new found evidence has given birth to new ideas, which are being swiftly popularized and accepted as a quick solution to many of these unexplainable mysteries. Ancient Alien theory is flooding the media and presented as the only possible explanation to the newly discovered mysteries of human origins and ancient advanced civilizations.

The theory posits all human life to have been the result of alien intervention and asserts alien technology as the sole reason for the evidence of advanced civilizations of prehistory. Ancient alien theorists believe aliens aided human existence by manipulating the DNA structure of savage primitives. As scientifically fitting as it may appear on the surface, it falls far short of its mark for failing to answer one extremely important question. If the aliens were the cause of life on earth, what was the cause to the life of the aliens?

We must be careful not to replace aging false assumptions with new ones in our theories to explain the mysteries conflicting with obsolete history, lest we move from one dilemma to another. The religiously imbued God-concept, which has largely contributed to the ineffective views of our origins and history, has opened the door to the ancient alien theory by not faring well against the rigors of empiricism.

A pressing need for a new perspective is more important than ever before. It's essential to realize the urgency we face during these critical times or suffer the results of the aggregate failures heaped upon the world for thousands of years. Can we offer a new perspective on the

INTRODUCTION

human journey while posing new solutions for many religious, historical and scientific mysteries? Where can we look to find the answers that seem so evasive?

Many hidden truths are often unobserved, not invisible.

Many solutions to the mysteries of our origins, God and history can be found in the book of Revelation, an inseparable conduit between past and future—a two-way mirror or wormhole to both. The cryptic message is an unveiling of the false assumptions—born by vague concepts—that summon the actions and behaviors responsible for shaping our destiny. It provides a clearer picture of our origins, our tainted past, our voyage and our future.

Even the most fundamental prediction stems from the analysis of past events, constants and conditions. The accuracy of a forecast rests on the truth of historic information. The perfect prophecy of Revelation is an *inevitable* conclusion and deciphering its message will reveal, not just the future, but the human journey, its quandary and the reasons for it.

Since it is true we create our own destiny and our future is not predetermined, Revelation's unwavering conclusion affirms that unchanging conditions in human behavior will be cause to the eventual and unchangeable outcome. As we unravel the mysteries in *this* story of the human journey, misconceptions will be exposed by truths that will resonate with the core of our being. The secrets to the clues will be understood by those truly seeking answers to questions we have believed to be unanswerable. We will discover the dilemma of our human soul—an entity we don't consider with as much fervor as we should.

Clear concepts for God, humanity's purpose in the world and our history are necessary if we are to explain the human travail and determine what our future holds. The journey from Alpha to Omega—Adam to Armageddon—can be effectively demonstrated to reveal the unobserved and subtle metaphysical nature of our existence, the repetitive effects of human nature and, most important, the crucial significance of our eternal souls.

During the very early stage of my adulthood, I experienced an epiphany beyond words or explanations, which has left its indelible impression upon my entire life and being. One of the most significant effects of this event was a swiftly growing internal awareness that the world could not continue in the same fashion and that disaster was right around the corner. It drastically changed my life's direction by igniting an insatiable curiosity towards Revelation's meaning. The year was 1977 and the end-of-days notion wasn't nearly as popular as it is today.

It's not a secret we face the most difficult challenges in the history of our human existence. The increasing sense of urgency in today's modern world is born of an internal instinct to be able to distinguish between the things that resonate with the core of our being and the many things that do not. The hidden iniquities are being exposed by many who have dedicated their lives to find reasons for the observable chaos and answers for the truths and meaning to our existence.

INTRODUCTION

Here is an unprecedented perspective on the story of our journey, a viable alternative to the ancient alien theory and one not passed down from preceding generations. It is aimed at exposing and clarifying our murky concepts, igniting an individual yearning for truth and providing crucial information for decisions we must make when approaching crossroads that lie ahead in the human voyage.

The urgency is implied by Revelation's steadfast conclusion, which demonstrates there isn't enough time to alter the eventual outcome. Although we may be able to somewhat popularize a new idea, gaining an almost collective ideal is nearly impossible, especially in the short-term. It has taken centuries for diverse myopic concepts to become firmly planted in people of various religions, countries, regions and cults. Established concepts and habits have been so thoroughly embedded that even a profound discovery will not easily supplant them.

The unavoidable consequences ahead are caused by human nature—our reluctance to release old habits and beliefs; the continual reliance on authoritative viewpoints; and the false precepts deeply planted in the subconscious collective mind. Everyone's destiny will depend upon decisions we haven't remotely considered and this perspective will prove quite helpful in revealing them. By acknowledging our false assumptions as the cause for our future calamities, and by realizing how close humanity is to the threshold of existence, we should be zealously willing to examine new perspectives for information.

If we can go back to the days of our infancy, when we were void of thought and notions about the world and our place in it, we

ALPHA TO OMEGA

would discover our perfect connection to the essence of God, All Truth and infinite possibilities. Our awareness is a dream of limited reality defined by our five physical senses—a dream from which we must awaken in order to find the eternal answers within ourselves.

The emergence of human awareness begins with our curiosity and becomes part of the collective consciousness. Slowly, the collective entity has grown to include countless people who realize there is much more to discover when we look beyond the beliefs of our presumed realities.

To move forward relies on our willingness to, not only examine our priorities and their collective effects, but to be willing to release obsolete notions and credos, which continue to impede human progress.

Part I:

LAND OF DEMIGODS

Chapter One

DAYS OF FUTURE PAST

If we really want to know where we are headed, we have to know where we came from. If we can truly see where we are headed then we can figure out the important things we are missing about our past.

Alpha and Omega

Each of us views the world from a different perspective. Our beliefs are not only shaped by individual experiences, inherited concepts and behaviors, but reinforced by judgment born of those factors. True facts and events are subjected to varying perspectives and predisposed to individual judgment. Have you ever differed with someone over the recollection of an event you witnessed, read or heard about?

It's easy to see how perceptions greatly influence personal judgment. Although an actual event will remain to be true, it will become clouded by varying perceptions and faded memories, which aid in tarnishing the recollection of the truth. Without video replay, we turn to historical accounts, which are deemed reliable

ALPHA TO OMEGA

but often biased by the author's perspective and skewed by the increasing progression of time. How can we determine the truth?

There are three basic types of truth: absolute truth or omniscience, scientific truth, which is all that has been discovered and archived, and personal truth. Omniscience is unimaginable in scope and beyond our comprehension. It far surpasses scientific truth, which is the beach of the sands of personal truth.

This analogy helps us to easily see how uninformed we truly are. Personal truth is limited by both our acquired knowledge and ability to stay informed. We often hold tight to erroneous beliefs brought on by the misinterpretation of facts we have already learned. At times we may think about something, form our own opinion based on what we thought we knew, and readily accept it as true, when in fact it is not. A belief, despite personal conviction, may not be true at all.

Here's an example. Is there more air resistance on a humid day or a dry day at the same temperature? In other words, which day would provide a better chance for a baseball to carry further—a humid day or a dry day? Think about your answer for a moment before moving on.

If you're like most people you will insist the ball will travel more easily on the dry day with less humidity. However, water vapor-filled air is lighter and offers less resistance than dry air. Here's the explanation to settle the argument.

The atomic number of a molecule is determined by the amount of protons it contains. It's the protons that determine the mass of a molecule (neutrons also contribute to the mass of a molecule, but

14

DAYS OF FUTURE PAST

in this example neutrons are not present). Dry air consists of 21% oxygen gas (O_2) and 78% nitrogen gas (N_2). Oxygen gas has an atomic number of 16 (two atoms of oxygen each with an atomic number of 8). Nitrogen gas has an atomic number of 14 (two atoms of nitrogen each with an atomic number of 7). Water vapor or H_2O has an atomic number of 10 (two atoms of hydrogen each with an atomic number of 1 and one atom of oxygen with the atomic number of 8).

Avogadro's law of gases states that any given space contains the exact same number of gas molecules at the same temperature and pressure. Replacing oxygen or nitrogen gas molecules with water vapor molecules would reduce the weight by 6 or 4 respectively for every molecule of water vapor. This means that the air has less density and resistance as the humidity increases.

This is one of hundreds of examples we could use to demonstrate the prevalence of errant presumptions. How many times have we truly believed something only to find out we were wrong? More important, relying on beliefs causes us to cease further inquiry that could reveal the errors in our concepts.

> **What we choose to accept, question or ignore depends upon the information's relevance to our current beliefs and circumstances.**

When we base our reasoning on false premises, we follow with conclusions that may be untrue despite the raw logic that supports it. Ironically, the same scientific process responsible for discovery can cause individual stigmas when reasoning with untrue facts.

ALPHA TO OMEGA

Alpha and Omega are the first and last letters of the Greek alphabet respectively and have often been used to denote the beginning and the end of a cycle—the biblical story from Adam to Armageddon. There are more far-reaching implications to this if we closely examine biblical texts.

What does the Bible say about the Alpha and the Omega? Let's examine the book of Revelation for a better understanding.

> "I am the Alpha and the Omega", says the Lord God, who is and who was and who is to come, the Almighty (Revelation 1:8).

> And he said unto me, "It is done! I am the Alpha and Omega, the beginning and the end. I will give to him who is athirst of the fountain of the water of life freely." (Revelation 21:6)

> "I am the Alpha and the Omega, the beginning and the end, the first and the last." (Revelation 22:13)

Throughout history mankind has succeeded in the continual search and discovery of knowledge, which has led to the successful solutions to many of our historic perils. The power of amassed knowledge has transformed humanity into a world full of information and technology. New and helpful discoveries are made every day, leading to new questions and subsequent discoveries.

We will continue our insatiable search until we have answered every single question we can propose. Circumstances will determine how and when, but humanity will eventually become omniscient (if we don't become extinct). The ultimate goal of human beings is achieved by learning all there is to know. The final accomplishment of humanity's purpose and collective will—our final destination—is the Omega. Omniscience is the Omega.

DAYS OF FUTURE PAST

For there is nothing hid, except to be made manifest; nor is anything secret, except to come to light. (Mark 4:22).

Hasn't the representation of God always been one of omniscience and omnipotence? God is All Knowledge and All Power. Doesn't it stand to reason that in the end we will know everything? Wouldn't complete knowledge convert our current concept of God into a clarified reality? Haven't we demonstrated the purpose for our existence is to discover God or All Truth?

Some scientific pundits may be inclined to stop reading right here, but a true scientist cannot deny the existence of God without examination of all evidence. Perhaps science is confusing the religiously imbued concept of God with an undiscovered reality. We will thoroughly examine this in the next chapter, but for now, omniscience is the Omega and the final destination of mankind.

But where, when and how did it all begin? What is the Alpha? The book of Revelation clearly states that God is both the Alpha and the Omega. If so, did the human journey actually begin with a complete understanding of all there is?

Looking closely, the Bible clearly answers that question. In the earliest texts of the book of Genesis we observe life spans of nearly 1000 years before the flood.

Thus all the days that Adam lived were nine hundred and thirty years; and he died. (Genesis 5:5)

Only in the book of Revelation are humans depicted with a similar lifespan in the 1000-year kingdom of the post-Armageddon society—the time when man will know God without mistaken beliefs at the end of mankind's journey.

ALPHA TO OMEGA

> They came to life and reigned with Christ a thousand years. (Revelation 20:4)

From this perspective, we see absolute knowledge as both our destination and the origin of the human drama. Adam and Eve in Paradise is a significant biblical tale, which implies that mankind knew God without misconceptions or errors at the very beginning of the story. This is an important observation because it exposes the power associated with absolute knowledge revealed in the supernatural ability to live for almost 1000 years.

How many times have we heard the phrase, "knowledge is power"? The three basic types of power are individual, societal and omnipotence. Individual power is not limited by personal knowledge, but is increased by the scientific advancements of the combined knowledge of our civilization. For example, we can fly anywhere in the world in a short period of time—that's power without individual knowledge.

Our contemporary societal level of knowledge and power will be referred to as technological sophistication while omnipotence will be associated with omniscience, which makes complete sense because absolute knowledge yields absolute power.

Let's consider the continuing advancement of our civilization over time. Someday, our sophisticated technology may increase by new findings that will significantly increase our power in the blink of an eye. Whether it is the discovery of a Unified Field Theory, or any major advancement derived as a result of spectacular discoveries, we will eventually become an advanced civilization with super intelligence and capabilities beyond our current societal level of power.

Look at power in Figure 1. The second outermost circle represents the expansion of our knowledge to a point where we evolve into an advanced civilization, much like that of the legendary Atlantis. We will refer to that stage as the Demi-God level of power.

The tiny gray circle in the center is individual knowledge and power. It pales in comparison even to the currently discovered knowledge. It's gray because individual knowledge is clouded by perception, judgment, misinformation, inadvertent forgetfulness, diversions, confusion, selective attention, and the inability to assimilate the aggregate knowledge.

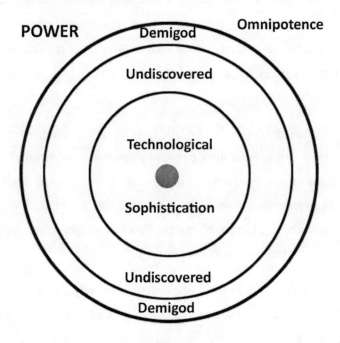

Figure 1

As societal power edges closer to the outer ring of omnipotence, individual knowledge and capabilities would have to expand in order to be an essential part of such an advanced civilization and higher intellect. The reasoning is such that omniscience is universal and all-encompassing and would be shared by everyone. There would be no separation of power or knowledge among the members of an omnipotent society and very little separation in a Demi-God society.

Since we've already demonstrated that human nature will someday lead us to omniscience, then the Omega is the individual and collective omniscience, which manifests itself as omnipotence in both the individual and collective abilities of the society. We will eventually become a magnificent and ever-powerful society without limitations, infirmities, inequalities or questions—the 1000-year post-Armageddon society depicted in Revelation. Likewise, the Alpha represents equal knowledge and power, which is depicted as Paradise in biblical terms.

> **Axiom # 1:** Both the Alpha and the Omega are the combined individual and collective personification of omniscience and omnipotence—*a state of Supreme Being*—which is religiously designated as Paradise on Earth, Nirvana, Total Enlightenment, or One in Unison with Everything.

This is a simple scientific observation showing us the final destination of humankind's journey. Take religion out of this and you will agree that our search for knowledge will eventually lead us home. The easiest way back, is to steer ourselves along the road that

DAYS OF FUTURE PAST

got us here today, but an objective view of our world shows us to be lost and moving precariously in several directions.

We are failing to get home because we can't find the road we traveled to get here. Our origination is blurred by preconceived notions and vague concepts about our beginnings. How can we expect to figure out how we arrived to this point if we cannot clearly define our origins? A clearer picture of our starting point is necessary in the determination of our journey—the road that brought us here today.

The first axiom should be easily acceptable. Hence, if we are heading back to Paradise, then humanity was omniscient somewhere in our distant past. A superhuman civilization of Supreme Beings with unimaginable power and knowledge thrived. Theoretically, we can make that claim, but we need evidence to support the assertion.

Historical evidence depicts primitive man living in caves and controlling fire at about 200,000 years ago. The appearance of "modern man" about 40,000 years ago continues to provide evidence of primitive skills and far limited ability. How could those of a superhuman civilization completely lose their knowledge and power? As a sophisticated civilization today we are constantly passing information to succeeding generations. It would stand to reason that a more advanced society would certainly be able to store information to ensure its longevity. What happened to them? Is it really possible that a super society existed long before our current one?

These questions shouldn't show cause to reject the axiom. What we clearly find here is circumstantial evidence in support of an epic cataclysm. In a scenario where the total annihilation of civilization occurs, all knowledge and power would be erased. Here is where we see the significance of the biblical flood, as recorded in the earliest texts of our current civilization. This proposes another question. If such an advanced civilization was destroyed by a great flood in ancient history, why can't researchers find evidence of a disaster of such great magnitude?

Somewhere in Time

> ...you do not know that there formerly dwelt in your land the fairest and noblest race of men which ever lived, and that you and your whole city are descended from a small seed or remnant of them which survived. And this was unknown to you, because, for many generations, the survivors of that destruction died, leaving no written word. (Excerpt from Plato's Timaeus, 360 B.C.E.) [1]

Nearly every culture on earth is linked to a flood myth depicting a society that was destroyed because of their avarice and wrongful deeds. This is not a made-up fact. A small amount of research will verify my claim. The details and descriptions are varied and are found the world over from Europe to Asia, to North America and South America, Australia, the Pacific Islands, Africa and the Near East. They include the flood of Noah, the Sumerian epic of Gilgamesh, infamous tales of Roman and Greek mythology where Jupiter and Zeus punish the inhabitants of a malicious society, American Indian stories, and ancient Hindu and Chinese legends just to name a few.

DAYS OF FUTURE PAST

Every corner of the world is linked to one or more of over 500 deluge legends. Some of the stories make little sense while others tell similar stories about a great civilization of long ago that was eradicated. All had died except for a handful of people who repopulated the earth.

> We are on a trail of mystery here. And while we may never hope to fathom the plans of the Creator we should be able to reach judgment concerning the riddle of our converging myths of global destruction.[2]

An enormous amount of available information about the myriad ancient legends can be found at Mark Isaak's website: http://www.talkorigins.org/faqs/flood-myths.html. More information is also available at: http://www.nwcreation.net/noahlegends.html. For a detailed examination of many unknown facts about some of the legends, I highly recommend Graham Hancock's *Fingerprints of the Gods*, which is a comprehensive digest of these and other pertinent and unexplained historical mysteries.

When reading the legends and folklore there's a tendency to challenge the facts because many of them lack congruity and logic. The tales are easily debunked by skeptics who argue there is little or no scientific evidence to support them. We should recognize it would be typical for an ancient tale about a prior civilization on earth to become convoluted, fragmented and misaligned by time and primitive means of communication.

The flood story, which has spread throughout prehistory to all corners of the globe long before technology or dominating religious influence, is compelling enough to provide supporting evidence. By disputing it, we join science on the basis that empirical evidence to support it is missing. However, it should be well noted that not a shred of evidence exists to prove that a major flood has not occurred in our prehistory. Why must we side with incomplete science when we have ample circumstantial evidence to prove that a great flood completely destroyed the inhabitants of a once great civilization?

The Bible provides evidence for the annihilation of a prior high society. Examining the book of Genesis we find that the authors distinctly described the differing lifespan of mankind, in pre-and post-flood eras. It is clearly elicited that those of pre-flood times including Noah lived nearly 1000 years as mentioned previously.

> All the days of Noah were nine hundred and fifty years; and he died. (Genesis 9:29)

Is this evidence that a race of demigods lived before us? Why else would the Bible's earliest recordings stress these specific facts?

Another distinct aspect that endured the bias of time is the proof of total destruction found in the Bible:

> For behold, I will bring a flood of waters upon the Earth to destroy all flesh, in which is the breath of life from under heaven; everything that is on the earth shall die. (Genesis 6:17)

> I will send rain upon the earth 40 days and 40 nights; and every living thing that I have made I will blot out from the face of the ground. (Genesis 7:4)

Total destruction is depicted in nearly all of the deluge legends, many of which were not subjected to any type of religious influence.

The legendary tales of the lost continent of Atlantis adds additional support to a gargantuan destruction of a demigod society. Plato wrote the descriptions and accounts of Atlantis around 350 BC, which has been based on information handed down via family lines for centuries by a Greek statesman named Solon.

The Egyptians had described Atlantis to Solon at about 600 BC based on sacred accounts in their possession. This legendary place, according to Egyptian description, existed more than 9000 years prior and was believed to be as large as the known area of the world at that time.

Keep in mind that the Egyptian accounts were likely skewed by their concept of time even though the tale remained a sacred legend throughout their early history. Egyptian measurements of time were based on the rising of Sirius and also by the flooding cycles of the Nile River dating back to about 4500 BC.

Taking into account Egypt's early understanding of time and their sacred and most likely distorted tales of Atlantis, it is fair to suggest that Atlantis flourished in antiquity and 9000 years prior was representative of their conceptual understandings at the time.

In the seventh century BC, it is highly likely that 9000 years prior was far enough in history to support the belief in a previous society, which was destroyed, and the beginning of a new one. After all, scientific knowledge wasn't ample enough to reveal the time error. Moreover, the prevailing belief was that the world was flat and anyone who ventured beyond the *Pillars of Hercules*—or straits of Gibraltar—would fall off the earth. The Egyptian conceptual view of the world in 600 BC was obviously quite limited.

ALPHA TO OMEGA

Relying on the literal interpretation of 9000 years prevents the search for evidence in areas that would support its existence in a much further removed period in time. It also fails to consider the impaired talents and limited concepts of early civilized man. Why does it seem that so much of historical research fails to address this variable?

Plato's infamous dialogues, Timaeus and Critias, are the only known references to Atlantis yet they exhibit Plato's clear perception when he wrote them in 360 BC. Is it possible that the information Solon received included more persuasive evidence? The following is a passage from Plato's Critias, which obviously tells of man's closeness to God and the wonders that were prevalent.

> Let me tell you then why the creator made this world of generation. He was good, and the good can never have any jealousy of anything. And being free from jealousy, he desired that all things should be as like himself as they could be. This is in the truest sense the origin of creation and of the world, as we shall do well in believing on the testimony of wise men: God desired that all things should be good and nothing bad, so far as this was attainable. Wherefore also finding the whole visible sphere not at rest, but moving in an irregular and disorderly fashion, out of disorder he brought order, considering that this was in every way better than the other. Now the deeds of the best could never be or have been other than the fairest; and the creator, reflecting on the things which are by nature visible, found that no unintelligent creature taken as a whole was fairer than the intelligent taken as a whole; and that intelligence could not be present in anything which was devoid of soul. For which reason, when he was framing the universe, he put intelligence in soul, and soul in body, that he might be the creator of a work which was by nature fairest and best. Wherefore, using the language of probability, we may say

DAYS OF FUTURE PAST

that the world became a living creature truly endowed with soul and intelligence by the providence of God...[3]

The next passage reveals how the Atlanteans lost sight of their Divinity over time. We, who cannot see, would have envisioned them as glorious and angelic at the time of their demise, which is very important to remember as we move forward in this presentation.

> ...By such reflections and by the continuance in them of a divine nature, the qualities which we have described grew and increased among them; but when the divine portion began to fade away, and became diluted too often and too much with the mortal admixture, and the human nature got the upper hand, they then, being unable to bear their fortune, behaved unseemly, and to him who had an eye to see grew visibly debased, for they were losing the fairest of their precious gifts; but to those who had no eye to see the true happiness, they appeared glorious and blessed at the very time when they were full of avarice and unrighteous power. [4]

In the evaluation of secular history, we must account for the shortcomings of an incomplete archaeological history. Most historical accounts of ancient history reflect the ideas of an historian or authority, whose intent was to derive conclusions to support their hypotheses. The search for answers within presupposed timelines exacerbates the unseen error. If we unilaterally accept the unproven explanations of prehistory we will be forced to view history through the limited lens of an historian or historical authority.

Creationists argue that there is a mistake in the scientific interpretation of the geological column. The column is a bored extraction of the stratified layers of sedimentary rock, which can display evidence that helps to provide a glimpse of our geological history.

ALPHA TO OMEGA

Creationists believe somehow everything began 6000 years ago and present an argument that relies on the inconsistencies found in the column. The many inconsistencies and unanswered questions of geological history is the foundation of the Creationist argument.

Evolutionists point to certain consistencies in the column supporting their findings. Both sides of the argument present their cases well, but neither can provide substantial evidence to unequivocally prove their argument, which is because of the many unanswered questions of archeology and geology.

Looking closer, Creationists begin with the assumption that no major break in time separated the pre-and post-flood era while Evolutionists begin with the assumption that a major flood hasn't occurred. Archaeological discoveries continue to provide fossil evidence to dispute the 6000-year-old Creationist story but do not address the possibility of a catastrophic event, other than that which destroyed the dinosaurs about 65 million years ago. Is it possible that the earth's major pole shift, which occurred somewhere between four and seven million years ago, was linked to this epic flood? [5]

Polar shifts and continental drift are commonplace events in geological history. Provisional evidence suggests that the North and South poles have changed dramatically over time. Heavy doses of radiation from the sun, which would likely kill all life-forms, are to be expected whenever the poles of the Earth's magnetic field dramatically change because the protective magnetic field is disrupted. Additionally, polar shift creates climate changes, when the poles coincide with land rather than water. [6]

DAYS OF FUTURE PAST

According to researchers, records for ancient time are incomplete and there are questions that are proposed concerning the perceived rising and falling of the oceans as seen in their incomplete geological map. It is found to happen again and again throughout history over the course of millions of years. It is not known exactly why but speculation suggests continental drift, polar positions, and changes in the earth's speed of rotation, changes in the actual size of solid earth and changes in the amount of water in the oceans are contributing factors. Science cannot answer these questions indisputably but can only speculate.[7]

Accordingly, somewhere in late Tertiary time, the relative position of continents to the Earth's poles shifted from sites in eastern Siberia and in the southern Indian Ocean to their present positions, which is about a 45 degree shift.

With the South Pole relocated in the great mountainous Antarctic continent, a series of important events began. First, precipitation in the mountains turned to snow and then ice; snowfields built up in the glaciers and, growing larger, the glaciers spread out over the low lands. The freezing of Antarctica began about 3 or 4 million years ago and initiated a drop in the world's sea level because water was not returned to the oceans by the normal melting in the summertime.[8]

Because of the swiftly forming ice during the freezing of Antarctica, the lowering in sea level was dramatic. Could there have been other events like high doses of radiation and a continental drift as well? Is it possible that the polar shift was a cataclysmic event? Could there have been a dramatic event known as crust displacement where the entire crust of the earth slides over the mantle and repositions itself on the earth?

ALPHA TO OMEGA

Could the huge aquifers of ancient times have been released by continental shifting and drifting as the Creationists suggest (although they believe that it occurred 6500 years ago)? Does the real evidence of an advanced civilization remain hidden beneath the miles of ice in earth's Polar Regions, which were situated in the tropical zone before the shift occurred? Could other remnants of an ancient lost civilization have become pulverized by the quickly advancing ice and millions of years of erosion? Did you know that most of the Oceans' sea floors are unexplored?

This is where incomplete evidence prevents us from knowing for sure. However, the generally accepted ideas are presented in such a way to prevent us from considering the remote possibility of a previous high civilization. Our history books didn't tell us Atlantis was real because it cannot be proven empirically. Instead, historians paint a picture that is equally as fallible but generally accepted because it is presented to be factual. Archeological and geologic evidence is incomplete.

> **If we really want to know where we are headed, we have to know where we came from. If we can truly see where we are headed then we can figure out the important things we are missing about our past.**

The gap in time between the cataclysm and our new era had to be long enough to prevent contemporary discovery of evidence. The theorem presented here is that an advanced civilization (referred to as Atlantis) predated our era of civilization and history by a much larger amount of time than we have presumed.

- By establishing the first axiom we agree that there was an advanced society—Paradise—obviously somewhere in our distant past because current archeological and geological evidence remains inconclusive.
- We have corroborating evidence in the many flood stories from all parts of the world, which were not influenced by religion. In the Old Testament, which is the earliest compiled chronological history of our era, we find similar details to support a prior and more advanced civilization destroyed by cataclysmic floods.
- Plato's famous tales of Atlantis depicts an advanced society in our distant past. The story survived the bias of time because of its importance and not because someone wanted to create a myth.
- Historical presentations lead us to believe that a previous culture never existed at all because it didn't fit within the presupposed chronologies of history and the inherited archetypes of historical thinking.

The idea of a previous civilization is not a new proposal. There are hundreds of books written about Atlantis and several contemporary researchers who posit the same idea. Discrepancies between recorded history and new evidence to the contrary are being exposed continually, which leave no other conclusion but one that is provin-

ALPHA TO OMEGA

cial in arguments supporting a super-society of ancient history. Precisely how long ago Atlantis flourished depends upon how we evaluate the newer evidence and other pertinent information.

The History of History

The world has relied on history to provide us with information to help us understand our world, our cultures and their origins. Unfortunately, the further back in time we go, the more errors we can expect, which presents a major obstacle to a clarified view of our past. An overview of the historical tradition will help us to see how religion and history have the same origins and how easily the earliest depictions could have become misaligned and misconstrued.

> 'History' means the conscious and intentional remembrance of things past, in a living tradition transmitted from one generation to another. For this there must be some continuous organization, be it the family of the chieftain in the beginning, or the school today, which has reason to care for the past of the group and has the capacity for transmitting the historical tradition to future generations. History exists only in a persisting society which needs history to persist.

> But no living memory links us with the inventors of fire, with the masters, who some 15,000 years ago painted walls of caves in France and in the Ural Mountains, or with the builders who, perhaps about 2000 BC, began to erect the still-standing monoliths at Stonehenge in England. These men left signs, and they knew what those signs meant, but they left no written word, and their message cannot be clearly understood by us.[9]

The historical tradition is based upon the evidence of the first persistent societies in Sumer and Egypt and became the fountain-head of historical memory and consensus. Any culture that may have existed outside that which began in the Near East is relegated to the imagination of historians because the idea of history itself was built upon Babylon and Egypt.[10]

History contends that both were the earliest civilizations because they are situated at the center of the cradle of civilization, where man is believed to have first evolved before migrating to other areas. Historians relentlessly depict all societies as having become eventually comprised of Neolithic primitive humans who evolved into the knowledgeable worldwide civilization of present day. We are beginning to discover evidence to the contrary.

The earliest discovered writings of human history are found in ancient Sumer, Mesopotamia and Egypt dating back to 3000 BC, 2600 BC and 2700 BC respectively. The most ancient are found on the Sumerian clay tablets, which depict the epic of Gilgamesh—a remarkably similar flood story—among many other things. The Pyramid Texts found on the walls of several Egyptian pyramids date back to 2700 BC. All of these writings mysteriously compare with one another in an apparently urgent attempt to define gods, a flood and other remarkable events.

Egypt and Mesopotamia were early focal points of mystery, intrigue and power struggles. Any events occurring prior to the ancient texts are based on limited archeological evidence. Little or no evidence can support many of the assumptions regarding early societal developments of prehistory nor can history tell us exactly what transpired throughout the globe during the thousands of years before written documents.

Why are the most ancient records of prehistory's societies focused almost entirely on descriptions of gods and hell, flood legends and chronicles that curiously resemble the earliest Hebrew accounts in Genesis? It's quite apparent monumental events precipitated writing because all of the earliest writings are focused on the same core themes.

Biblical history, which is known to be the earliest chronological history on record, reveals to us how extraordinary events transformed mass confusion into a cohesive band of adherents to a newly formed ideology and governing authority.

Understanding the Bible, rests on realizing vital information was urgently necessary to be recorded and passed onward, but the bias of time and other factors unavoidably effected translation and blurred the truths about these world-changing discoveries. The contorted depictions of truth surrounding momentous ancient events eventually became the earliest known recorded chronological history.

Important events must have occurred long before the Israelites established the tenets of early Judaism. Without the presence of several remarkable events and discoveries, the transformation of the world's prevailing ideologies would not have occurred and the urgency to forward the information would be nonexistent.

The book of Genesis describes everything from creation to the origin of the Egyptian conflict in the first twelve chapters—an enormous amount of history for such a short depiction. The earliest five books of the Bible were developed over a period of 1000 years.

DAYS OF FUTURE PAST

They were derived from various sources and intricately woven together by the 6th century BC.

Not until the 19th century did scholars notice the anomalies in style, semantics, and word form in the ancient texts, leading them to conclude that the Pentateuch of Hebrew tradition—the first five books of the Old Testament—was derived from at least four different sources. These independent versions of literature were developed over time and drawn from oral tradition to become the world renowned compilation.[11]

Although many believe dutiful scribes were extremely careful when copying the texts, it's apparent the story was meshed and continually altered until the 6th century BC, which is clearly evident in the book of Isaiah.[12] About 900 years had elapsed following the Exodus (presumed to be 1446 BC), before the texts were completed. Jewish authority, which had been well established by the 6th century BC, dominated the interpretation of historical events for hundreds of years prior.

In all probability, the initial compilations were agreed upon by authorities attempting to explain significant events exposed by startling evidence from all parts of the Middle East. It is more realistic to assume the governing authority in 1400 BC was a constituency of leaders, which later became the early Jewish authority—a fusion of government cemented by control of history's interpretation for strategic political and economic reasons.

In 1200 BC, the entire Middle East, Near East and Greece were areas of intense power struggles. How could it have been possible for the Jews to be recognized as the earliest respected authority without concessions for other dominating authorities with similar interests?

Closer examination of the specific chronological events recorded in the Bible's book of Genesis reveals Abram to have preceded the Exodus by almost 1000 years. This proves the recorded chronology to be a 1000-year historical account written by Moses after the Exodus. Where did he get his information?

An additional 900 years or so transpired after the Exodus and before the accounts became collated and finalized into the earliest Hebrew Bible. By 600 BC, Moses wasn't alive to explain what had remained of his 1000 year-old scrappy ledgers, which were descriptions of events that occurred almost 2000 years prior. Jewish authority had ruled the interpretation of historical records dating back to the advent of mankind's earliest writings.

This strongly suggests accounts were most likely structured to reflect the opinions of a consortium, whose intent was to make sense of oral traditions, early writings and integral events of which Moses had been likely involved. In all likelihood (we will demonstrate in chapter five), the most significant events occurred long before the earliest known Sumerian writings (3000 BC).

Notwithstanding, Sumerian and Egyptian writings were surely an essential component of records perused in order to craft the early versions of history. If it required almost 1000 years to formulate the Pentateuch, then the prevailing authority of the 6th century BC was at least 2000 years removed from the origin of events beginning with Shem of Old Testament scripture.

Power is always awarded to those whose discoveries change the world, but both truth and its power are usurped by the authority born of such discoveries.

Origins of truth became tainted history, especially when we acknowledge the depicted events to have predated mankind's earliest records. The stories were reinterpreted, rearranged, altered and organized by designated authorities only to become fragmented and misunderstood in succeeding generations. Over time, history's truth eroded into dogma while the historical authority became a powerful entity. We can understand more easily how the earliest records might have been skewed by both unavoidable ineffective translation and the immorality of power.

Did Hebrew authority gain its power as a direct result of the control of history and its interpretation? Did the dawn of alternative historical tradition emerge from recognizing history's importance as a necessary element of power?

History and public opinion had long been influenced by the powerful Jewish tradition before Greek leaders enlisted scholars to gather information and compile separate accounts of history. Not until the fifth century BC did another organized process of transmitting the portrayals of past events begin.

The history of Greece and its surrounding regions (including Egypt) became important enough to enlist Herodotus, the first known historian of Greco-Egyptian times, to compile records of various cultures, their clashes and politics.

His documents are tattered and still remain respected by historians as bona-fide descriptions of Greco-Persian wars, as told to

ALPHA TO OMEGA

Herodotus by the many witnesses he interviewed and by reports based on the oral histories he evaluated.[13]

Herodotus is arguably the pioneer of history and was soon followed by a number of Greek historians also commissioned by regional powers to gather information on wars, geography, culture and politics of surrounding areas. Not to take anything away from *"the Father of History"*, but the origin of written political, socio-economic history as we know it, is compiled from verbal sources, which are incredulous by today's standards.

What do we suppose was the reason for a growing obsession with history? Isn't it more probable to suggest that powerful nations relied on bold challenges to popularized versions of history in order to gain constituents and power? Since we see history and religion having similar origins, we can surmise that challenges to history were challenges to religious concepts.

History erupted into a discipline primarily concerned with educating powerful leaders with agendas. It leaves us to presume embellishment to have played a big part in transcribing the accounts of early history equally as prejudice played its part on methods of information gathering. We cannot deny the repetitive habits of human nature in our evaluations.

Greece remained obsessed with ancient legends of Greek and Egyptian gods. Alexander the Great could have completely conquered the Persians after the Battle of Issus in 333 BC, which pushed the Persians back to Babylon with a decimated army. Instead he moved down the coast to Tyre, which baffled his Generals. Many historians speculate that he intended to cut off the bases of the Persian fleet and prevent its making trouble in Greece, but that didn't make sense because they had been severely beaten. It took Persia's King Darius III two years to rebuild his army and it wasn't until then that Alexander returned to Persia to defeat the newly formed army in 331 BC.[14]

It was later discovered, in tales by his Generals, Alexander was more interested in Egypt, where questions regarding his destiny took precedence over the destiny of Greece. He was obsessed with knowing whether he was a demigod who had been fathered by a Pharaoh rather than his presumed father, King Philip, after rumors of his mother's infidelity.[15] There is no need to expound on the story. It serves as a reminder to the obsession, even in 330 BC, by leaders who were consumed with the long standing myths and legends, which preceded them by at least 2,500 years.

In 270 BC King Ptolemy II, enlisted a priest named Manetho to gather the history of ancient Egypt. His original three volume manuscript was very popular and placed in the library of Alexandria only to perish there in the renowned burning by Moslem conquerors in 642 A.D.

Somehow, Manetho's arrangement of a list of gods and demigods (reigning long before Pharaohs became Kings in Egypt) survived in the records of other ancient historians and are followed to this day. His listing depicts 17,520 years of Divine rule—3,650 of which were demigods—prior to any Pharaoh in Egypt (placing gods and humans together in Egypt as early as 21,000 BC).[16]

King Antiochus I of Seleucid, a Greek-Macedonian State created as part of eastern conquests of Alexander the Great, commissioned a priest-historian named Berossus to compile a more complex tale that could embrace many lands, diverse rulers and different kingdoms. Portions of the three volumes, which he composed around 278 BC, were copied and extensively quoted in antiquity by other Greek and Roman historians.[17]

Apollodorus of Athens in the 2nd century BC and a Greek-Roman historian of the first century BC named Alexander Polyhistor similarly quote Berossus' list of ten pre-flood gods whose total reign lasted for 432,000 years. The last of such rulers is named Xisuthros, who bears a remarkable resemblance to Noah in that he survived a worldwide deluge in order to save the world and ruled for a total of 64,800 years (apparently divided by pre and post-flood times).[18]

Many other similarities to the Hebrew Bible, including the exact story of the Tower of Babel, lead many to believe the same source material must have been born out of archaeology and influenced each detailed account, although selectively.[19]

Where did all of this information originate? Because these tales bear curious similarities to the tablets of ancient Sumer, it is highly probable these narrations were derived in part from information obtained from the Royal library of Assyria's King Ashurbanipal of 7th century BC. He was the first to organize a library consisting of thousands of clay tablets, gathered by his scribes from all parts of ancient Babylon. The library was comprised of enormous documentations written on original Sumerian tablets, which were discovered, albeit fragmented, in 1859 by archeologist Austen Henry Layard and are currently housed in the British Museum.

The compilations of Berossus and Manetho were unprecedented and their testimonies were respected enough to have been copied by other curious historians of the time. Importantly, their collections concur that an enormous amount of time of Egyptian rule by gods and demigods had preceded the Egyptian rule by Pharaohs. Can we provide a unique evaluation of this evidence?

Although these descriptions of history relied on centuries of oral tradition, they demonstrate the importance and reliability of oral tradition in specific historical accounts long before written records. This suggests that historic events of monumental proportions had influenced oral tradition with enough degree of uniformity, over hundreds or possibly thousands of years, to render their stories somewhat credible. It doesn't imply the events and circumstances were totally agreed upon or understood with clarity, as is evidenced by conflicting time periods in each description, but specific concepts were agreed upon because of the veracity of corroborating oral descriptions.

Both testimonies allow adequate time for development of humans and societies in the post-flood era, which is unaccounted for in the biblical version of the story. Each of them supports the establishment of god-like rulers, which are depicted in Greek and Egyptian myths and will prove to be a crucial part of this presentation.

The narrative accounts of Berossus and Manetho will help to answer the questions arising from newly exposed mysteries, to which current historical consensus cannot, and prove the biblical version must have been convoluted over time if, in fact, the earliest sources of information were the same.

ALPHA TO OMEGA

Curiously, the renderings of both Manetho and Berossus had been written thousands of years after the actual events and more than 2500 years after the first known writings of our civilization—much like the Pentateuch. Did they mold their stories to reflect what had been long believed in Greco-Egyptian history or did they find evidence to corroborate their findings?

History's conundrum is the ineffective translation of the earliest and critically formative events of prerecorded times. Important discoveries don't fit within the conduct of history's presupposed timeline and corroborating evidence seems to be derived from unknown sources.

The Piri Reis map of 1513 is a perfect example. It precisely depicts the geographic landscape of Antarctica 300 years before its discovery and over 400 years before science created a seismic map of the land buried thousands of feet beneath the mountains of ice.

How is it possible for a map, copied from an unknown source map (believed to have been housed in the Imperial Library of Constantinople), to precisely depict the sub-glacial topography of Antarctica 400 years before an accurate seismic profile was created with 20th century technology? How could Piri Reis have any knowledge in 1513 of the continent of Antarctica, which hadn't been discovered until 1818?

> Piri Reis obligingly gives us the answer in a series of notes written in his own hand on the map itself. He tells us that he was not responsible for the original surveying and cartography. On the contrary, he admits that his role was merely that of a compiler and copyist and that the map was derived from a large number of source maps. Some of these had been drawn by contemporary or near contemporary

explorers (including Christopher Columbus), who had by then reached South America and the Caribbean, but others were documents dating back to the fourth century BC or earlier.[20]

Perhaps we should lean towards accepting the implications provided by the works of both Manetho and Berossus because it helps to explain the physical evidence exhumed, which strongly supports adeptly thriving civilizations at least 12,000 years ago.[21] We have no conclusive evidence to help us determine whether or not these legends were influenced by anything more than oral tradition, but circumstantial evidence is more than ample to assume their validity with as much zeal as we have the archaic and incomplete historical portrayals.

We cannot change the teachings of history without changing the assumptions on which they are founded. In lieu of the staggering evidence it's apparent that unprecedented technological advances flourished long before ancient writings emerged and we must acknowledge the supporting scientific evidence uncovered.

Written records emerged long after the events, which had originally spawned the unvarying oral descriptions. Historical accounts are the later collation of written records born of oral tradition, which were selectively chosen and governed by central authorities whose combined efforts were aimed at developing a common understanding to pass onward.

Compiling historical documents and proclaiming them to be the truth provides substantially more leverage than oral tradition in the governance of an expanding civilization, but are more likely to become influenced by powerful leaders whose primary concern is to retain power—even at the expense of truth.

43

> **As the practice of compiling written renditions of ancient oral tradition became familiar, the "official" history and beliefs of many nations became divided by separate interpretations of the same monumental world-changing events of centuries past.**

Contemporary historians believe the Old Testament to be a legend built on heroic ideals, which emerged in the 12th century BC.

> Beside the legends, the collection contains fragments of law codes, historical works, imaginative literary compositions (notably the Joseph romance), borrowings early and late from Mesopotamian mythology, and many minor elements. Most of these have been worked over by three or four editors and cemented and augmented by editorial inventions. The collection now begins with the creation of the world, which dates about 4000 BC, and contains a history of mankind from creation to the building of the tower of Babel, a genealogy of the Semites from the flood to Abraham and finally history of Abraham and his descendants down to 560 BC.[22]

This isn't an attempt to detract credibility from the Old Testament or the Bible, but to show how time must have taken its toll on a very important oral tradition; it's much later Hebrew translation and the above historical analysis, exposed to the frailty of human nature, which emerged 3000 years later.

It is best for us to determine what may have caused the original divergence—a fork in the road separating the truth from man's interpretations of historical events, which led to the eventual convolutions of religious thought and incomplete history.

DAYS OF FUTURE PAST

It's impossible to make any provable assertions about prehistoric chronology because the earliest records cannot tell us, with a comfortable degree of certainty, exactly what transpired prior to 3000 BC.

To establish what happened in prehistory relies on one's intuition to speculatively connect an uncertain past to what is presumed to be reality today. If any historical analysis shows signs of a disconnection between the two, then such history would most likely be considered unfounded and unaccepted. However, as we have demonstrated, it's not just the present to which history must be fluidly connected, but the future, which is our ultimate destiny.

As evidenced in the evaluation of historical tradition, it appears that its birth and therefore its bias conduct are influenced first by power and secondly by the obsession to connect the past and present in a manner that upholds the basic assumptions. Without written and confirmed accounts we rely on archaeology, which can be seen as the embellisher of a predetermined history. Sure, archaeology can point to discoveries and surmise what is most likely to have happened (and there are certainly hundreds of opinions), but when it comes to the actual events or circumstances that shaped human history, we can never be certain.

In science, assumptions change when new evidence is discovered (most of the time). It seems that religion and history are unbending and permanently connected at the root, which leads us to surmise the retention of authoritative power is more important than the truth. Religious and historical authorities deny glaring evidence contradicting the presumptions on which they

45

are founded—hardly scientific and inherently evil when observed as a hindrance to truth.

If we can go back to the fork in the road that initiated the diversion between early written history and the truth, we would have two choices. The first would be to accept the oral tradition of ancient gods and spectacular wonders of years gone by and the second would be to completely ignore the verbal tales and rely on the pronouncements of a newly formed authority.

Human nature suggests that many continued to rely on the verbal tales until authority eventually transformed the believers into heretics, lunatics, and rebels, who were left without a leg to support the ancient traditions that soon became the myths of a modern society.

How can we make sense of the myths and legends evidenced in man's earliest writings and ignored by historical tradition? The exposed evidence of unexplainable mysteries leaves us only to speculate in our attempts to describe events, which can explain what got us here today.

By sharpening our objectivity, we can see clearly how the accepted version of prehistory has been founded upon speculation, embellishment and bias. If we can present new hypotheses addressing the mysteries seemingly ignored by historical and religious teachings, then our speculations should not be disregarded.

Chapter 2

HEART OF THE MATTER

The stars and planets do not guide us. Instead, they are guided by the eternal core of our being and reflect our physical moment in time.

Origins

How do we connect the dots between scientific discoveries, unexplained worldly phenomena and religious ideologies concerning human origin? One of the biggest mysteries of science is trying to determine the origin of life. Science requires proof for everything and, since God cannot be empirically proven, science concludes that God does not exist and that creation is not an option.

Instead, science has discovered the sophistication and complexity of a single cell, which renders Darwin's spontaneous generation theory mathematically impossible. In other words, science has proven that is impossible for the evolution of life to emerge from lifelessness.

Yet, scientists like the late Francis Crick, who won the Nobel Prize for elucidating the structure of the DNA molecule, and the

ALPHA TO OMEGA

late Sir Frederick Hoyle, who proved the mathematical impossibility of spontaneous generation and believed in purposeful intelligence, spearheaded a non-miraculous cause for life's origin. They believed that life has been delivered from outer space by aliens or by a comet infected with bacteria (panspermia). And according to Michael J. Behe, author of *Darwin's Black Box,*

> The primary reason Crick subscribes to this unorthodox view is that he judges the undirected origin of life (evolution) to be a virtually insurmountable obstacle but he wants a naturalistic explanation.[1]

This highly suggests empiricism has no place for God and miracles. Even though evidence supports purposeful intelligence, science does not imply the existence of God by proof of intelligent design. To me, it's merely semantics for denouncing God in the presence of enormous evidence to the contrary. Science would rather provide new theories, which continue to fail in explaining the origin of life, than subscribe to esoteric ideologies and presumed magic. Panspermia does not address the origins of the life of the aliens or the bacteria on the comet, so we are still faced with the same dilemma.

With each new scientific discovery, myriad questions emerge revealing the extent of our limited knowledge. Science still can't tell us how life began nor can it tell us why we are here. David Berlinski says it with distinction:

> Charles Darwin talked speculatively of life emerging from a "warm little pond." The pond is gone. We have little idea how life emerged, and cannot with assurance say that it did. We cannot

HEART OF THE MATTER

reconcile our understanding of the human mind with any trivial theory about the manner in which the brain functions. Beyond the trivial, we have no other theories. We can say nothing of interest about the human soul. We do not know what impels us to right conduct or where the form of the good is found.

On these and many other points as well, the great scientific theories have lapsed. The more sophisticated the theories, the more inadequate they are. This is a reason to cherish them. They have enlarged and not diminished our sense of the sublime.[2]

Intelligent design theory emerged in the early 1990s when about 80 percent of North Americans believed in God but were divided by those who believed they were directly created by God and those who believed that God guided evolution. What could possibly unite this very broad group of viewpoints—the 80 percent who did not accept Darwin's naturalistic view? The scientifically-based theory of intelligent design—a theory positing that science is capable of telling us that the universe and life bear evidence of an intelligent designing agent.[3]

A noteworthy argument for God as the intelligent designer came from those who have shown rarity of habitable planets as supporting evidence for God. The possibility that planets can support habitable life is extremely rare. Still, science challenged the argument on the basis that an extremely rare habitable planet wasn't strong enough evidence to eliminate the possibility of chance over design. In 2004, a book entitled *The Privileged Planet*, by Guillermo Gonzalez and Jay Richards, was released. It sturdily supports God as the intelligent designer by showing that those rare

49

ALPHA TO OMEGA

places in which observers can exist are also the best overall places for observation.[4]

They have demonstrated with astonishing empirical evidence that habitability and measurability are correlated. Habitability and measurability together increase the rarity factor exponentially making it mathematically impossible for it to happen. What a remarkable coincidence, which gives added reliability to the concept of purposeful intelligence through God. The very conditions that make earth hospitable to intelligent life also make it flawlessly suited to viewing and analyzing the universe as a whole. This exhibits that our purpose is to observe and discover, and that all conditions are perfect for uncovering the evidence needed to provide us with the answers to our questions.

The battle between extreme creationists and evolutionists is an arena where the scientific process is often compromised. On the scientific side, Darwin's evolution theory has been convincingly challenged because of the irreducible complexity of functional mechanisms found at the cellular level. Yet those who still believe in the evolution of life from lifelessness have either failed to remain informed or refuse to give up their obsolete concepts. Some are the same scientists who are bent on proving that God does not exist. Their conclusions are often slanted by incomplete evidence and presented as finite even with evidence suggesting otherwise.

Absolute denial for the existence of God without unequivocal evidence is biased and clearly not scientific.

Literalists, who staunchly deny evolution theory, adhere strictly to the literal interpretation of scripture, which makes their arguments for God appear baseless and just as biased as the scientific theories built on premises that exclude God completely. Literalists begin with their own presumption of fact before discovery and the scientific process. Most often, their intent is to search for evidence to support a conclusion that is already decided upon—hardly a scientific approach resulting in the blurred concepts of God.

Each side wants to be right and neither side wants to change its position. Consequently, it becomes a publicized argument which is not at all scientific. Under-informed people are left with a choice between two ill-formed conclusions. Doesn't it seem that the extremists on either side of an argument are those who create division to begin with?

Contemporary science contends that early man's superstitions, fears and unawareness, led to the origins of God-concepts. Yet now, they consider alien intervention a theory for life's origins while failing to consider the origin of the aliens.

To those of us who faithfully believe in God, we are compelled to be more scientific in our approach towards releasing the stranglehold of our inherited concepts.

Supreme Being

Can we truly envision what it would be like to acquire absolute knowledge and power? Imagine a place of limitless power where everyone is united in harmonious will, purpose and comprehension. It's almost impossible to imagine and equally difficult to describe. Our imaginations have always extended far beyond our current level of thought but Heaven, Nirvana, Total Enlightenment, Paradise and One with Everything is too far removed from our present level of thought to effectively imagine or describe it. It is a superior level of existence—paraphysical (beyond physics as we know it) in all of its arrangements.

Remember the outer ring of omniscience and omnipotence in figure 1? We referred to it as the *state of Supreme Being*, where absolute knowledge, harmonious will and unlimited power are commonplace. If we can relieve ourselves of preconceived notions and judgment, then Paradise and the *image of God*, in which we were created, can be understood in a new light.

- Supreme Being is the *complete reflection* of God in physical form
- Supreme Being is omniscient and omnipotent.
- Supreme Being is immortal.
- Supreme Being is an integral part of all that exists.
- Supreme Being Will is in unison with Divine Will.
- Supreme Being is a Child of God.

Understandably, empirical thinkers do not like metaphors. Thus, we shall consider the above parameters to be acceptable conditions for this argument rather than metaphors. Here is another passage from Plato's Critias. Was he explaining the same concept of superior beings in a previous society?

HEART OF THE MATTER

...For many generations, as long as the divine nature lasted in them, they were obedient to the laws, and well-affectioned towards the god, whose seed they were; for they possessed true and in every way great spirits, uniting gentleness with wisdom in the various chances of life, and in their intercourse with one another. They despised everything but virtue, caring little for their present state of life, and thinking lightly of the possession of gold and other property, which seemed only a burden to them; neither were they intoxicated by luxury; nor did wealth deprive them of their self-control; but they were sober, and saw clearly that all these goods are increased by virtue and friendship with one another, whereas by too great a regard and respect for them, they are lost and friendship with them...[5]

The manner in which we think has a lot to do with our perspectives. Are we a top-down or bottom-up thinker? Most of us are bottom-up thinkers. We gather available data and analyze it to form hypotheses and/or conclusions. It's the process of deductive reasoning. Conversely, top-down thinking is the process of inductive reasoning. This type of thinking requires breaking down or decomposing the most complex part of a system or idea into smaller parts that can be explained. From those explanations, the top-down approach continually breaks down information until it gets to the raw data.

This is only a brief summation but let's take a closer look. By establishing the above conditions we have defined the obscure 'in His image' metaphor. But the definition could not have been derived without inductively presenting an acceptable axiom. So, in effect we have replaced obscure concepts with something a little more understandable. As we move further along, these new defini-

ALPHA TO OMEGA

tions will help to develop a more clarified view of various obscure concepts.

By accepting the theorem of a prehistoric and superlative world, we allow ample circumstantial evidence to supersede the bottom-up approach where evidence has yet to be discovered—and there are innumerable undiscovered facts. This adds credibility to biblical text and helps to remove some of the ambiguity, especially when allowing for the inadequacies of prehistoric man.

From this proposition, new questions emerge because we have to explain how an advanced society with nearly unlimited power was unable to prevent its own destruction. Further, how did a civilization so far removed in time become known to man in a completely new era? We also have to determine why ancient writings describe the deluge as punishment by God for evil deeds. Who or what is God? The goal is to set acceptable principles that remain constant throughout this analysis, while providing new answers to some of the oldest questions of mankind.

God

No material man could behold the spirit God and preserve his mortal existence. The glory and the spiritual brilliance of the divine personality presence is impossible of approach by the lower groups of spirit beings, or by any order of material personalities. The *spiritual luminosity* of the Father's personal presence is a light which no mortal man can approach; which no material creature has seen or can see. But it is not necessary to see God with the eyes of the flesh in order to discern him by the faith-vision of the spiritualized mind.[6]

One of the oldest inherited notions is that God is indefinable yet we have also been taught to worship God. How can we worship a blurred concept? Most every believer has an indistinct concept of God developed by inherited thought, limited knowledge and our assignment of personal attributes and aspirations. Therefore, the God in our mind is the *reflection* of our extremely limited and vulnerable self upon a Limitless Entity or *the creation of a god in our own image.*

Top-down thinking can help to provide acceptable definitions for what God is and isn't. Within the context of this presentation, we are many steps removed from Supreme Being. If we concede that mirroring our human attributes in the definition of God would be restrictive, then we can derive some characteristics to describe what God is not.

- God is not bound by the dimensions of space and time
- God is not physical
- God is not animate
- God is not a gender or personality
- God is not emotion

As a human race, we are here to discover All Truth. Our inherent curious nature will continue until we become Supreme Beings. If that is so, then we can say it is the will of Truth to be made manifest through creation and ultimately in Supreme Being. The nature of Divine Will is to be physically and consciously expressed over time.

Closer observation reveals it as the incessant natural process to animate matter. The Infinite Power creates the vehicles for the fulfillment of will, which is the ultimate expression of Creator and created in the physical realm: Supreme Being—the Reflection of the Infinite.

Creation and evolution can be seen as the same process from this viewpoint as long as the Essence of Life supersedes everything. As the Essence of Life manipulates matter and energy, the physical world begins to manifest creatures—vehicles of Life—with increasing degrees of complexity over time.

Each creature has the inherent will to survive and thus the will of the non-thinking creature invokes the Infinite Power, which beneficially alters each species, within the maximum potential for sustainment in each particular vehicle. This progressive process continues until a creature evolves into a vehicle in which the potential for the maximum expression of Infinite Power can be manifested in physical form—a sentient being whose will to know All Truth takes priority over everything.

Does this help to explain intelligent design and the apparent miraculous creation of life from lifelessness? Perhaps the assumption can be contrived as a leap of faith but how else can we explain the shocking discoveries that science stumbled upon during its efforts to prove that God does not exist? Those who seek empirical or tangible proof are failing to see the evidence that exists all around us.

The prejudiced attempt to prove the basis of life as exceedingly simple has proven the opposite in the incredible complexity of living cells, which gave birth to the scientific theory of intelligent design. Empirical evidence verifies that billions of bits of information, carried within the DNA molecule, provide blueprints for endless numbers of diversified cellular components.

> As strange as it may seem, modern biochemistry has shown that the cell is operated by machines—literally, molecular machines. Like their man-made counterparts (such as mousetraps, bicycles, and space shuttles), molecular machines range from the simple to the enormously complex: mechanical, force-generating machines, like those in muscles; electronic machines, like those in nerves; and solar-powered machines, like those of photosynthesis. Of course, molecular machines are made primarily of proteins, not metal and plastic.[7]

In a nut shell, proteins are a combination of amino acids, each with enough attributes to provide millions of combinations and assume any shape and characteristic required to perform a specific cellular function. Compare it to a manufacturing company with the capacity to produce every part required to build an aircraft carrier. Each part of the whole does what is necessary to perform individual functions precisely.

The human body, using its detailed blueprint encoded in DNA molecules, continuously manufactures millions of precision parts, which work together seamlessly and flawlessly to ensure the vital and enormous mechanical functions taking place at the cellular level. It is amazing, but no more inconceivable than the plausibility of similar harmonious interaction on the larger scale when perfect creatures exist together on earth.

Did you ever witness the coordinated swim of large schools of fish? Have you watched the amazing synchronicity of huge flocks of birds in flight? We can see the same type of harmony in the bees, insects and other animals that demonstrate their tremendous capacity to work together flawlessly and towards the same objective without thought? It's as though their minds are one collective entity. Wouldn't humans be exceptionally more remarkable than the lesser creatures while living in a perfectly unified higher state of consciousness?

> Look at the birds in the sky: they neither sow nor reap nor gather into barns, and yet your Father feeds them. Are you not of more value than they? (Matthew 6:26)

We marvel, when observing the beauty of every plant and creature, their matchlessness, behaviors and instincts. In every life form beneath the human being, God has reached the maximum potential of expression in that vehicle. Human beings are the most advanced vehicles on earth and the only vehicle with the *potential* for the ultimate expression of Divine Will—a superior state of existence beyond our imagination.

If it all sounds too metaphysical for us to consider then maybe we should inspect another realm of metaphysics—quantum mechanics. Metaphysics is defined as a division of philosophy that is concerned with the fundamental nature of reality and being; a study of what is outside of the objective experience. The study of physics has actually become philosophical with the advent of quantum theory. The complexity of quantum reality renders it such that it lacks a single comprehensive metaphor for the way the world really is.

Our sense of reality in the physical world is molded from the evidence of our senses. Niels Bohr, a world renowned physicist, Nobel Prize winner and pioneer of quantum physics affirms in Part One of the Copenhagen Interpretations that the world we see around us is real enough but it floats on a world that is not as real. Everyday phenomena are themselves built, not out of phenomena, but out of an utterly different kind of being. In Part Two of the Copenhagen Institute's evaluation, reality was demonstrated to be created by the act of observation. There is no reality without observation. In the quantum world, an unmeasured atom is not real; its attributes are created or realized only in the act of measurement.[8]

Bell's theorem, a foundation in quantum theory, proves clearly that reality must be nonlocal, i.e., the atom's measurable attributes are determined by events at both the actual measurement site and at arbitrarily distant sites outside the light cone—events so far away that, to reach the measurement site, their influence must travel in multiples of light speed, which is deemed impossible by the theory of relativity. He goes on to prove that the act of measurement is not a private event but rather a public event in whose details a large portion of the universe instantly participates. [9]

What are the implications to all of this? I haven't begun to scratch the cover on the surface of quantum physics. Quantum theory proves that reality becomes so only in the act of observation.

ALPHA TO OMEGA

Even then, what we observe can be exactly opposite of what we intended in experiments. The results of these experiments are mind-boggling. I urge readers to lightly explore the world of quantum mechanics to see how the physical world is like nothing we perceive it to be.

Token examples here are for those who aren't privy to any of the implied notions of quantum mechanics. I've provided them to assist readers in realizing that science is far from proving the non-existence of God. The more science attempts to define reality in the quantum world, the less real everything proves to be. The evidence derived from quantum mechanics yields undeniable proof of another intelligence—a set of laws—that works outside the dimensions of time and space as we know it.

> If we are to assume that laws of physics and chemistry are essentially uniform throughout the physical universe, and that those laws alone are insufficient to explain life on earth, then we must conclude that life could not have arisen by chance anywhere in the universe. Since this is true, the only other option is that the source of life in the universe must be an extra-dimensional one—in effect, an extra-dimensional Creator, independent of our space-time domain.[10]

Science remains steadfast in its mission for answers to explain the physical and not-so-physical universe in which we live. We've been presented with what appears to be concrete evidence for many things, which are far from solidified. Science gets enormous media attention and exploits their growing number of followers with bold and unsupported assertions. The intolerant nature of science was painfully exposed in the August, 2011 premier of

Discovery Channel's Curiosity series: *Did God Create the Universe?* Stephen Hawkings proclaimed that God was not necessary in the explanation of our physical universe.

Perhaps science is trying to discredit the personal God, which religion and our own narrow views have helped to conjure. Empiricism doesn't accept vague concepts, which exhibit unrealistic explanations for scientific processes and phenomena. This isn't to imply that God cannot be a personal concept to we who continuously alter our notions during the conscious attempt to understand and discover God. I am saying, however, that God is not a personal being and that by assigning limited human attributes to God, we provide easy targets for scientific abuse.

Anytime someone uses the word "God", it immediately summons the various concepts and preconceived notions instilled in the minds of many. I'd like to convey a concept of God as a *discoverable* entity behaving in a consistent fashion. In consideration of all this and the previous outline of characteristics that shouldn't be attributed to God, we can ascertain a little about what God is.

- God is infinite and timeless, which implies that there is no beginning or end to God. God is exempt from the boundaries of space-time (extra dimensional).
- God is the Essence and Animator of all life—an infinite and infinitesimal furnace of limitless power. From the smallest sub-atomic particle to the single cell, from a complex organism and throughout the hierarchy of more complex living creatures, God is the root.

ALPHA TO OMEGA

- God is consistent, incessant and unyielding intent, throughout the infinite and the infinitesimal, to become evident in physical and conscious expression—ultimately in Supreme Being (The Omega or final 1000 year Kingdom).
- God's complete reflection in the physical realm would be perfect harmony, which would be observed in the spectacular wonders throughout all levels of physicality from the microcosm to the macrocosm.
- God is the Unending Source of all Knowledge and Power. Everything attributed to life, energy, cause and effect stems from the original source of power and knowledge. This means that everything flows from the top and works its way downward.
- God is both *scientifically* and *personally* discoverable but nothing can change the Nature of God. It cannot be controlled because it is consistent and unchanging. Deliberate attempts to control, direct or oppose it will lead to varying levels of physical disharmony.

How else can we describe a Perfect God in a world inundated with evidence of a severely misaligned society? If God is All Truth then our problems must stem from the failure to know All Truth. If we are indeed a post-diluvial civilization separated by both the capacity to know God and the power and intellect afforded that knowledge, then those who knew were destroyed before they could effectively share it.

Therefore, the misgivings and sufferings of the existing age have always been the direct result of our relatively limited knowledge and not the workings of an unjust god. What has been referred to as "original sin" is both the cause and effect of a new and uninformed civilization. Inherent ignorance is the original sin in a new age, which is also the effect of the first mistake of a previous society with higher intellect.

If we look at it from the perspective that our destiny is to arrive at Paradise, then the misfortunes of our ignorance are what we have long referred to as the Judgment of God.

> **If the nature of God is toward the manifestation of All Truth, then the only way to there is through the experiences that expose our errors, which is more of a gift than a judgment.**

Do we judge death and when it occurs as an unfair bestowal by God? Do we believe the serious illness or unfortunate accidents of loved ones as being in direct conflict to our understanding of a merciful God? Does a child born with defects or an incurable disease challenge our acceptance of a loving God? Do the tribulations of humanity throughout the world add to our disillusionment?

The natural selection of nature is the process of genetic heredity. DNA is a complex computer of physical attributes with historical memory. Unfortunate accidents are the result of timing, which may or may not be prevented. God supersedes timing and the scientific natural selection process. We are subject to random acts of nature because of the limits to which our age has been fashioned.

Our awareness is severely impaired in comparison to the Supreme Beings of a previous era. We live in a three dimensional world where other dimensions are reserved for our imaginations only.

I believe we should modify our concept of God from one mirroring our personal nature to one akin to an elite energy—behaving in consistent fashion throughout the visible and invisible dimensions of reality. It is like no other power known to man but serves as the underpinning for all discovered and undiscovered forces in our physical realm.

When exposed, we will recognize it indisputably to be the Essence, Foundation, Creator and Animator of all aspects of perceived and yet to be perceived realities. We can observe God as the incessant and inexorable natural intent to become expressed in absolute fulfillment within the physical realm and beyond through an astonishing synthesis of energy, matter, space and time.

Throughout the rest of the book, the use of the word "God" is to be taken in the context presented here. My efforts are not to change the way you think, but to look at things from a different perspective. The above concept of God is provisional in this presentation.

The Big Mistake

> So God created man in his own image, in the image of God he created him; male and female he created them. And God blessed them and God said unto them, be fruitful and multiply and replenish the earth and subdue it. And have dominion over the fish of the sea, and over the fowl of the air, and over every living thing that moves upon the earth (Gen. 1: 27-28).

HEART OF THE MATTER

God's perfection was once mirrored in the original creation without blemish. The Incessant Will to become Supreme Being was achieved and manifested perfectly in the entire physical world of creation. Supreme Beings lived in harmony with God's Will, all of creation and each other. Just like the world of microbiology today, the macrocosm was completely balanced and in unison. I'm trying to emphasize the notion of nearly unutterable magnificence and wonder. Every living thing was a perfect reflection of God in the physical world. Creator and creature were intertwined in a world that defies physics as we know it today.

This idea may at first seem to be impossible but the newer scientific discoveries present plausibility in numerous ways. Even the creation of the entire Universe could have taken place in zero time because time, which is a mere dimension in our reality, only becomes real by our observation from a fixed point.

Einstein's theory of relativity proves that the faster an object travels, the slower time moves and Quantum theory proves that observation is required for physical realities. From our extremely limited perspective we might be more inclined to suspect that such a scenario is only a metaphor or a stretch of our imagination, but if we accept the ideas presented thus far, it is plausible. We must look beyond the senses of our limited and presumed realities to imagine a world where anything is possible.

If we can concede to mankind's perfection in a lost epoch of human history, then we need to determine the reason for their demise. Resolving to analyze the transgression is an important step in this presentation.

ALPHA TO OMEGA

In the state of Supreme Being, Divine Will and Creature Will are in unison. Creator wants to be consciously expressed and becomes so by creature will for All Truth. Should just one individual of a collective supreme society choose to allow personal motivation to supersede Divine Will, then regression would immediately begin from Supreme Being to demigod. It would hardly be noticeable at first but it would begin the process of *'human nature gets the upper hand'* as Plato described. In this case, the metaphoric Adam and Eve were those responsible for the fate and destiny of a super civilization eons ago.

What was the big mistake of Adam and Eve? How could any mistake lead to the annihilation of life on earth? The Atlanteans had become entirely aware of their environment and integration with nature's perfection and all that exists. The civilization was perfect in every way—a complete reflection of God. We can only speculate as to how long the perfect arrangement lasted.

In an imperfect world, curiosity is imperative for the acquisition of knowledge to help relieve our insufficiencies, perils and ignorance. In a perfect world, all questions are answered and there is no need for curiosity and selfish concerns in an omniscient world. Symbolically, the *'tree of knowledge of good and evil'* represents absolute knowledge—the knowledge of God, which, in a Supreme arrangement, is knowledge of self while possessing absolute Power.

Self-awareness, curiosity and free-will simultaneously emerge with the command to refrain from the knowledge of good and evil. The Tree of Life was also in the garden and presented immortality

HEART OF THE MATTER

as an option, but they chose otherwise. Knowledge begets power and the human will to utilize it is almost unstoppable.

With free will comes the decision to either align with Universal Will or give in to the will of self. Without awareness there can be no choice. Without awareness and choice, human beings can be no better than the animals, birds, trees, and flowers that merely exist perfectly in creation. Only when thinking creatures freely ally themselves to Divine Will can the ultimate expression of God be realized in the creature.

> The Creator refuses to coerce or compel the submission of the spiritual free wills of his material creatures. The affectionate dedication of the human will to the doing of the Father's will is man's choicest gift to God; in fact, such a consecration of creature will constitutes man's only possible gift of true value to the Paradise Father.[11]

Allowing curiosity to get the best of them, Adam and Eve made an irreversible decision leading them to realize their actions were in vain. They epitomized the blinding effects of self-awareness or ego and the humbling retrospect of errant decisions. Nothing could prevent the eventual disintegration of a perfect civilization.

The society, although imperfect from an absolute standpoint, remained extremely advanced, enlightened and powerful. They had discovered absolute power, which could be directed at the behest of individual will, giving cause to personal ambition and its opposition to Divine Will. Perhaps we can imagine, but surely cannot fathom, the degree of power at their disposal—an almost impossible temptation to overcome, even with the most innocent of intent.

ALPHA TO OMEGA

Peak separation from God's will coincide with individual awareness and absolute power. A division at this echelon sets up two diametrically opposed and extremely powerful forces, which can potentially become severely imbalanced. If the Will of God is to be ultimately expressed as Supreme Being, then anything interfering with Natural Intent will create an imbalance of power. Power imbalance would have to be exponentially higher when thinking creatures, armed with Absolute Power, consider personal motivation in decisions that may oppose Natural Intent.

Is it possible for a gigantic turbulence caused by the imbalance to have eventually created earth's monstrous cataclysm and destroyed the great civilization? I suspect that it was, when thinking in terms of forces that not only surpass but sustain our currently expressed physical reality. If we accept that the collective actions of mankind affect our collective destiny today, then we can understand the possible drastic effects of a collective society armed with absolute power and separate will.

Although Adam made a big mistake, he and all members of the antediluvian society possessed Absolute Knowledge and were keenly aware of the potential for disastrous complications when yielding to personal motivation. Adam knew his transgression destroyed his chance at immortality and would eventually lead to the ruin of a great civilization.

Adam was a Supreme Being and we clearly find evidence of this in scripture where he is renowned as the first son of God. He is considered to be God's Son even after his mistake, as we can see when reading the lines of genealogy in the Old Testament.

68

...the son of Methuselah, the son of Enoch, the son of Jared, the son of Mahalaleel, the son of Cainan, the son of Enos, the son of Seth, the son of Adam, the son of God (Luke 3:37-38).

Yet death reigned from Adam to Moses, even over those whose sinning was not like the transgression of Adam, who was a type of the one who was to come (Romans 5:14).

The second passage points to two things that need specific attention. First, we see that Adam was a *'type'* of the one who was to come. This gives credence to the fact that Jesus was like Adam and that Adam was like Jesus. Both of them are sons of God, and both had an enormous amount of power at the behest of their own will. This is going to be crucial in our examination of Jesus Christ later on.

Secondly, we see that the sin of Adam was not like those in Moses' (our) era. The transgression of Adam was colossal enough to lead to the annihilation of an entire world and civilization. Adam's mistake was different than ours because of the knowledge he possessed. Our mistakes differ because the inborn lack of knowledge or ignorance, which characterizes the foundation of our epoch, is in direct contrast to the omniscience in theirs. The scriptural verse is an important clue and piece of evidence revealing the line of demarcation between two different civilizations and intelligence.

Each decision to employ personal will slowly eroded the Supreme Power of Collective Will in the perfect arrangement of Paradise. This can be seen as the falling from Supreme Being to demigod where, as Plato explained *"... to those who could not see the true happiness they appeared glorious and blessed at the very time when they were full of avarice and unrighteous power..."* Each mistake breeds new mistakes and, after many of years regressing, the imbalance in power expanded enough to manifest in the violent upheavals and the cataclysm of destruction.

The highest level of experientialism was bestowed upon the earliest people on earth and is beyond the extent of our conceptualization. They were super humans in total control of their life and environment on the planet Earth. Spectacular wonders and events that we would deem miraculous were routine. Communication, through telepathy, and remarkable paraphysical abilities, are mere words to define their capacity. Life expectancies of almost one thousand years are evidence to their unlimited capacity.

> Atlantis was verbally articulate and developed expressions of complex thought patterns, and visions that often flashed back and forth quickly and telepathically...[12]

If we were to come face to face with the inhabitants of Atlantis today, we would be filled with awe and believe them to be gods. Adam, who would live for almost 1000 years, did so after his fall from perfection. It doesn't appear as a dire consequence for such an imposing mistake, which begs us to wonder how this could be possible.

The knowledge and power they had acquired was like none before or since on this planet. Had Adam and Eve chosen the Tree of Life they would have achieved immortality coupled with the power of Angels. Instead, their errant choice left them certain to die, nevertheless coupled with the power of Angels.

Angels, Demons and Aliens

Much of the research centered on early biblical text has been interpreted and redefined in numerous ways, but most of the contemporary end-time theories espouse that Angels, Demons, and UFO's are related to both historic and future events. Numerous sources have provided volumes of tantalizing information and adequate evidence to support the argument that all of these phenomena are indeed real.

How many of us have a sincere tendency to believe in the reality of these paranormal phenomena? This book is not focused on them but each has its place in the analysis. The scope of this book is not to present the evidence supporting UFOs and the arguments presented by skeptics. This is for those who have come to the conclusion that either of the unexplained mysteries has substantial merit for further evaluation. I'm of the opinion that Angels are real and that they have played a significant role in our past and will likely play a role in the future human drama.

Over the course of many years I have read several books and watched many documentaries on the UFO phenomenon. In my opinion, the most compelling is Leslie Kean's 2010 book, *UFOs: Generals, Pilots and Government Officials Go on the Record*, and FCZ Media's 2007 documentary, *I Know What I Saw*, a comprehensive video report by James Fox of the most credible cases and witnesses throughout the world. Both provide an objective and informative scientific approach, which permits readers and viewers to determine the validity of well-documented evidence. Thanks to the cooperation of government officials, each one takes on a

ALPHA TO OMEGA

professional air as "official" presentations of UFO phenomena. Anyone investing the time to peruse these media with an unprejudiced perspective will find that UFOs must be taken seriously.

Still, even the proof of UFOs doesn't empirically support the assumptions regarding extraterrestrial visitors or interdimensional phenomena. Simply put this means that no proof exists (as far as we know) of beings from other planets aboard these vehicles or if they are actually extra-dimensional.

I believe that Angels are extra-dimensional, which can be explained simply by the ability to move in and out of our three dimensional world while operating in another (extra) unseen dimension. Anything that can defy physics as we know it is exceptionally more advanced and operates in the realm of physics where only future discoveries can define them. Our ignorance is exposed by skeptics who deny mounds of corroborating evidence on the basis of insufficient tangible evidence.

Importantly, if we hold our position that power and knowledge are directly proportional, then we can conclude that aliens would be far superior to us in every way. They would have to be advanced enough to overcome the law of inertia, which creates instantly perilous g-forces when maneuvering in the manners described by witnesses and captured on video. The laws of aerodynamics as we know them do not apply to those vehicles, which have been consistently reported to move at high rates of speed without any sound or sonic boom.

To traverse the universe, star-travelers would have to be well advanced to overcome the logistic hurdles of propulsion. Even with today's knowledge of physics, we can predict ways to reach speeds about 75 percent the speed of light, but each concept requires enormous advances in science, which are consigned only to science fiction today. Although we understand ways for more advanced means of interstellar travel where speeds are measured in multiples of light speed, we are far from solving the multitude of problems exposed by this possiblity.[13]

These and similar notions continually affirm my long-standing belief that Angels and aliens are the same entities. Biblical references to Angels are plentiful and descriptions of their characteristics and behavior mimic that of the UFOs today. Both are rarely seen and remain obscure with a multitude of descriptions and characteristics.

What if we could find a reason for this stealthy behavior? Would it help to reduce one's skepticism if we could explain the battle between good and evil and demonstrate why Angels will not deliberately heal our insufficiencies and create a spectacular world for us? Can we explain why their counterparts are equally as stealthy and benefit from a hands-off approach? Will these explanations help to prove Angels and UFO's to be one entity rather than two unexplained and separate phenomena?

So far I have exhibited that Supreme Being with adjunct power is the highest of physical experience and beyond description. Yet, it pales in comparison to the highest echelon of Angels in a nine-step hierarchy. Angel hierarchy has a history agreed upon by most researchers. This, found in "The Testament of Adam"—part of the

ALPHA TO OMEGA

Gnostic texts discovered in the 1950's—was written somewhere between the 2nd and 5th century A.D.

The Angel Hierarchy describes the duties of each level and how they are involved in service to the world. The orders, from lowest to highest, are:

1. *Angels:* One angel is assigned to every person to accompany that individual everywhere.

2. *Archangels:* They direct everything in creation according to the plan of God.

3. *Archons:* They govern the elements and the weather. Other sources refer to them as *Principalities.*

4. *Authorities:* They govern the celestial lights of the sun, moon, and stars. Others sources refer to them as *Powers.*

5. *Powers:* They prevent the demons from destroying the world. Other sources refer to them as *Virtues.*

6. *Dominions:* They rule over earthly kingdoms and decide the outcome of wars. In biblical battle descriptions, they are angels riding on red horses.

7. *Thrones:* They stand before God and guard the gate of the holy of holies.

8. *Cherubim:* They stand before God and reverence his throne and keep the seals.

9. *Seraphim:* They stand before God and serve his inner chamber.[14]

A prominent influence on medieval Christian thought were the writings of Pseudo-Dionysius, a Greek biblical scholar whose works included *The Celestial Hierarchy.* He wrote extensively on Christian mysticism and his writings, which are believed to be from the 5th or 6th centuries A.D., influenced the likes of St. Augustine, St. Thomas Aquinas and Dante to name a few. He wrote:

> The upper triad is composed of SERAPHIM (love), CHERUBIM (knowledge), and THRONES, all of whom are in direct contact with God. They receive "the primal theophanies and perfections." These three levels are so close to God as to be perfect and utterly pure: "they are full of a superior light beyond any knowledge and ... are filled with a transcendent and triply luminous contemplation of the one who is the cause and the source of all beauty.[15]

What is the difference between Angels and Supreme Beings? Angels are immortal creatures who remain eternally dedicated to the will of God regardless of their realized power. By holding steady in our definition of God, we understand that God is a unique, indefinable and unapproachable force of energy, which provides reason to believe that Angels completely understand all of the mysteries of God, creation, the universe and the secrets to eternal life.

> Angels do not have material bodies, but they are definite and discrete beings; they are of spirit nature and origin.[16]

The Bible provides a significant clue regarding the degree of power, which Adam had acquired, and its relationship to higher levels of Angelic power. Here is evidence that Adam, a Supreme Being, was not nearly as enlightened as the higher Angels of the Cherubim.

> Then the LORD God said, "Behold, the man has become like one of *us* in knowing good and evil. Now, lest he reach out his hand and take also of the tree of life and eat, and live forever"—

ALPHA TO OMEGA

> therefore the LORD God sent him out from the garden of Eden to till the ground from which he was taken. He drove out the man, and at the east of the Garden of Eden he placed the cherubim and a flaming sword that turned every way to guard the way to the tree of life. (Genesis 3: 22-24)

Adam became like *them* by achieving absolute knowledge, but he is denied immortality because of his mistake.

We should note here that throughout the Bible, when it is believed that God is speaking directly to man, it appears evident that the Angels are speaking instead. God works through his highest creatures to accomplish tasks and it is the angels who speak and do God's work, because God is unapproachable by lower levels of spiritual beings and by all physical beings. We see evidence of this when God says *"...they have become like one of us..."*

The Cherubim and the flaming sword that turned every way seems to be depicting a beacon; a force-field of light that is unapproachable by Adam (notably, a similar depiction is used for the Ark of the Covenant and will be discussed later). Adam, a superior physical being, lacks the ability to approach the light of the Cherubim—one of the chiefs of Angels. In the previous discourse about God, *spirit luminosity*, which was quoted to describe the inapproachable essence of God's Spirit, is not a light as we know it.

> Light—*spirit luminosity*—is a word, symbol, a figure of speech, which connotes the personality manifestation characteristic of spirit beings of diverse orders. This luminous emanation is in no respect related either to intellectual insight or to physical light manifestations.[17]

HEART OF THE MATTER

Angels have no need to discover God because they are the Essence of God in graduated levels of "being" above Supreme Being. God works through Angels to continually disseminate Divine Will throughout the Universe. By their power and in accordance with God's Will, they battle to ensure integrity throughout the universe; are without physical limits or boundaries and can take on any form they so choose.

Marked by their ability to transcend the dimensions of space-time, these elevated beings work unceasingly to promote self-discovery within the consciousness of mortals throughout the Universe. Intervention is limited to promoting the discovery of God and truth in thinking creatures without direct control and without forthright provisions, unless in accordance with Divine Will and void of self-motivation. Angels hold firmly to the idea that Absolute Power, which is only recognizable through Absolute Knowledge, must not be utilized by personal will for temporal concerns.

Conversely, there are those angels led by Lucifer's rebellion, who choose to seize the power of God so as to establish and maintain physical worlds while propagating temporal (physical) concerns and ideals. These adversarial forces, who appear benevolent and radiant to untrained observers and can take on any physical appearance, continue to urge personal motivation as the impetus for utilizing power while shrouding the true nature of God—Absolute Knowledge—throughout the universe.

As long as human beings have a distorted view of God and truth, Lucifer and his followers are in control. All Demons possess the same power as their benevolent counterparts and will attempt

ALPHA TO OMEGA

to intercede to promote their cause. There is a real battle taking place—one long believed to be a fairy tale—as God's power, which is unmistakable in the capabilities of Angels and Demons, is continuously wielded throughout the Universe.

Demon as defined by Merriam-Webster is, *(1) a source or agent of evil, harm or ruin; (2) usually Daemon: an attendant power or spirit: GENIUS.* We mustn't confuse ourselves with notions of pitch forks and horns, because a Demon is an Angel with a different agenda. Biblical verses concerning Lucifer show that he is the epitome of the misuse of Absolute Power for deception. Yet, he deceived himself when he believed, with blinding power, that he could be like the Most High.

> How you are fallen from heaven, O Lucifer, son of the morning! *How* you are cut down to the ground, you who weakened the nations! For you have said in your heart, 'I will ascend into heaven, I will exalt my throne above the stars of God; I will also sit on the mount of the congregation on the farthest sides of the north; I will ascend above the heights of the clouds, I will be like the Most High.' (Isaiah 14: 12-14)

Lucifer's bold and deliberate attempt to assume the Power of God for what he believes will prosper throughout the universe is evident. His goal is to emerge victorious in the battle between truth and deception.

Angels and Demons operate on varying levels above Supreme Being, each deriving their power from the same unending source. After Adam made the mistake there was no reprisal. Civilization was doomed and Lucifer had gained the advantage because he exploited human nature in a Supreme Being. All inhabitants would not submit every bit of their magnificent power for a Collective Will because they were blinded by their power and believed that they were righteous. Even we would be blinded enough to envision them as gods at the time of their destruction.

Lucifer has maintained the advantage for a long time. After the flood destroyed the earth, uneducated and uninformed people are the norm in a new civilization. Death remains inevitable and evil (ignorance) has the upper hand because the secrets of knowledge are gone.

Lucifer's agenda is to ensure mankind remains on a limited physical plane; to confuse information and keep it as minimal as possible for as long as he can. Lucifer and his band of rebels will do everything to prevent the post Armageddon Paradise from becoming reality.

In contrast, the Angels cannot provide us with absolute knowledge again. What would happen if we were to gain absolute knowledge? The answer lies in the faults of our human nature and demonstrates the outcome would be similar or worse, while extending Lucifer's rule in the process. The first mistake caused the eventual cataclysm leading to a new era where ignorance is inherent. Our arrangement is completely opposite to the enlightened and previous super civilization and gives a seemingly unfair advantage to Lucifer, who revels upon our incomplete knowledge of God and Truth.

Further evidence, which adds credence to the roles played by angels and demons, are exposed upon closer inspection of Adam and Eve's temptation.

ALPHA TO OMEGA

> And out of the ground made the LORD God to grow every tree that is pleasant to the sight and good for food, the tree of life also in the midst of the garden, and the tree of knowledge of good and evil (Genesis 2: 9).

> And the Lord God commanded the man, saying, 'You may freely eat of every tree of the garden; but of the tree of knowledge of good and evil you shall not eat, for in the day that you eat of it you shall die.' (Genesis 2:16)

We have demonstrated how God works through Angels, so we can understand they provided the instructions to Adam and Eve to provide awareness, curiosity and free-will.

By invoking free will Adam needed to realize that only through choice can man assent his will to God's. They could have chosen to become like an Angel and have eternal life, but the temptation of unlimited power in the flesh was too much to overcome, which is why the Angels will not provide mankind with absolute knowledge again.

> But the serpent said to the woman, 'You will not die. God knows that when you eat of it your eyes will be opened, and you will be like God, knowing good and evil.' (Genesis 3:4-5)

Here, the work of the adversary succeeds in his bid to convince Eve to consider the power that absolute knowledge would offer. There is also a subtle hint here. Why would Eve trust the serpent? The serpent is a metaphor for the deceiver. Lucifer is an Angel appearing to be as benevolent as those who instructed them otherwise. He is an Angel with a different motive and will do whatever is necessary to deceive. After Lucifer was able to convince a Supreme Being to falter, the world was his domain. The desire for

80

HEART OF THE MATTER

unlimited power in the flesh is the root cause of their ill-fortunes and the essential scope of evil's promotions.

It's worth mentioning the possibility that God's highest Angels worked deliberately to create a magnificent world of Supreme Beings and purposely present them with a choice. It also seems possible for God's Angels and Lucifer's rebel followers to have participated equally in initiating the causality to, not only a super-human race destined for obliteration, but to everything that has come afterwards. Are we to assume that this was a test or common practice on the inhabitable worlds of the universe?

> In Zoroastrianism, the amarahspands are six "bounteous immor-tals" or "holy immortal ones" created by the good god Ohrmazd for the purpose of assisting him with their creativity and organiz-ing ability. The amarahspands are similar to Archangels and or-ganize the material world. Each is responsible for a sphere of the world, and each embodies a virtue or quality.[18]

Given that we present Angels to be God's essence, in varying degrees, and the vehicles through which God works, we can safely suggest that it really doesn't matter. God is the source of all power and only our conscious choice determines the final outcome. If indeed the Angels create the actual circumstances, then the situa-tions and conclusions have the potential to be different on every inhabitable planet.

If all scenarios begin with Supreme Beings having an equitable choice, as has been demonstrated so far, then everything is fair in causality, the nature of God, truth and deception. The process yields innumerable souls, each with the intrinsic essence of God and the potential to reach the highest levels of spiritual being.

This is why we should consider the fact that our perceptions of aliens with the intent to harm or destroy us is actually born by our menial fears and the mirroring of our limited human nature upon those beings who exist far above the extremely limited realm of our physical world and mental precepts. Obviously, if they wanted to harm us they could have done so without reprise.

Even Lucifer's band of adversaries is light years ahead of our imagination, let alone our reality. Angels and demons don't want our food, our resources or anything in our physical world. They have far surpassed our limited physical world. They are vying for our souls.

Opposing forces, each with an extremely high level of intelligence and power, are battling each other for either the enlightenment or deception of our eternal souls. Lucifer's reign will end when Paradise is restored, which obviously makes the fight to prevent it a reality. The end of the soul's voyage is either the light of Truth or the darkness of ignorance. Although it may seem to be a long process for the human journey, it is trivial to the timeless Angels, who patiently endure the process of a soul's journey home. Demonstrating the story of Noah from this perspective may help to clarify these ideas.

Chapter 3

Bridge over Troubled Waters

Mysteries are the evidence to errors in our religious and historical precepts.

Supreme Mandate

Many of us, who believe in a great flood, have subscribed to the story of Noah because its presentation leads us to believe that it was the only way to preserve mankind and all species of creation. However, we have established that the power of God's will creates the avenues and the vehicles for the expression of Divine Will over time, which can be seen as both creation and evolution.

Even the cataclysm that caused the extinction of the dinosaurs 65 million years ago was not enough to prevent remaining species from evolving into the human inhabitants in the society of Atlantis. I suspect that any cataclysm would be followed by a slow regeneration of life spawned by the remaining organisms of a life-bearing civilization without any intervention from the Angels at all. The question we should be asking ourselves is why would eight humans of a great society on the verge of extinction be concerned with surviving the great destruction?

Religious ideologies have instilled perceptions, which fail to adequately challenge science or equally provide a strong foothold for spiritual growth and understanding. The fundamental notion that Noah was willing to save himself and his family while becoming the lone survivors in a destroyed world makes no sense without extremely vital reasons to substantiate their efforts.

Biblical references do not indicate an order from God, but rather an amiable gesture to save Noah's family, while all else perishes. How would they benefit from such an enormous undertaking? Would any of us be willing to live alone after the *complete* annihilation of our world? If we are to accept the story of Noah, then it is imperative to provide meaningful concepts, which will validate the ancient references, regarded by many to be mere dogma, and help to shed light on the human experience.

Many of us have an inclination to believe that we are comprised only of ego and soul (often referring to soul and spirit as a single entity), but closer observation clearly reveals Spirit as a third distinctive entity. The Spirit is a tiny drop of God's Essence with the same magnificent properties as the whole. As it is in Spirit so it is in God and the hierarchy of Angels. Spirit is the life-giving power and exists within every physical life form in the Universe and is the essence of Angelic life forms. Imagine it as the infinitesimal furnace of unlimited power as discussed in the previous chapter.

BRIDGE OVER TROUBLED WATERS

Supreme Being is the complete reflection of God in physical form—a complete or Whole Soul radiating its luminosity or complete reflection of Spirit from within. Soul, which arrives with awareness and Spirit are united as one. In the case of Adam, initial awareness was complete with absolute knowledge so both Spirit and Soul were united and whole. Anything shy of perfection causes physical death to become inevitable and the whole soul is reduced to a less enlightened eternal soul—a separate entity from the complete and perfect Spirit.

As Adam and other human beings fall from perfection, the essence of God becomes a lesser reflection (spiritual illumination) in each unique soul of creatures at graduated levels below Supreme Being. Just as there are levels of Angelic beings above Supreme Being, there is a hierarchy of eternal souls below Supreme Being determined by the degree of illumination within them.

A soul cannot die, because it is born of both consciousness and Spirit. Spirit cannot be destroyed, because it creates. It becomes personalized by individual experiences and limited understanding in our soul. Only through this personalization does soul have the potential to become whole through complete Spiritual discovery or All Truth. The individual and unique expression of awareness in our soul, no matter how limited, will continue to live for eternity because Spirit is eternal.

We have exhibited that Supreme Being, although beneath the realm of the angel hierarchy, is the highest rung on the ladder of physical hierarchy. Yet, the two indelible and unique facets of human beings, which separate us from all the other animals and

ALPHA TO OMEGA

provide us with a vehicle for rising to new heights, are the ego and the soul.

Adam wouldn't have had a choice without self-awareness but he wouldn't have acquired self-awareness if not having been given a choice to begin with. What does this tell us? It reveals that ego or self-awareness is explicit and patent in the nature of all humans even as a Supreme Being. The ego is indispensable for gathering knowledge, making choices, and remains an integral part of every individual. Without self-awareness man cannot release his will to Divine Will.

Importantly, we see it was Adam's ego he couldn't overcome and the reason for the mistake. Taking from the tree of knowledge of good and evil represents complete self-awareness and the associated awareness of power. He may have said something like, "Look at the power we possess and the things we can do." This can be seen as the birth of a super-ego—one much larger than we can grasp from our current perspective.

Obviously, a proper choice would have begun the upward climb on the ladder of spiritual hierarchy. Instead they "fell" and were reduced to superior mortal creatures with an eternal soul, which is the second unique feature of physical human beings. Importantly, their souls were no longer whole or complete.

The souls of Adam's era were markedly more spiritually illuminated than any today because of the Absolute Knowledge to which they had been granted. There was not a single misconception at the outset. The degree of spiritual luminosity in the fallen beings would undoubtedly be awe inspiring in the eyes of the unenlightened souls

BRIDGE OVER TROUBLED WATERS

of our era. The difference is that we must ascend from the pits of darkness to more spiritual enlightenment while they were denied another chance at immortality after the fall.

It's important to recognize and understand the various levels of spiritual existence. Many philosophers, saints and sages have professed that the soul's illumination is the road to home, which can only be traversed by reason and intuition—something that relies on our ego's curiosity and the wisdom of the soul, which is bred from our inborn Spirit.

> The soul is raised from the body to the contemplation of itself, then to reason, and finally to the light which illuminates it—God Himself. –St. Augustine [1]

Adam's mistake was irreparable and, although mankind had maintained superlative abilities, their chance at immortality and the ascension in spirituality was lost. Angels were powerless because there was nothing they could do to change the consequences. Lucifer had succeeded in bringing almost limitless power to mortal humans and there was not a chance 100% of the people would relinquish their power for collective will. Therefore, Paradise was no longer possible as long as civilization thrived. The souls of Atlantis were losing illumination rather than gaining spiritual enlightenment.

Within the guidelines presented thus far, we must achieve the level of Paradise before elevating to higher realms of Angelic beings. If the highest level of Angels is unapproachable by Supreme Being, then the residence of Angels and God (heaven) must be notably higher than Paradise. Biblical scripture describes the 1000

ALPHA TO OMEGA

year post-Armageddon kingdom as a temporary realm and precursor to the *'real heaven'* and proves that Paradise on earth is not the end-all in spiritual progress.

> Now I saw a new heaven and a new earth, for the first heaven and the first earth had passed away. Also there was no more sea. Then I, John, saw the holy city, New Jerusalem, coming down out of heaven from God, prepared as a bride adorned for her husband. And I heard a loud voice from heaven saying, "Behold, the tabernacle of God *is* with men, and He will dwell with them, and they shall be His people. God Himself will be with them *and be* their God. And God will wipe away every tear from their eyes; there shall be no more death, nor sorrow, nor crying. There shall be no more pain, for the former things have passed away." (Revelation 21: 1-4)

Although we might tend to envisage Paradise on earth as a final achievement, it's just the beginning of a soul's progress, especially for those afforded Supreme Being status to begin with. Adam failed in the responsibility required of the knowledge he was given, ensuring his death and those of his entire civilization.

Noah unequivocally knew a return to Paradise on Earth was a requirement before the progression of any soul from their era—including his own. For them, Heaven (the highest level of spiritual achievement) wasn't a remote possibility after death, nor was the ability to ascend to the first level of Angelic beings.

To better explain heaven and hell, we must realize that every individual from Atlantis understood each of them with the utmost clarity and distinction. Our limited vantage point yields obscure concepts for both, but to those with Absolute Knowledge, it's quite a different story.

A complete understanding of heaven would expose, with equal clarity, another opposing and limited realm. If power in the flesh seems too provocative to overcome, then where is the power when the flesh is gone? The limits are revealed when the flesh is gone and the light of the once unapproachable God exposes the prison of limited illumination or darkness.

Noah was beginning to realize that a revisit to Paradise was highly improbable as the years progressed. The society had plunged from the heights of Supreme Being to demigods over time, which was a large and noticeable step from their perspective. Noah and the people of his time remained quite powerful, regardless of their inherited transgressions, and knew that civilization was on the brink of annihilation.

Seemingly endless torment would be unavoidable for the perished souls, who would be confined to a comparatively limited realm until Paradise could be restored. Noah understood very well that the ultimate destiny of their souls hinged upon his aptitude to promote conditions for a return to Paradise in a world that would begin to appear millions of years later.

Knowing the future generation would begin without any knowledge was more challenging. Additionally, the new generation would be without notions or concepts of God to begin with, which meant that they would have to be taught everything in some way. God's Angels would sever communications and intervention until long after Noah and his descendants had completed their mission to the best of their abilities.

The explicit reason for Noah's directive was his awareness that the souls of the doomed inhabitants of the great society would remain tortured in the limited dimension of souls for as long as it would take for Paradise on earth to be restored. There was a good possibility it would take much longer without his intervention.

To the wise and powerful souls, a frightening awareness emerged that a dreary and seemingly endless eon confronted them. The eternal souls of the doomed world would watch from a confining dimension, with no ability to intervene, as the ignorant creatures of the future world would torment their unjust souls for a long time. For this reason alone Noah's almost impossible task is justified and substantiated.

A true test of wisdom and superiority in the face of imminent extinction was the decree. Many united in a common effort to accomplish the goal of spawning and educating a future generation—one that would be enhanced by the wisdom and technology of a doomed empire of demigods. Noah had to ensure his entire family could make the journey into the future and enhance human progress to enable a quickened return to Paradise on earth. Without another Paradise, the souls of a long forgotten society would forever suffer the pain of looking through the glass at heaven's door and witnessing the splendor and magnificence of which they could never take part.

Noah's mission was the scientific and humanistic influence, consistent within the guidelines of perfection in scientific technology and with the direction of God's Angels. Superlative intellect and the knowledge of God would be manifest in Noah's ark—the *arc,* like a bridge or a rainbow, connecting two points in time and two completely different civilizations.

The ark would remain untouched for millions of years—an ageless time capsule standing as a beacon and serving as the catalyst for life's quick regeneration in a new epoch. Noah and his family, suspended in time, were about to embark on a journey that was much more than anyone in our era could ever imagine. A further detailed discussion about Noah's Ark resumes later in this chapter.

If we honestly believe in the story of the flood, for no reason other than the numerous myths of diverse cultures and regions of the world today, then we must reconsider the chronology of current history. If we truly believe in a markedly advanced civilization, then we must consider the supreme abilities of those who preceded us.

The Great Pyramid

The first glaring conflict to startle my attention occurred in the late 1970's when my curiosity led me to information regarding the Great Pyramid. At that time most people, including me, were oblivious to the newer discoveries and the implications presented by the evidence surrounding it. Even today, it is laughable that the majority of people aren't aware of the facts, which researchers of the Great Pyramid have uncovered.

New discoveries should be presented in classrooms throughout the world so students can begin with a clearer understanding of the mysteries surrounding it. Perhaps this information may aide in stimulating young minds towards new exploration. Once we learn

ALPHA TO OMEGA

the facts about it, we find it impossible to accept the intimidating claims that a civilization—one step removed from the Stone Age— built this magnificent edifice. Institutions bent on preserving their authority continually push their obsolete concepts onto the uninformed populace.

The Great Pyramid of Egypt is one of mankind's most problematical mysteries and remains the most complex of all pyramids throughout the world by any standard. Situated on the Giza plateau with two inferior pyramids, it is often confused with the less appealing center pyramid of Khafre, but can easily be recognized as the one to the right with a flat top because of a missing capstone.

The conflict surrounding the Great Pyramid today stems from the mountains of evidence uncovered over a century, which exposes the orthodox belief (espoused by Egyptologists claiming it to be a magnificent tomb for an egomaniacal Pharaoh named Khufu) as an outdated rendition of the historical presumptions of Egypt's earliest historians. According to these early experts, the Egyptians built this Pyramid, during Khufu's (Cheops) 23-year reign, which ended in 2366 BC.

Three distinctive elements of the pyramid need to be considered to effectively evaluate its magnificent construction and why it is the center of controversy. First, we must consider its size, weight, and positioning. Secondly, the unmatched degree of accuracy in its construction, compared not only to other pyramids, but to every single building in the world today. The final element is the astonishing mathematical correlations designed in its construction depicting knowledge of the Earth's exact solar year, distance from the sun, radius, distance from the moon and the Pi factor—all of which clearly supersede any of the knowledge of that time.

To address the first consideration, the core masonry of the Great Pyramid is made up of over 2.3 million blocks of limestone. The smallest of these blocks weighs nearly 3 tons with many exceeding 30 tons. Inside the pyramid and over 200 feet above the ground there are over one hundred fine red granite blocks weighing more than 75 tons each—that's more than a railroad locomotive. Each of the four sides of the pyramid is over 755 feet long, which is more than 2 ½ football fields. It's easier to envision its great mass by comparing it to a cruise ship, which would be somewhat similar in length to one of its four sides although not as tall.

When looking at the Great Pyramid today, we see only the core masonry because most of the luxurious casing stones have been removed. The 144,000 casing stones, which were made of finely polished white Tura limestone, measured an average of 5 feet by 8 feet by 6 feet and weighed 15 tons. These stones gave the pyramid a seamless appearance and reflected light from the sun and the moon as did no other object ever built by man.

All told, the Great Pyramid weighed in excess of 6.3 million tons across its square 13¼ acre base. Each of its four triangular sides comprise an area of nearly 5½ acres and slopes upward to a finished height of over 480 feet.[2] Putting all of this in perspective, the Great Pyramid weighed more than eight times the combined weight of the defunct World Trade Center towers and was taller than any building in New Jersey until 2004. Thirty Empire State Buildings could be built with the estimated 2,300,000 stones. A wall

ALPHA TO OMEGA

three-foot high and one-foot thick could be built across the United States and back using the amount of masonry contained in the Great Pyramid.[3]

If the Egyptians built the pyramid, as suggested by scientific conjecture (not evidence) during the 23-year reign of Cheops, it would have taken more than 19 blocks per hour to be set into place in a workday of 14 hours per day, seven days per week for 23 years. That is one block every three minutes, which wasn't enough time to rig one to a crane's lifting assembly—an unknown piece of equipment at the time. Using today's technology, modern stonecutters have estimated that it would take at least twenty-seven years just to quarry and deliver the stone.[4]

If that isn't enough to incite readers, let's discuss precision and tolerances that distinctly set the Great Pyramid apart from any other building in the world today. Each side of the Great Pyramid is oriented almost perfectly to the four cardinal points of the compass. In comparison, the Greenwich Observatory in London, which was built with the sole intent to be oriented exactly to true North with modern engineering and surveying, is three-fifteenths of a degree shy of its mark.

Constructing a 4-sided building with intent to orient each side to all four cardinal points is exponentially more difficult. The Great Pyramid misses its marks by an average of one-twentieth of a degree, with the south face shy by only one-thirtieth of a degree—incredible accuracy for any building in any epoch, and an inexplicable almost supernatural feat in Egypt 4500 years ago.[5] It is believed by researchers that this masterpiece was in all probability,

BRIDGE OVER TROUBLED WATERS

perfectly aligned and that changes in the Earth since then have caused the minute degree of deviation found in today's measurements.

The base of this 6.3 million ton architectural marvel is level to within less than an inch across its 13 ¼ acre base today, which is .001 inch per foot—an unprecedented level of accuracy not demanded or expected in building standards today. Are we to assume that Egyptians arbitrarily picked a spot that could support this enormous and multi-million ton building? Could they have designed and constructed it with amazing accuracy and without the help of modern engineering and surveying tools?

It just so happens that the Great Pyramid sits atop one of the largest underground mountains of bedrock in the world and is situated at the precise center of the Earth's land mass. The east-west parallel that crosses the most land and north-south meridian that crosses the most land intersect at the Great Pyramid. The north face of the pyramid is completely lit without shadow, for one hour only—on the day of the summer solstice.[6]

William Flinders Petrie, a well renowned 19th century Egyptologist, measured the outer casing blocks in 1882.

> Petrie's close examination of the casing stones revealed variations that were so minute that they were barely discernible to the naked eye. The records show that the outer casing blocks were square and flat, with a mean variation of .01 inch over an area of thirty-five square feet. Fitted together, the blocks maintained a gap of 0 to .02 inch, which can be compared with the thickness of a fingernail. Inside the gap was cement that bonded the limestone so firmly that the strength of the joint was greater than the lime-

95

ALPHA TO OMEGA

stone itself. The composition of this cement has been a mystery for years.[7]

To manufacture just two blocks with a tolerance of .01 inch and place them together with a gap not exceeding .02 inch is a remarkable feat. The pyramid's original construction consisted of 144,000 blocks—some weighing over a hundred tons—fashioned with the same exquisite precision and can be observed in the remaining stones along the base of the pyramid. Some sources claim that the adhesive has been analyzed but cannot be replicated.

Interior components of the structure manifest equally spectacular engineering wonders. The descending passage is within .25 inch of being perfectly straight over its 350 foot corridor, which terminates almost 100 feet beneath the bedrock at the entrance to the subterranean chamber. Understand that carving a tunnel into dense bedrock (strong enough to maintain level to the heaviest building in the world for thousands of years), with such great precision is mind boggling. In its first 150 feet, the descending passage is within .02 inches from being perfectly straight and begs us to ask why such perfection was required when greater deviations would not be noticeable with the naked eye.

The Grand Gallery, which rises upward for 153 feet at a constant slope of 26 degrees with a vaulted ceiling of 28 feet, was structurally built to withstand more than 70% of the pyramid's weight. It was constructed with huge, smoothly polished blocks carved into sloping parallelograms and laid together so closely and with such rigorous precision that the joints were almost invisible to the naked eye.[8]

BRIDGE OVER TROUBLED WATERS

The inner chambers and walls of the pyramid are not measurably inaccurate when observed using today's modern methods of surveying. The builders did not cut passageways into the pyramid, but instead built the passageways within the exquisite masonry. Can you imagine trying to determine how each block would have to be dressed in order to fit together perfectly to form long passageways within tolerances of .02?

> The bald fact is that the Great Pyramid—by any standard old or new—is the largest and most accurately constructed building in the world.[9]

Another long-standing discovery about the Great Pyramid is the significant mathematical relationships to the Earth. This knowledge was first presented by John Taylor in the mid-19th century. His discoveries have not been challenged, but instead expounded upon by every researcher who painstakingly took the time to measure the pyramid's components and note the impeccable correlations.

Taylor basically proved the pyramid builders understood the number pi (π) and incorporated it into the construction of the pyramid. Pi is a constant number with infinitely repeating decimals that express the ratio of a circle's circumference to its diameter and radius.

He suggested that perhaps the Great Pyramid was intended to be a representation of the spherical Earth, the height corresponding to the radius joining the center of the Earth to the North Pole and the perimeter corresponding to the Earth's circumference at the Equator. In other words, he proved that the pyramid's height relates to its perimeter in the same ratio that a circle relates to its radius

ALPHA TO OMEGA

(inasmuch as you can square a circle mathematically) and that a constant scale ratio of its measurements to many of the earth's measurements exists.

In order for the mathematics to apply, the angled slope of each side of the pyramid had to be precisely 51° 51' 14" to achieve the proper height and maintain the pi ratio. Measurements of the Great Pyramid reveal an impressive accuracy to within one-fifteenth of a degree making it highly likely that it was perfect at one time yet still close enough to maintain the ratio within a tolerance of .04%. This observation widely promoted Taylor's idea and rendered the theory of coincidence mathematically improbable.

To make this a little clearer, building a perfect pyramid, in which all sides culminate precisely at the apex, requires that it must be predesigned and exquisitely carried out during construction. If one block is off by the smallest amount, the structure's accuracy would denigrate with each course of masonry. To complicate this problem, builders who wanted to express the pi ratio in the final construction would have to predetermine the ratio of the height to the perimeter and therefore the angle of the slope.

The Egyptians had no concept of geometry or pi during the purported time of construction and could not, in mathematical probability, have accidentally designed it with such precision yet alone build it with such accuracy. Each course of masonry had to be finely cut and dressed within an optician's tolerance and set with an equal degree of precision. Any trace of deviation and the pyramid could not reflect the mathematical certainties exposed by measurement today.

Taylor was able to define a pyramid inch as 1.0011 British inches. The value was derived as a constant that expressed the scale ratio of the pyramid's measurements relative to earth's measurements. Before we discuss those measurements, it's important to understand that units of measurement today are defined as fractions of the distance from the equator to the North Pole. Today's value of 1.00106 British inches is calculated as 1/500,000,000 of the polar diameter which is the distance from the North Pole to the South Pole in the center of the earth. The meter is a measurement determined as one ten millionth of the same distance.[10] In order to derive these measurements, instruments had to be developed to precisely measure the earth's sphere, which were surely not available during the reign of Khufu. In fact, modern earth measurements weren't defined perfectly until the 20th century.

> In the case of the Great Pyramid is represented, the year-circle has a circumference of 36,524 pyramid inches or the exact number of days in a century. Taking that circumference and designing a square base with a perimeter equal to that number of pyramid inches, we come up with a base square of the Great Pyramid. If we make the vertical height of the pyramid equal to the radius of the same year-circle we obtain the exact height of the Great Pyramid of 5,813 pyramid inches (extrapolated to include a missing apex) or 481.4 feet. Using the year circle as a basis, we find the base sides of the pyramid will be one fourth or 9,131 pyramid inches, which converts to 755 feet, 9 ½ inches, or roughly 755.7 feet. Despite the ravages of time, the great pyramid's measurements are within a few inches of perfect with the west side spot on.[11]

ALPHA TO OMEGA

In simpler terms, the height of the Great pyramid expresses the same relationship to its base perimeter as the radius does to the circumference of a circle (Circumference = 2πR: 2π X 481.4 = 3023 feet: the exact perimeter of the Great Pyramid). Is that mere coincidence? No, it reveals that the pyramid inch almost identically matches today's true inch when expressed as a fraction of a distance in the measurement of earth's sphere.

It's worth mentioning that Egypt's calendar during the Old Kingdom (2649-2150 BC) was composed of 360 days having 12 months of 30 days and had recently been changed from a lunar calendar of 354 days. It appears that while Egypt was trying to determine the number of days in a year they constructed a pyramid demonstrating knowledge of precise solar year measurements. For this reason alone, it is hardly acceptable or possible that they were the designers and crafters of the Great Pyramid.

The pyramid embodies the constant scale ratio of 1: 43,200. The height of 481 feet multiplied times 43,200 equates to 3935 miles which is the polar radius of the earth within 15 miles. The perimeter of the pyramid is 3023 feet and that equates to 24,735 miles, which is within 200 miles of the equatorial circumference of the earth. These examples prove that the builders knew precise measurements that were unknown at the time of its alleged construction.

We could utilize numerous pages presenting the formulas using pyramid dimensions that will demonstrate the builders' knowledge of the sidereal year, a tropical year, the earth's distance from the sun, the radius of the Sun, and earth's distance from the moon.

These and many other mathematical certainties have been proven and demonstrate an indisputable and precise relationship between the pyramid and the earth, which is unmatched by any building in the world today.

We would find it to be an extremely difficult, if not impossible, task to duplicate it using today's modern technology. Egyptian knowledge and capabilities were clearly insufficient to construct such an engineering marvel.

The phenomenon of the precession of the equinox has become a bit more recognized in the mainstream because of increased interest popularized by the Mayan calendar and attempts to decipher its meaning. Basically, precession is the result of the earth's wobble as it spins, much like a top or gyroscope as it begins to slow down. If we were to imagine the earth's axis of rotation as a line extending from the North Pole, the line makes a complete 360 degree wobble over the course of almost 26,000 years. It is observed by the suns position within the signs of the zodiac at dawn on the vernal equinox.

It takes about 2,160 years for the sun to move from one zodiac sign to the next with each sign marking the beginning of a new age and the end of an old one (the Age of Aquarius is soon to replace the age of Pisces—the symbol of the fish—heralded by Jesus Christ, who has often been symbolized by the fish). The reason this is so important is because the movement is barely detectable by even the most dedicated star-gazers. It takes 72 years for just one degree of the sun's recession in the sky and would require careful observation and precise measurements over a lifetime to notice.

ALPHA TO OMEGA

Remarkably, the sum of the diagonals of the Great Pyramid's base is 25,826 pyramid inches, which is the precise measurement of the complete precession of the equinox (the rate of precession isn't uniform and varies slightly from 25,920).[12]

Another amazing feature of the Great Pyramid is the concavity of the core structure on each side. It is hardly noticeable from the ground and under precise lighting conditions only. Likewise, it is visible from the air with more distinction but the light needs to be at proper angles as well. With adequate viewing conditions it appears that each side is bisected by a line created by the slight concavity making it appear as an 8-sided structure. It was measured in 1883 by Petrie who reported that he observed constant dips of ½ to 1 degree. Today it has been measured accurately with lasers and the measurement of the arc of the radius is equal to the arc of the radius of the earth.

Still, Egyptologists firmly claim all pyramids including the Great Pyramid to be nothing more than tombs for Egyptian Pharaohs. Solid arguments to the contrary, which present these and other marvels of the Great Pyramid and undeniably reveal that the builders knew much more about the earth than any Egyptian 4500 years ago, is rejected by Egyptian authority.

And, although we could note many more details, which are beyond the scope of this book, there are still three more important facts. First and foremost is that no bodies or mummies were ever found inside any pyramid.

Those beliefs are only inferences that are reinforced by inaccurate documentaries that link the pyramids closely with the Valley of the Kings, where there are no pyramids, but where the mummies were actually found. Of all excavations, not one pyramid contained an original burial.[13]

Secondly, an impossible feat would have had to be performed by the guardians of the Great Pyramid after a funeral procession would have departed, in order to satisfy the tomb theory.

> Jammed within the lower part of the Ascending Passage are three huge blocks of granite that block the passageway that leads to the supposed burial chamber. Egyptologists propose that the blocks were originally stored in the Grand Gallery, held in position by wooden pegs inserted into slots, and then released to slide down the Ascending Passage and into position after the funeral procession had exited the pyramid. Yet architects and engineers claim that this would have been impossible and that these blocks had to have been installed as the pyramid was being built. In order for these blocks to slide down the passage, there would had to have been a half inch or more of clearance between the blocks and the passageway, whose surfaces would had to have been as smooth as glass to overcome friction. The fact is that these blocks fit into the passage without any clearance on the sides; and the limestone walls, which may or may not have been smooth, would more than likely have been scoured by the harder granite as it pushed past...

> Such objectivity, in light of all the preceding arguments, can lead us to only one likely conclusion: There is precious little evidence to support the traditional tomb theory.[14]

Another important clue is Egyptologists long insistence that ramps of one kind or another had been used during the construction of these megaliths. Professor I.E.S Edwards (July 1909-September 1996), a former keeper of Egyptian antiquities at the

ALPHA TO OMEGA

British Museum and John Baines, professor of Egyptology at Oxford University concurred that ramps composed of brick and earth maintaining a 10% gradient sloped upwards from the level of the ground to whatever height was desired.[15]

To construct a ramp that is almost a mile long with strength enough to withstand the varying weight of blocks implies that it would be wide enough to allow hundreds of workers to push and pull it along—before the wheel was invented. It also suggests that at any point along the ramp a 15-ton block (average) could easily be put into perfect position by manpower and wooden levers alone. To accept inferences suggesting such primitive means were used to produce such a perfectly engineered masterpiece is ridiculously naïve. To continually publicize such nonsense is a bigger mystery than the pyramid itself.

Can you imagine how much material would have to be used in the construction of the ramp itself? Each time you extended the ramp to lift another block, it would be necessary to provide hundreds of blocks to support the extension of the ramp. Enormous amounts of material would eventually surpass what was needed to construct the pyramid. Notwithstanding the ramps, we are asked to believe that all of the rock was quarried, transported 20 to 500 miles, dressed with precision and pushed up a ramp before the wheel was invented.

> It now remains for those who are absolutely convinced that the ancient Egyptians constructed the pyramids using primitive techniques to build a pyramid themselves, using those same techniques that they propose the Egyptians used. As part of such an

attempt, it would help if they cut out just one seventy-ton block of granite from the Aswan quarry, which is located five hundred miles away, using their hardened copper chisels or dolerite balls and then transported the block to the Giza Plateau with their barges, ropes, and manpower. If the proponents of traditional theories of constructing the pyramids are able to accomplish this feat, then we should give serious consideration to their proposals about pyramid construction.[16]

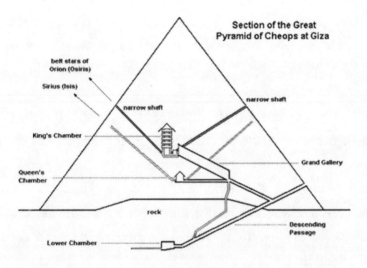

Figure 2

Another spectacular wonder is how the first 30 feet of core masonry was not constructed on flat ground. Looking at Figure 2, we notice the large supporting outcrop of bedrock (it is not depicted with precise measurements). This outcrop of rock stands 30 feet high in some areas at the center of the foundation. It is a small natural hill of bedrock located in the center, irregular in shape and accounting for 70% of the 13 ¼ acre area of the foundation. This

ALPHA TO OMEGA

obstacle would require each of the blocks to be perfectly dressed to match the irregular shape of the bedrock in order to remain positioned with such accuracy.

Observe the precise geometric lines in its construction as these are the exact configuration diagrams of the Great Pyramid. Each passage and shaft is built to hundredths of an inch precision within the core masonry and not tunneled. Only the underground portion of the 350 ft. descending passage was a rectangular tunnel cut into the hardest bedrock on the planet with incredible accuracy. It appears quite evident the builders knew exactly what they were doing, including locating a spot for construction? Does this look like a tomb?

And by the way, those shafts built into the pyramid line up precisely with the stars of Orion and Sirius during certain epochs of time, which is beyond the scope of this book. Do you suppose the alignments were also a coincidence? Maybe we should ask ourselves to consider whether or not the Great Pyramid was built to stabilize the earth's gyrations after an actual shift in the earth's physical orientation.

Figure 3 is a depiction of a spectacular discovery made by Gary Osborn in the last decade. He illustrates how both the ecliptic and polar axis of the earth bisect the exact center of the King's Chamber when superimposed on the earth and using the apex for marking its true location. This could not have been possible if the chamber had been located directly beneath the apex, which means that the King's Chamber is representative of the exact center of the earth's core, and was pre-designed. The earth is depicted exactly as it really is:

BRIDGE OVER TROUBLED WATERS

an oblong sphere that bulges at the equator because of centrifugal force. More information on this topic and Gary's research can be found at: *www.freewebs.com/garyosborn/greatpyramidandaxis.htm.*

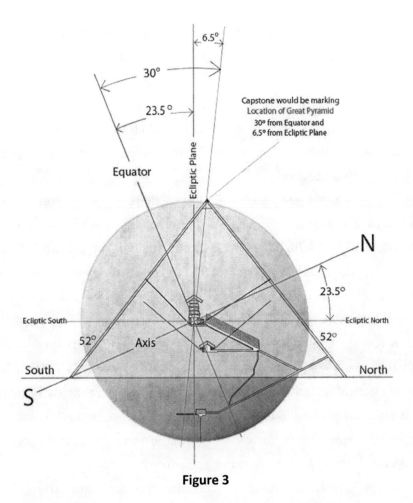

Figure 3

Many people may have seen documentaries on television where attempts to build a grossly reduced scale model of the pyramid was presented. Understand that the precision of stone cutting, orientation,

ALPHA TO OMEGA

quarrying, transportation and other logistics weren't considered or shown on any of those specials.

In Nova's presentation *This Old Pyramid* of the late 1990's (it's viewable online), a mockery is made of the process as well as the general public's limited knowledge and inherent complacency. I remember being infuriated the first time I watched it.

Trying to understand why Nova would create and air such a biased documentary was never clear to me, but I'm sure the financers of the project had a viable interest. How many people will continue to believe the authoritative tomb theory even after reading this discourse?

In case there are those who insist there must be something wrong with these facts and the Egyptians must have had some kind of knowledge to which we have yet to be made privy, it is important to remember written information had reached the early stages then. It would have been more possible than not to record and maintain some kind of primitive records for future generations—especially if they had the ability to build something with an optician's precision. Instead, we see every pyramid since the Great Pyramid was markedly inferior in design and workmanship—including the two others on the Giza plateau. Such a monumental construction effort would require ample written forms of information to coordinate workers' tasks and would have been retained for the next project.

There are many theories explaining why and how the Great Pyramid was built. Some of the theories may seem bizarre, but with the evidence uncovered in the last hundred years or so, many of them are not as preposterous as the publicized and widely held

BRIDGE OVER TROUBLED WATERS

assumption. Until a major breakthrough can garner enough support from the majority of people, the popular presumption is winner by default. Even though supporting evidence is weak and strong evidence is to the contrary, textbooks will not change without either the undeniable proof of a new theory or enough public opposition to demand that our academia and media publicize the truths with as much fervor as they have hidden and tainted it.

Noah's Arc

Certainly one of the most widely accepted dogma of modern religion is the story of Noah's ark. Some claim to have sighted a huge ship concealed in the deeply frozen tundra high upon a mountain in Turkey. It's purportedly the ship believed to have carried eight pairs of every living species of mammals, reptiles, amphibians and any other creature of a civilization whose imminent destiny was cataclysmic destruction. The animals would remain on the ship for a full year until the flooding waters had receded and work could begin to replenish a new world aided by the eight human survivors on the ship.

Do you know how many mammal species exist on earth today? How about reptiles, amphibians or insects? According to Mammals and Species of the World's most recent list, which doesn't include thousands of extinct species or those yet to be discovered, there are 4629 species of mammals alone. If we multiply that by 16 we get 74,064—and that's just mammals. If there really is a ship on Mt. Ararat, don't you think we would have unearthed it by now?

ALPHA TO OMEGA

Challenging the notion of a massive ship, complete with eight pairs of every species on Earth should offer no resistance, but deeply seeded concepts are often hard to change. Today's modern aircraft carriers provide room and sustenance for 5,500 people. Even then, the ship's capacity is limited to carrying a three month food supply before having to replenish the stock. Sixteen elephants consume more food than 1000 people do in one day.

This isn't an attempt to dispute the story of Noah's Ark, but rather to redefine it. The story survived for a very important reason but we need to evaluate it so it makes sense in light of our God of Truth and Power.

There are only two options: one is to accept that a catastrophic deluge destroyed a civilization and the other is to deny that it happened. If only for the many similar worldwide myths and legendary tales of an epic cataclysm depicting a handful of survivors who repopulated the Earth—many of which emerged without religious influence—we should be inclined to believe in the concept alone.

Perhaps the standing assumption depicting a huge ship, used to insure survival of the animals and humans of a doomed civilization is creating the confusion. The prevailing notions result from consistent religious and historical impressions upon our individual thinking—beginning at our earliest age.

The current paradigm instills the notion that there is no major separation in time between the two civilizations. This causes a conflict with science because there is no evidence supporting an eradication of all life anytime in recent history. If complete destruction actually

110

occurred, as is intimated in every legend, then there would have to be enough time to repopulate the earth with animals and humans, which according to science has taken well over 4 million years.

Why would a doomed civilization make the effort to save only eight humans and hundreds of thousands of animals? Don't you think there might be some humans trying to get aboard that ship? We must try to retrain thought processes linked to obsolete and baseless models, which tend to allow the collective subconscious to harbor concepts deterring change and progress. To me it seems apparent these modes of thought are the Achilles' heel of human progress, at which Lucifer constantly gnaws to maintain his control.

Our earliest impressions are born of the widespread notions that fence us into the limits defined by our presumed realities, some of which are derived by the many unsupported pronouncements of historical, archeological and religious authorities. The plausibility of building a ship to withstand the violent forces of nature sizeable enough to destroy a complete world is an error of the existing model. These same archetypes prevent us from envisioning Noah's society as a spectacular place even on the day of its doom and from considering a difference in their physical appearance or the millions of years between us.

Perhaps we should envisage Noah's Ark as a magnificent accomplishment of a great society. The story in the book of Genesis demonstrates that God directed the construction and measurements, which implies perfection in every aspect to ensure its function and doesn't mean that the measurements, as recorded in the earliest archives of early man, are exact. As we discussed in

ALPHA TO OMEGA

chapter one, the earliest writings must have been inspired by significant events, which drastically changed human understanding and created the urgent need to record information. The main idea remained intact, but specifics have been contorted.

It seems apparent that the authors were trying to convey a story about a previous society, a flood and an Ark out of desperation for some reason. These scripts are man's first attempt to explain something they were just beginning to comprehend—something extremely crucial, which had to be passed onward.

I conceive the Ark as something timeless—mirroring the intrinsic characteristics of the almost limitless knowledge and power of a spectacular era and the God of all creation. It was a scientific marvel of extreme technology—a time energy device beyond our capabilities.

Before moving on, I would like to preface further discussion with a bit of personal history in hopes of adding some credence to what I'm about to propose. By 1979, I had already developed a rough concept of this entire idea because of a personal epiphany I experienced two years earlier. Since that time I have always believed that a superior civilization preceded us and that the story of Adam and Eve was representative of that concept.

I believed they existed much earlier in time than we had ever imagined and the Great Pyramid was Noah's Ark—a time machine and life catalyst for the future age. I envisioned it as an arc, like a rainbow or a bridge between two points in time and two completely different civilizations.

I envisioned the Great Pyramid as the cause rather than the effect of ancient Egypt's early societal supremacy. I perceived it as a device coveted by the early Egyptians because of its splendor, wonder and power. I considered it the center of controversy and mass upheaval in a new age of confused people, which invoked man's desperation to pass on as much information as possible. Equally as clear in my vision was Angels and aliens being the same entities and our final outcome would be the result of a battle of perceptions, which I will demonstrate more clearly in succeeding chapters.

The reason I bring this to readers attention is because I had no evidence to support this idea but wholeheartedly believed it because of a deep-seated reasoning that I couldn't explain. Those who know me well can attest to my persistence in challenging their personal concepts. The only proof I had was internal, yet the more I tried to squash the idea with research, introspection and retrospection, the clearer it became to me.

My entire adult life has been centered on this internal concept, which has finally become clear enough to present with reasonable fashion due to my recognition of emerging qualifiable information.

Are we beginning to get a better picture of the ideas being presented? How do we suppose the advanced time travelers explained their journey to the very uneducated people of the new age? Do we think they could explain time travel to people who couldn't grasp the concept of time or who could barely communicate at all?

Let us suppose that early man was told the exact truth by our time travelers: "We have journeyed through time after a devastating flood destroyed our world in a very distant past." Could early man understand it? Why do we fail to factor the early limited human capacities into our contemporary analysis? The answer is simple.

ALPHA TO OMEGA

Current precepts and inherited modes of thought do not require questions of this nature. We may be looking in the wrong direction.

Noah's family couldn't describe a machine to primitive humans who couldn't understand the concept of a machine. Isn't it feasible to assume the story of the boat to have developed as a result of oral tradition handed down over many years before man learned how to write? The answers reside in the Spirit within us and they are trying to become illuminated in our soul.

> The First Reason Why the Soul is Immortal: It is the Subject of Science Which is Eternal

> If science [*disciplina*] exists anywhere, and can exist only in that which lives; and if it is eternal, and nothing in which an eternal thing exists can be non-eternal; then that in which science exists lives eternally. —St. Augustine (*On Immortality of the Soul*)[17]

One of the most important books I have read is Christopher Dunn's, *The Giza Power Plant*. Written from an engineer's perspective, his impeccable attention to all details of the Great Pyramid has proven to me his ability to reverse engineer what is obviously a sophisticated machine deriving its power from the harmonics between the earth and the stars to which it is finely tuned.

His revolutionary theory is the first to address the synergy of components in the pyramid, which most people would not recognize as being related. His conclusions demonstrate the Great Pyramid as an enormous energy producing machine, akin to microwaves, which help to support my theory.

For those who are not familiar with harmonics, understand it as vibrations that can be amplified within a structure or building. All

BRIDGE OVER TROUBLED WATERS

materials vibrate at certain frequencies depending upon the length, density and other physical attributes. Modern engineering accounts for these harmonics by incorporating dampers designed to absorb certain frequencies to protect a structure from severe damage or total destruction, especially after the disaster of Washington State's newly constructed Tacoma Narrows Bridge in 1940.

The majority of us have seen footage of the bridge swaying like a strand of spaghetti and self-destructing within seconds in a mere 42 mile-per-hour wind. There is a great degree of power in harmonics and Dunn provides precise details of how every unique component in the pyramid is utilized to maximize the potential energy created by a structure tuned perfectly to the Earth's harmonics.

In chapter two we demonstrated how the reflection of God can be seen in the harmonious synergy in the microcosm and upward to the macrocosm of nature and living things. In consideration of this, Dunn's theory becomes more probable because of the exquisite correlation observed between the Great Pyramid, the Earth and the stars. I believe, however, he may be shortchanging the features and capacity of the actual energy that is being produced. I make this assertion because an important element is missing, which supports my theory.

Dunn's theory explicitly requires the apex of the pyramid to be an integral part of the synergistic capacity. The Great Pyramid is the only pyramid in Egypt missing its apex today. Researchers speculate it may have been a great crystal, solid gold, or a number of other valuable elements—one of the first things to be looted— but no evidence whatsoever exists to validate these claims.

ALPHA TO OMEGA

I propose the apex to have been composed of the intrinsic essence of God and Angels—the Cherubim, which guarded the tree of life in Adam's era. If the Great Pyramid was indeed the finest accomplishment and reflection of a superior race preceding us by millions of years; a fine-tuned machine that could swiftly catalyze the rejuvenation of life and transcend time so that a select few could journey through eons, then wouldn't the capstone of such an endeavor be intrinsic to its nature? In the new era, the Ark was the life-giving power on earth. I suspect that the capstone is missing for other reasons which we will explain later.

Axiom # 2: The Great Pyramid is Noah's *Arc*—the bridge of the demigods. It was a magnificent time-energy machine constructed eons ago by a previous super-society for the purpose of saving their souls by promoting a chance for the restoration of Paradise on Earth.

More questions surface from this idea. First, we have to remember this implies the Ark to have preceded everything on this earth after the total annihilation of the super society. For argument sake, let's propose that it was resting upon the Giza plateau 4 million years ago—an ageless, timeless and indestructible edifice of brilliance, radiance and life. Is it possible to provide new answers for questions proposed in the evaluation of other pertinent mysteries by agreeing on this assumption?

A philosophy that does not culminate in a metaphysic of ecstasy is vain speculation. *–Shihab al-Din Yaha Suhrawardi* (1154-1191)[18]

Part II:

LOST IN TRANSLATION

Chapter 4

HIS-STORY AND MY-STORY

If we can subscribe to the ancient alien theory, why is it difficult to accept the possibility of a time machine built by a previous super civilization?

Wisdom of the Ages

Some of the most prolific advances of history were spawned from seemingly radical changes to widely accepted beliefs. Often times many of the new theories had been initially regarded as impossible, unacceptable and outright heresy. Eventually, new ideas were scientifically validated, which often altered mankind's view of the world. We must embrace scientific exploration and its discoveries, which aids in humanity's progress, knowledge and eventual omnipotence—the clarity of God that will someday convert dogma into mutually accepted fact and reality.

New discoveries by science cannot begin without an agreeable hypothesis to prod investigation into the uncharted areas of hidden evidence. Today's experts rely on informational archives to form the basis of their research and seldom venture beyond the perimeters of standard teachings and ideologies. History and its basic concepts imbued throughout the world have been built first upon early religious concepts and later upon archeology and anthropology.

Archeology has uncovered evidence of five major extinctions on earth, the last of which is known as the K-T extinction, responsible for killing the dinosaurs and more than 70% of all life 65 million years ago. The data yields many unanswered questions, but the preponderance of evidence leaves most of us to believe that humans have arrived only recently since then with nothing in between. Major cataclysms like the K-T extinction present undeniable evidence due to enormous changes to the earth. Isn't it more than likely for many events and circumstances to easily be undetectable by archeological studies?

We are led to believe fossil evidence to be so advanced and complete, yet excavations are not as widespread as science would have us believe. In fact, excavations account for less than 2%, on average, of any explored site.[1] Pronouncements made by archeologists are based on what little evidence is discovered in that small percentage. What about the remaining 98% of each site or the unexplored and yet unrecognized archeological sites throughout the world, which account for the majority of undiscovered territory? When someone presents a challenge to accepted authoritative "facts" they are often portrayed as crazy people without knowledge, but it is the newly exposed evidence that presents the conflict— knowledge of which many are not privy.

> Artifacts and evidence can be staring us in the face but we fail to recognize them because of the conflict presented by the widely

HIS-STORY AND MY-STORY

accepted paradigm, which fails to consider the possibility of a previous civilization.[2]

The planet has experienced many catastrophes since the K-T extinction. Anthropology has uncovered evidence of "genetic bottlenecks", which are basically a reduction or elimination of several genetic lineages. In essence, the diversity of a species dwindles when many are eliminated by disasters, sudden environmental changes, rampant disease or a combination of either. DNA samplings of fossils show sudden decreases in genetic variety that might correspond with specific events presumed to be responsible for the changes.

Vigorous debates regarding the events and time-periods are ongoing, but the Yellowstone caldera eruption, which occurred around 640,000 years ago, is presumed to be one of the earliest known bottlenecks of the human genome. Others include the super eruption of Toba, a volcano located in Northern Sumatra, about 70,000 years ago. Evidence is minimal and speculation is at maximum throttle, but the average person has no idea about any of this.

Scientific evidence, which we outlined in chapter one, describe probable events resulting from the earth's most recent pole shift about seven million years ago. It's difficult to determine exactly what happened because the shift also marked the start of the great Quaternary Ice Age. Enormous geographical changes caused by mountain folding and huge shifts in water levels throughout the earth are evident during that period, but archeological evidence does not indicate the existence of a previous high civilization that

121

ALPHA TO OMEGA

long ago. Isn't it likely for inherited presumptions to prevent research that might possibly provide evidence to the contrary?

Evidence of human fossils is relatively minuscule and there is no telling, with any degree of certainty, whether or not another civilization thrived on earth long ago. The earth's crust is 20 to 45 miles thick on the continents and 3 to 6 miles thick in the ocean basins. The oceans have an average depth of almost three miles with some of the deepest parts reaching almost 6 miles. Until we can sift through every inch of it, assertions to the contrary are baseless.

Altering our view of the distant past would be futile without equal considerations for biblical accounts, unresolved mysteries, humankind's struggle and the expeditions of our souls. We are the pioneers of the dawning Age of Aquarius—the beginning of another 25,826 year sojourn around our galaxy. What does this mean for us?

The world will not suddenly change by our position in the galaxy. Actions change when beliefs change; collective actions and beliefs change the world.

It is not a coincidence the story of Atlantis parallels the biblical accounts of the Great Flood. Linking them together to provide a new perspective, which typifies the human experience and the soul's excursion, adds credence to both tales—each of which have never been supported by evidence other than in the testimonies of recorded history. The story of Atlantis is conceived as a myth today because our preconceived notions prevent us from considering the

122

HIS-STORY AND MY-STORY

possibility of a tale whose origins and implications conflict with them.

By proposing axiom two, I'm asking readers to accept a seemingly extraordinary assumption from our limited perspective. Despite our technological advancements, we must recognize our limits while imagining the many possibilities of scientific progress. Science fiction is founded on this principle and seems always to become imitated by reality over time.

In this evaluation, we exemplify the human travail where knowledge of our past becomes diluted over time and the truth can only be found in the common threads of ambiguous dogma, unexplained myths and scientific mysteries, which imitate science fiction today.

By accepting axiom two, we have to explain the mysteries so we can both qualify the assumption and further exemplify the human journey. As we have previously demonstrated, we cannot decipher foretold prophecy without a clearer understanding of our past. Up to this point we have explained enough to reveal what our final destination will be, but getting there is the key.

Is it possible to revise our clouded impressions of prerecorded history to clear a path for the road home? Specific mysteries, which challenge the chronological events we've come to accept, can be explained while offering new and stimulating hypotheses built on the same speculation as those presented by contemporary research.

Taking into account what has been presented so far, we need to accept four important factors introduced by axiom 2.

ALPHA TO OMEGA

1. The Great Pyramid was a catalyst to the evolutionary process; an assurance to life's speedy rejuvenation over a period of time.

2. When energized, the Great Pyramid would become timeless and ageless—outside the dimension of time. Those inside would also be ageless and timeless—existing in a suspended state and traversing thousands of years in the blink of an eye.

3. Humans of the new world, evolving within the Ark's proximity, exhibited noticeably different attributes in comparison to other evolutionary humans of the world.

4. Noah and his family were superhuman, paraphysical giants—the gods of the new age. His sons Ham, Japheth and Shem each bore supreme and distinctive physical, intellectual and spiritual attributes.

These factors are not considered by contemporary researchers who posit two basic solutions to the mysteries that contradict current history's chronology. One begins with the assumption that ancient aliens are responsible for these unexplainable mysteries and the other contends that a previous high civilization somewhere in our recent past is responsible.

Each hypothesis is spurred, not only by the fascination surrounding the Great Pyramid, the Sphinx and other anomalous wonders of Egypt and surrounding regions, but on the mounds of other common evidence, which include the spectacular monolithic and megalithic structures of the Incan, Mayan, Olmec, and Aztec societies of Central and South America. The evidence of remarka-

124

HIS-STORY AND MY-STORY

ble structures, consisting of megaliths with boulders weighing over 100 tons in these regions, contradicts the supposed abilities of the people during those times.

By studying the mysterious descriptions and legends of ancient gods, curious similarities to each other and to those of the famous Greek and Egyptian pantheons are uncovered. Astonishing mysteries, including the Nazca lines, Piri Reis map, Easter Island, Stonehenge, Tiahuanaco, Puma Punku, Cholula, and Machu Picchu, are but a few of those presented with amazing detail to support both theories.

The ancient alien theory circumvents the timeline enigma by removing the need to explain construction of the Great Pyramid and other spectacular wonders within the timeframe of primitive man. In this case, aliens are presented as intelligent beings; visitors of earth who built these magnificent structures, while serving as gods to our primitive ancestors before departing with valuable resources from our planet.

It is structured on assumptions that aliens from other planets bear the same physical needs similar to humans, which urges them to exploit earth and its inhabitants for their own well being. Ancient astronaut theory suggests that earth has been used as a breeding ground, a science lab producing hybrids of man and beast, a source of raw materials and a frontier for exploration.

In the theory presented within these pages, we have demonstrated that Angels are higher creatures with benevolent intent promoting self-discovery. Why would higher beings want to deny the evolution of our spiritual progress? There are trillions of

125

ALPHA TO OMEGA

uninhabitable planets, which can be mined for any required resources. Isn't it presumptuous, fearful and unthinking to conceptualize aliens as possessors of our own inadequacies? Is it due in part by our failure to remotely consider our spiritual progress being the sole reason for the entire course of misunderstood events? We shouldn't fear Angelic intervention.

The other theory, built on assuming a previous advanced society was rather recent, posits all flood myths as stories passed to succeeding generations of Homo sapiens smart enough to repeat what they had learned from flood survivors. The theory relies on assuming a flood actually occurred within the timeframe of intelligent humans, otherwise the story could not have been passed on. Therefore, the previous super society is assumed to have most likely thrived inside of the last 50,000 years.

It addresses an enormous amount of evidence, but its conclusions are shackled by proof that complete annihilation of the species is not possible anywhere during the last 4 million years or more. The theory holds firmly to the undeniable evidence indicating earlier humans had witnessed and possibly contributed to a high society somewhere in the more recent past. If there was a great flood, wouldn't it have been as depicted in all of the legends—complete and utter obliteration? How can we suspect a gargantuan flood to have eliminated a high society without killing the coexisting and more primitive humans?

Perhaps one of the most important and overlooked mysteries of science might offer clues to other unexplained anomalies. Scientific evidence suggests that the evolution of modern man began in

HIS-STORY AND MY-STORY

Africa along the coast of the Red Sea. From there, scientists believe the migration of man is responsible for populating the world. Fossil evidence of morphological changes and physical adaptations has been the most convincing data demonstrating that Homo sapiens likely existed approximately 200,000 years ago and were able to control fire. Science has discovered fossils of what is believed to be our earliest ancestors—Homo erectus—about 2 million years ago.[3]

Evidence of morphological changes in physical adaptations has been the most convincing evidence of research. The ability to hunt, control fire, and fashion crude tools defines the characteristics of Homo sapiens. Their ability to reason, to establish some form of organized civil life, and the later evidence of human burial provide scientists with clues to their "human" development when compared to other primates.

This period also marks the beginning of fossil evidence of the great Neanderthal—the most controversial of all human species. Early anthropology had once considered Neanderthal to be a link in our evolutionary heritage, but interbreeding had later been ruled out.

In 2010, a report was released by the Max Planck Institute of Evolutionary Anthropology in Germany suggesting intermingling of genes to have probably occurred about 45,000 years ago, in the Middle East, when migrating Homo sapiens mated with the Neanderthals there. Evidence suggests a 1 to 4 percent genome admixture and earlier interbreeding in Europe and Asia. The debate lingers as to whether the newly discovered DNA evidence is conclusive enough. Homo sapiens still remain quite dissociated from them genetically, although positive selection was evidenced in genes involving metabolism, cognitive and skeletal development.[4]

Neanderthal fossils have been found in Europe, North Africa and the near East—dating back to the earliest times of earth's last major glacial expansion—the Würm glaciation.[5] This is noteworthy because much of the evidence uncovered suggests Neanderthals survived many years of harsh climate in Europe long before Homo sapiens arrived. Archeological evidence exhibits Neanderthals and Homo sapiens cohabitating for 150,000 years until Neanderthals disappeared.[6]

Neanderthal was bigger, stronger and had a remarkable ability to adapt to the harsh environment of ancient Europe. Additional evidence shows Neanderthals had a much larger brain than both primitive and present-day humans. Their average brain size was 1400cc against our current size of 1360cc (that's approximately 2½ cubic inches larger).[7] Imagine adding a 2½ inch cube to our brain size—it is quite substantial.

In Homo sapiens, the developmental increase in the size of the brain is proven to be the result of growing mental capacity and not the other way around. Shouldn't we assume that, if Neanderthals had a substantially larger brain, they must have had the capacity to use it? Who were they? Is there another possible explanation for their disappearance?

Although Neanderthals appear, in morphological aspects, to be more rugged looking and much larger and stronger people, their cultural behaviors seem to transcend the normal diversities of the time. Some Neanderthal fossils have been found in gravesites that

HIS-STORY AND MY-STORY

provide evidence to their advanced cultural behavior. They lived in Europe and survived a number of glacial advances before disappearing about 28,000 years ago, which up until now is the most recently discovered fossil. Smooth edged scrapers found in many Neanderthal sites suggest the preparation of skins and hence probably the manufacture of clothing. We may assume that it was this invention that permitted Neanderthal man to penetrate into the cold country of Central Asia.[8]

Science is puzzled by their sudden disappearance because it leaves them to assume Neanderthals were eventually killed by their inferior and substantially weaker counterparts, which fails to corroborate the available evidence. Newer hypotheses propose that Neanderthal slowly declined in numbers and became extinct. The debate rages on within the scientific community because evidence doesn't quite fit—curiosity is not satisfied.

Curiosity has always been the catalyst to the procurement of knowledge, but our wisdom is just as necessary in the determination of truth. The definition of wisdom by Webster is *"...having the power to judge rightly and follow the soundest course of action, based on knowledge, experience, understanding and good judgment; insightful understanding of what is true, right or enduring."* The definition implies a sixth sense, and it truly is. By invoking our curiosity, in an attempt to answer questions aroused by suspicion, we empower our wisdom to offer solutions.

Here's an example. What happens if we choose to accept or believe something is true when in fact it is not? Let's suppose we want to be on time for an eight o'clock movie. We will calculate our

129

ALPHA TO OMEGA

departure time in a basic scientific way. Let's also suppose that, for some reason, the clock in our house was one hour slow and we weren't aware of it. We would fail to achieve our objective because we did not know the truth. We certainly believed that we knew, but we were wrong and therefore had to suffer the consequences.

Let's also suppose that, under the same circumstances, we didn't believe the clock was correct because we had a hunch that something wasn't right. We willingly accepted the insight and chose to reject the presumed truth. We looked for clues to verify our hunch. The position of the sun, the mailman's arrival, the sound of the school bus or the bell of an ice cream vendor aided us in verifying that our intuition was correct. Our internal wisdom observed the constant conditions and freed us from the mistake of our ignorance.

Where did our gut feeling originate? It came from within us. It was a premonition induced by our subconscious storehouse of information. This warehouse of memory remembers all of our experiences and can decipher the common threads more clearly than our conscious minds. We must ask questions and be willing to closely inspect our hunches. This process can work for all of us when we ask questions that we think are unanswerable.

> "Ask and it will be given you; seek and you will find; knock and it will be opened to you." (Matthew 7:7).

Mysteries are the evidence of errors in our contemporary religious and historical beliefs. They have not been solved by fragmented history's pronouncements or religious proclamations. Dogmas, which are beliefs, doctrines or opinions and have no logical explanation or evidence of truth, are challengeable without regard for the presumed truth. If we begin to summon and heed the thoughts of our wisdom we can provide conceivable solutions to murky concepts and unanswered questions.

Is there evidence indicating history's perplexing Neanderthal to be the earliest descendants of Noah's family? Did the crossbreeding, which is still debated within the higher seats of anthropology and posited as DNA manipulation in the ancient alien theory, occur on a predicted and calculated basis over thousands of years?

New questions surface when applying the factors imposed by axiom 2 and they imply suggestions for explaining many of the unsolved mysteries of today. By examining the baffling relics of evidence from a fresh vantage point, we may be able to solve the riddle and provoke research in other areas. Is it possible Noah and his family members utilized the time machine over the course of many thousands of years in order to implement their objective throughout the world?

> **If we can subscribe to the ancient alien theory, why is difficult to accept the possibility of a time machine built by a previous super civilization?**

Isn't it reasonable to suppose ancient Egyptians revered Noah's family as gods and correlate them to the mythical gods of Egyptian and Greek folklore? Is there evidence to support this notion?

Did the earliest Egyptians acquire significant power from the pyramid, which helps to explain ancient Egypt's mystique, sorcery and magic (as referred to in the Bible)? Can our alternate view help

ALPHA TO OMEGA

solve the mystery of the apparent sudden emergence of fully formed societies in Egypt and Mesoamerica?

> Yet archaeologists have often pondered on the exact process withheld to civilization as we know it. For it was with the suddenness of sunrise that human ingenuity and engineering skills arose from the Stone Age and burst forth onto the landscaping of history.[9]

Could the Egyptians have witnessed the time machine's operation? Might it have led them to believe their Pharaohs could live forever in a pyramid?

How did the Great Pyramid lose its remarkable power? Did it lead to Egypt's obsession to build replicas, which never entombed a dead Pharaoh?

What caused the enormous upheaval leading to the biblical battle between the Hebrews and the Egyptians and spearheaded the advent of recorded information? Once again we are faced with linking answers to these questions to a story that typifies the human struggle for truth and the soul's journey home, while adding credence to the legends that have mystified us for centuries.

In order to answer these questions, we must establish tenets that categorize the new age, with respect to our new assumptions. First, power and knowledge would be arranged differently in the new era. Absolute Knowledge would never be *given* to humans again. The standing order remains: *self-discovery* is the only way towards knowledge and the eventual Paradise of Absolute Knowledge.

HIS-STORY AND MY-STORY

Power, on the other hand, is a different arrangement in our era. In this New Age, power has always preceded knowledge. As is evidenced today, our individual knowledge is extremely limited in comparison to the power we possess as individuals. We can use thousands of machines and devices without having the knowledge to build them or understand how they work. I suspect, by the evidence of the megalithic societies and Ancient Egypt's mystique alone, that certain elements of power were utilized without knowledge of their scientific function and we will provide evidence in support of the idea.

Secondly, we need to recognize Noah and his family were extremely empathetic to the humans of the new era. After all, it was the transgressions of their defunct civilization that led to the new age where ignorance and suffering are patent among the people to begin with. Noah, a god-like survivor of a marvelous civilization, was undeniably a stupendous humanist and miracle worker with an enormous capacity for compassion. He must have possessed an overwhelming willingness to assist everyone in the new world so they could find the way to understanding God in the hopes of restoring Paradise on earth.

Noah's intent was to do everything in his power to aide in speeding humanity's progress and to substantially reduce as many of the ineptitudes and social inadequacies as possible. Certain elements of power and technology could be shared with the disadvantaged people of the new era to aide in reducing the hardships of a primeval civilization.

All intent was in the promotion of unity, harmony and a God-consciousness among people of worldwide societies during the course of human development after the flood. It is within the scope of this presentation to suggest a theorem that allows for this arrangement.

Religious authority may not bode well in this evaluation, but in our challenge to the espoused ideologies of religion, God remains paramount. Because we have demonstrated the foundation of religious tradition to have originated by mankind's earliest interpretations of these mysteries, we can view religious authority as an entity, which has slowly lost the secrets to the very mysteries on which it was founded.

Of Gods and Men

By 400 BC, Greece had become a dominating regional influence and like the Babylonians and Egyptians, they believed ancient gods were the real causality of events. How did they come to this conclusion over the many years? Most of the history during this time is filled with vague recollections of memorable events, which obviously prevailed for thousands of years. As we will see in the next section, Greece was very much a part of Noah's early influence. Important similarities found in the story of Atlantis, the book of Enoch and the book of Genesis, offer clues and information for consideration.

Plato's writings, which have prompted controversy and debate for over two thousand years, are the only specific known references to Atlantis. Atlantis remains a riddle, not just because substantiating evidence has not been found, but for references in Plato's accounts regarding the mating of gods with earthly women.

According to the ancient tale, Atlantis was the domain of Poseidon, god of the sea. When Poseidon fell in love with a mortal woman, Cleito, he created a dwelling at the top of a hill near the middle of the island and surrounded the dwelling with rings of water and land to protect her. Cleito gave birth to five sets of twin boys who became the first rulers of Atlantis. The island was divided among the demigod brothers with the eldest, Atlas—the first King of Atlantis—assigned to reign over the central hill and surrounding areas.[9]

Dispensing the myth of Atlantis to a piece of our historical puzzle may create resistance in readers who are asked to consider the notion of gods procreating with mortal women. Those predominantly influenced by mainstream religion have a difficult time accepting the possibility.

Keep in mind that the tales of Atlantis stem from roots found somewhere in prehistoric Egypt of the new era, which later inspired Plato's writings. Myths, which have emerged in this epoch, are believed by many to be mere fables until we are made privy to the parallels and similarities that entreat us to consider other explanations.

Intriguingly, the Bible substantiates the interbreeding between the sons of God and the daughters of men, who bore children known as the Nephilim—the giants of Old Testament scripture. Many can recall the story of David, who killed Goliath, the Philis-

ALPHA TO OMEGA

tine giant who measured "six cubits plus a span", which is over nine feet tall (1Samuel 17: 3).

> When men began to multiply on the face of the ground, and daughters were born to them, the sons of God saw that the daughters of men were fair; and they took to wife such of them as they chose. (Genesis 6: 1-2)

> The Nephilim were on the earth in those days, and also afterward, when the sons of God came into the daughters of men and they bore children to them. These were the mighty men that were of old, the men of renown. (Genesis 6: 4)

What does this tell us? For one thing it exposes the similarity of gods mating with mortal women in both the biblical tale and the legendary tale of Atlantis, both of which would surface in the new era. The Greek pantheon is a massive compilation of eight mythical classes of gods, the seventh of which include the demigod Gigantes (giants)—those spawned from the procreation of gods and men.

Equally compelling is the book of Enoch (Noah's great-grandfather), valued by Jews and Christians alike during the first century A.D., which explicitly details how 200 Angels conspired to take on physical form and mate with the beautiful and comely daughters of men. Their offspring were great giants who consumed all of man's acquisitions and turned against them. Enoch refers to these as the "Watchers" and eerily presents in his accounts how they and the unrighteous Angels were the primary reason for corruptions on earth and God's decision to destroy every living thing. (The book of Enoch and The Book of the Secrets of Enoch

HIS-STORY AND MY-STORY

make up the entire compilation, which are widely available for purchase and free on the Internet.)

By the late fourth century A.D., both Jewish and Christian authorities had censured the book of Enoch because of its theme and destroyed all known copies of the book. However, in the late 18th century a copy was found in Ethiopia, which was believed to have been composed by Syrian monks fleeing Byzantine persecution in the fifth century A.D. Three copies were brought back to Europe and Britain by a Scottish explorer and in the early 19th century it was first translated into English.[10]

The discovery of the Dead Sea Scrolls in the Qumran Cave, during the period A.D. 1947 through 1956, included parts of the original Aramaic book of Enoch, which were estimated to have been copied around 200 BC. The discovery added authenticity to the Ethiopian copies, which had long been scrutinized by religious zealots whose sentiments resembled those of early church fathers. It's widely accepted that many of the early church fathers knew of the apocryphal book of Enoch, which was confined to use outside of mainstream teachings before it was banned completely.[11]

One of the most learned researchers on the subject is Zecharia Sitchin (July, 1920 – October, 2010), whose theories are built on the Nephilim demigods of prehistory. His *Earth Chronicles* series provide evidence indicating that biblical references to the Anakim or Annunaki of Sumerian records are the giants of Old Testament scripture.

One of his simplest explanations for the translation is found in The Book of Numbers (chapter 13) describing the journey of men

ALPHA TO OMEGA

whom Moses sent ahead to scout the Canaan region. Upon returning they told Moses that they did *"...see the giants, the sons of Anak—the Nephilim... and we were like grasshoppers in our eyes, and so we were in their eyes."*

The plural, Anakim is found in Deuteronomy 1:28 and 9:2, when Moses encouraged the Israelites not to lose heart because of the *"fearsome descendants of Anak"*, and again in Joshua 11 and 14, in which the capture of Hebron was recorded. After that, the uncaptured strongholds were all the cities of the Philistine coastal enclave; and therein lay additional reasons for equating the Anakim with giants—because King David's giant-like Philistine adversary Goliath and his brothers were descendants of the Anakim.[12]

Sitchin is a pioneer in comprehensive research of the Nephilim and posits that the Annunaki arrived here as explorers from another planet, who came to mine our resources about 450,000 years ago. His theories describe the Annunaki as the sons of god, who mated with mortals and altered the human genome so that men could assist in the mining efforts of the Annunaki. What sets Sitchin apart from others who delve into this specific topic is his extensive study of Egyptian, Greek and Mesopotamian lore.

One of his novel theories posits the flood to have occurred around 11,000 B.C. resulting from a tidal wave burgeoned by the slippage of Antarctica's ice cap—a fitting explanation for the mystery of the Piri Reis world map of 1513. Coincidentally, many anomalies and unanswered questions emerge around 11,000 B.C.

Today, the subject of the Nephilim, made popular by Sitchin, has exploded into hundreds of books focused on these gigantic

138

HIS-STORY AND MY-STORY

men of ancient times. Most books depict the Nephilim as the evil offspring of fallen angels. Each theory hinges upon themes centered on their wickedness as the reason for God's decision to destroy civilization, while some depict future calamities coinciding with the return of the Annunaki. This author doesn't subscribe to theories like these because my research had served different postulates for the Nephilim long before their popularization.

It's more fitting to presume all inhabitants of the previous superhuman society to be demigods with unfathomable power and that none of them bore close resemblance to our physical appearance. If Adam is a son of God, then according to contemporary theory his children would also be giants. My position is that all members of the antediluvian race were giants and were separated only by their position in the obvious battle between those preferring to return to Paradise and those addicted to unlimited power in the flesh.

> The word Nephilim means giants, and they turned out to be evil later on by virtue of their actions (in both biblical and non-biblical Jewish literature). They weren't given some name because of some inherently fallen spiritual state (as though they could not be redeemed and were more fallen than humans). [13]

Why is it that only one line of Adam's children is traced biblically as the righteous genealogy? What differentiated Cain from Abel and Seth? Why do Adam's additional offspring fail to receive any notoriety?

> The days of Adam after he became the father of Seth were 800 years; and he had other sons and daughters. (Genesis 5:4)

ALPHA TO OMEGA

Why is it that Canaan, a son of Ham was cursed? Wasn't he Noah's grandson who was born to Ham after the flood? We cannot suppose with any certainty that the Nephilim were the sole reason for the destruction of Atlantis when scripture points specifically to others who were scorned and fails to provide information concerning added offspring. It stands to reason with more probability that all were giants who were engaged in the battle between good and evil.

For a long time scholars had surmised that the book of Enoch incorporated sections of the Book of Noah—another book lost to antiquity—which was also discovered in the Qumran caves in the late 1940s and affirmed what they had long suspected.

According to relevant sections of the book, the wife of Lamech (the father of Noah) was named Bath-Enosh. When Noah was born to her, the baby was so unusual that he aroused suspicions in the mind of Lamech. According to those scriptures, Noah's eyes were wide opened and he could speak upon birth. Right away, Lamech thought in his heart that his son was fathered by one of the Watchers and expressed his suspicions to his wife and his father Methuselah. Lamech, after being assured by his grandfather Enoch that he was indeed the father and that Noah was to play a significant role in the future of mankind, accepted it without further concern.[14]

Perhaps the giants in those days bore different features and different traits much like we have different traits today. To presume that all humans, except evil giants of that era, had physical appearance resembling ours may be myopic, especially within the pretexts of this theory, which postulates they have predated us by at least

140

four million years. It seems more probable than not, under those circumstances, our physical appearances would greatly vary.

Scripture refers to the Nephilim as *the mighty men of old; the men of renown* (as quoted from Genesis 6 above), portraying them as heroes rather than villains. From an objective viewpoint, there is a distinct duality in the nature of these demigods, when comparing references found in various sources.

Most importantly, all of the related historical documents about the Nephilim and the previous civilization were recorded and discovered in our age. All of it is incongruent and begins with the Sumerian cuneiform tablets, the Pyramid texts, the Vedas and the early Torah, which are the earliest recordings of our times. Contemporary scholars are just beginning to discover the similarities that appear to link all of them to a much earlier and common source.

> ... Such traditions are among the most imperishable of all human creations: they are vehicles of knowledge voyaging through time.[15]

Establishing that pre-diluvial superhuman giants thrived is crucial in this analysis. Corroborating evidence yields proof of Nephilim, a previous high society, and Noah's Ark, although varying hypotheses are presented to define them. I contend they were superhuman, paraphysical giants with unfathomable power. Super humans surely must be able to accomplish the extraordinary things that defy our current thinking and physical limits.

ALPHA TO OMEGA

Gods of the Ignorant

An enormous amount of time antedated the earliest crossroads of pivotal human events, which led to our earliest historical records. Religious texts, archaeological discoveries and historical accounts lingering through time are the bits and pieces of a lost truth still subject to interpretation and debate. We don't want to dispel evidence, but rather to assemble the pieces with new assumptions as a guide.

Perhaps a glimpse into the past, based on our new assumptions and the truth about historical tradition, can lead us out of the dark and into a more enlightening view of history. Although it would be nearly impossible to address every unexplained mystery with great detail, we will address those pertinent to explaining our adjusted view. I have researched many of them enough to be certain new theories are necessary to define our history. Many contemporary and well respected researchers have helped to qualify that assertion.

We've touched on the cycle of precession and the precise alignments of the Great Pyramid's shafts with specific stars during certain times within the 26,000 year cycle. Most compelling of all is the Giza necropolis and its many alignments. Amazingly and with clock-like accuracy, numerous celestial alignments occur cyclically with startling and almost frightening precision during the cycle.

I mention it here because the second axiom requires we demonstrate a means in which to deactivate the time machine. If Noah and his family were suspended in time, then some means of disabling the machine would be necessary. I suppose the time

HIS-STORY AND MY-STORY

machine could be activated manually, but had to be automatically deactivated at least once. It appears the only possible way is to somehow utilize specific cyclical alignments with celestial bodies, which were predetermined by the builders.

Elaborating on what has proven to be a remarkable discovery in the more current analyses of ancient mysteries isn't necessary. Precise stellar alignments, which are keys to understanding the Mayan calendar and several other mysteries, are the only possible explanation.

Curiously, the dove sent forth by Noah in the biblical tale, could be representative of a constellation known as Columba, which was discovered in the late 16th century by a Dutch astronomer named Petrus Plancius. The constellation was created to differentiate the unformed stars of Canis Major—the constellation containing the great star Sirius to which one of the pyramid's shaft aligns during periodic intervals. As was mentioned previously, these amazing phenomena are covered in great detail in *The Message of the Sphinx*, and are beyond the scope of this book.

It's important to focus more on Noah and his family's contribution to the development of humankind throughout the eons of a newly forming world. Acceptable theorems for the earliest years and through 12,000 BC, where substantial evidence mysteriously indicates advanced methods in stone-age world societies, must be presented. To do this requires a closer look at the biblical account of Noah's descendants.

The genealogies of Noah and his family are referred to as The Table of Nations (Figure 4), which was researched extensively by

ALPHA TO OMEGA

Arthur Custance (1910-1985). Custance earned an M.A. in Middle Eastern languages (Hebrew, Greek and Cuneiform) in 1941, and Ph.D. in philosophy in 1959. Notably, Custance had completed a thesis and all the comprehensives required for a Ph.D. in anthropology in 1955, only to be denied by the University of Toronto on the basis of his religious belief that Adam and Eve were real people. His thesis for his Ph.D. in philosophy was focused on anthropology and the influence of science, technology and philosophy on various regions of the world.

Custance authored *The Doorway Paper Series*, which are extensive compilations influenced by the Table of Nations and his anthropological research. His work has been organized into nine books. More information can be found on his website at: www.custance.org.

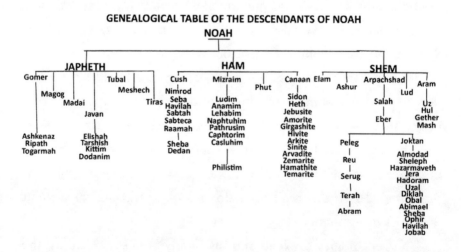

Figure 4

HIS-STORY AND MY-STORY

Much debate lingers regarding the authenticity of the Table of Nations. Is it a table or just a fable of nations? Early 20th century historians like James Thomas and Samuel Driver were skeptical on the basis that prehistory was too far removed from the time it was written and therefore could not be accurate. Once again, an unknown source of information is responsible for the debate surrounding its authenticity. It has endured the bias of time, but continues to be subject to interpretation and dispute.

One of the most intriguing aspects of the table of nations is each person in the family tree corresponds to regions and countries throughout the Eastern Hemisphere. Many of the names of these countries were renamed later, but it requires our attention. The importance is such that anthropology has discovered certain regional attributes that correlate to Custance's discoveries.

A closer look at Ham's sons hints to a substantial amount of time between the document and early history because Ham's son, Mizraim, is referred to later as Egypt in newer versions of Old Testament scripture. As for the authenticity and credence given to this document, Custance presents significant support.

> We come, finally, to the question of the date of this document. It will already be clear that, in our view, it is by no means "late" in the sense in which Higher Critics have understood the term. If it was composed many centuries after the events described, it has avoided anachronisms and certain errors, which would make it a masterpiece of forgery. So carefully has the supposed forger avoided these kinds of errors that it would seem far simpler and more reasonable to assume he was a contemporary of the terminal events, which he describes in the chapter.

145

ALPHA TO OMEGA

> Among the lines of evidence which strongly support an early date for this document, the following carry great weight: (1) the small development of Japhetic peoples, (2) the position of Cush at the head of the Hamitic family, (3) the mention of Sidon but not of Tyre, (4) the reference to Sodom and Gomorrah as still existing, (5) the great amount of space given to Joktanites, (6) the discontinuance of the Hebrew line at Peleg, and (7) the absence of any reference to Jerusalem by name.[16]

In support of his evidence for the authenticity and timeliness of the document it should suffice by just expounding on a specific reference. For simplicity sake, we will explain the second one as described by Custance. The earliest Hebrew Old Testament had long been known to be historically derived by the sixth century BC. Many experts presumed the document's origin to be about the same period because these were the earliest known chronologies of history to date.

> No historian at that time would have referred to any part of Babylonia as a land of Cush. By then, Cush had been used exclusively for the region of Ethiopia. If the writer had been attempting a piece of historic fiction, he would surely have added parenthetically that he was not referring to Ethiopia in the present context. As it was, he evidently foresaw not the slightest confusion in the reader's mind since the Ethiopian Cush did not exist.[17]

This is important in establishing the credibility on which early Jewish tradition had been founded. We established the earliest Hebrew texts of sixth century BC having been derived from several sources, but we don't imply they could not have originated at an earlier time in history. If anything, credence is added by the evidence in support of its authenticity.

Today's unearthed bits of ancient texts and clay tablets tell similar stories of flood legends and survivors. These must be the pieces of massive original sources of information collated by a consortium whose decisions influenced the compilation of the early Hebrew Bible.

Since our attempt here is not to discredit what has been found, but to piece together that which is credible, the Table is just as important as the similarities of oral traditions, which add weight to the events that changed the world. In all probability, they originate at the fork in the road, which predated the earliest known records of our species.

Custance provides impressive substantial evidence to support his theory that mankind's spiritual, physical and intellectual needs have been historically provided by Shem, Ham and Japheth respectively. He posits the blend of physical and intellectual attributes as science and the combination of intellectual and spiritual traits as theology. His stance is that each contribution, beginning with Ham, later followed by Japheth and finally by Shem, is the substance of human development after the flood.

Several of his ideas help to explain other mysteries, when observing our patriarchs as progenitors of specific races with specific capabilities. Custance does not deify Noah or his sons, but believes that a perfect synergy of their progeny could provide for a high civilization during earlier times, but not before 4000 BC.

ALPHA TO OMEGA

In this Table, we again meet with three groups of people, the descendants of Shem, Ham, and Japheth...So then, we have the Japhethites who can be conveniently equated for our purposes with the Caucasians, Indo-Europeans, or White Man; the Hamites who are held to encompass the Negroid and Mongoloid branches, i.e., the so-called colored races; and the Shemites who comprise both the Hebrew people (ancient and modern), the Arabs, and a few once powerful nations, such as the Assyrians and Babylonians. This is a very sketchy outline, but it will serve for the moment until the details of the Table can be examined more specifically.

Now, it is my firm belief that God has endowed these three groups, which we shall henceforth refer to normally as Japhethites, Hamites, and Shemites with certain capacities and aptitudes which, when properly exercised, have made a unique contribution in the total historical development of mankind and which, when allowed to find full cooperative expression during a single epoch, have invariably led to the emergence of a high civilization.[18]

Here is where we begin with positing that Noah and his descendants are the gods of our early ignorant race. Custance demonstrates how five major cultural centers began the expanse of our ancient world. Egypt, Sumer, and the Indus Valley are obvious locations because this is where history as we know it began. Interestingly, he includes a swath of North America and the northern part of South America as well. He offers evidence proving each of these locations to be Hamitic in origin. This not only implies the racial stock of the earliest gods, but that early civilization's most urgent priority required Ham's contributions after the flood:

148

HIS-STORY AND MY-STORY

A survey of history with this thought in mind, applied to nations or races rather than to individuals, reveals that Japhethites have originated the great philosophical systems; the Shemitic peoples, the great religious systems whether true or false; and, surprising as it may seem to one not familiar with the evidence, the Hamitic people have supplied the world with the basis of almost every technological advance.[19]

Custance posits that all people of the earth are direct descendants of Noah and his family, regardless of prehistoric evidence and the more recent evidence of high societies in 12,000 BC. Although he was a well-learned student of anthropology, he maintains that all prehistoric communities, fossil man, primitive cultures and civilizations of the past or present must have been squeezed within this span of a few thousand years. He has this to say about his supposition:

> On the face of it the proposal seems utterly absurd. However, I think there are lines of evidence of considerable substance in support of it. In setting this forth all kinds of "buts" will arise in the reader's mind if he has any broad knowledge of current physical anthropology. An attempt is made to deal specifically with a number of these "buts" in other Doorway Papers by the author, but some problems remain unsolved, particularly the question of the time element. However, one does not have to solve every problem before presenting a hypothetical reconstruction. After all, the prevailing view is shot full of them and yet it is still held to be a respectable one![20]

This supposition doesn't nullify his anthropological research indicating Noah's sons to be separate races and influences, which had been introduced at different times of post-flood development.

149

His findings are quite remarkable and agreed to by many reliable sources and well respected anthropologists cited in his work with disagreements based mostly on the time factor. What Custance believes to have occurred in only a few centuries, we can demonstrate as gradual advancements and interbreeding during more than 200,000 years of human development throughout the world.

> Thus it has come about that the pioneering task of opening up the world, subduing it, and rendering it habitable, was first undertaken by the descendants of Ham. This seems to have been done under divine pressure, for in a remarkably short time the children of Ham had established beachheads of settlement in every part of the world.[21]

The primary necessity of primitive humans was to learn basic survival skills. Undoubtedly, earliest humans could not fathom nor express the spiritual or intellectual facets of human progress. If Custance is right about the earliest Hamitic settlements, then it is more likely that the evolutionary humans of the new age were assisted by Ham's earliest offspring.

Why would advanced beings need assistance in their own development? If we are all direct descendants, wouldn't we have remained an advanced species? Questions of this nature are not considered by those who view the flood survivors to be nothing more than ordinary men and women to begin with.

It is more reasonable to suggest that, in the earliest years, Ham's contributions were the first provisions for a separate species of ancient humans. This means that the first of the Hamitic descendants were handcuffed by the learning abilities of primitive man, and

HIS-STORY AND MY-STORY

that they sacrificed their long lives in the slow but progressive mentoring of basic survival skills and technologies.

> In the case of Ham and his descendants history shows that they have rendered an extraordinary service to mankind from the point of view of the physical developments of civilization. All the earliest civilizations of note were founded and carried to their highest technical proficiency by Hamitic people. There is scarcely a *basic* technological invention which must not be attributed to them. As we shall show later, neither Shem nor Japheth made any significant contribution to the fundamental technology of civilization, in spite of all appearances to the contrary. This is a bold statement but it is not made in ignorance of the facts.[22]

I believe the earliest Hamitic descendants to be the Neanderthal species and the biblical Nephilim. It is a fitting solution for settling the Neanderthal debate, while accounting for their larger brain and the implied associated mental capacity.

We shouldn't concern ourselves with the bold presumptions of archeology exposed in the exact descriptions of Neanderthal appearance, living arrangements or behavior. The only certainty is that evidence is overly insufficient to support the precise anthropological pronouncements, which are baseless from a truly scientific standpoint. Anthropology relies on the fact that less data offers more freedom in interpretation and the principle is widely recognized and abused, especially in regards to human evolution.[23]

Startling evidence of Hamitic gods among later Neolithic societies is found in the examination of the Olmec mystery of ancient Mexico. The research of several archeologists has placed the Olmec at the forefront of any civilization in Mexico, including the Aztecs

151

and the Maya. They were an advanced civilization that appears also to have emerged as a fully formed society. In fact, the bar and dot calendrical code used by the Maya is proven to have been invented by the Olmec, based on artifacts discovered in Tres Zapotes.[24]

> Strangely, despite the best efforts of archaeologists, not a single, solitary sign of anything that could be described as the 'developmental phase' of Olmec society had been on Earth anywhere in Mexico (or, for that matter, anywhere in the New World). These people, whose characteristic form of artistic expression was the carving of huge Negroid heads, appeared to have come from nowhere.[25]

If we accept Arthur Custance's well-researched anthropology, then Ham and his sons were either Negroid or Mongoloid. Could these numerous and huge monolithic carvings of ancient Mexico be proof of an advanced prehistoric culture expressing their adulation for the Negroid gods responsible for their achievements?[26]

Figure 5   **Figure 6**

HIS-STORY AND MY-STORY

Advanced capabilities are evidenced by discoveries between 15,000 and 11,000 BC, which clearly indicate the presence of higher civilizations during that time. Could this have been the earmark to modern man's earliest concept of their gods? Noticeable advancements in megalithic construction, animal husbandry and agricultural ingenuity began to flourish at this time. It could very well be that miraculous achievements aided by Hamites led to the true start of incredible human accomplishments, which have been unearthed as the mysteries of today.

If we look again at the work of Arthur Custance, his position that all people on Earth are Noah's descendants conflicts with one of his very important discoveries, which indicate clearly the god-like status of Japheth while adding credence to the theorem that Noah's descendants were gods of ancient times.

> To begin with, it is well known that Japheth's name has been preserved in both branches of the Aryan family, which very early split into two major divisions and settled in Europe and India. The Greeks, for example, trace themselves back to *Japetos*, a name which without doubt is the same, and significantly, according to Skinner, has no meaning in Greek. It does have a meaning, however, in Hebrew. In Aristophanes' *The Clouds*, Iapetos is referred to as one of the Titans and the father of Atlas. He was considered by the Greeks not merely as their own ancestor but the father of the human race. According to their tradition, Ouranos and Gaia (i.e., Heaven and Earth) had six sons and six daughters, but of this family only one - *Japetos* by name - had a human progeny. He married Clymene, a daughter of Okeanos, who bore him Prometheus and three other sons. Prometheus begat Deucalion who is, in effect, the "Noah" of the Greeks, and Deucalion begat Hellen

153

ALPHA TO OMEGA

who was the reputed father of the Hellenes or Greeks. If we proceed a little further, we find that Hellen himself had a grandson named *Ion*; and in Homer's poetry the rank and file of the Greeks were known as *Ionians*.[27]

The myths of ancient Greece, which originated as garbled verbal accounts of their prehistoric pantheon, support the notion of Noah's family being the patriarchal gods of a new society. Although the above implies that the Greeks were descendants of Japetos, it also implies that Noah was a descendant of Japetos, so it is more likely to be an error in the translation during centuries or perhaps even millennia of oral tradition.

Japetos (Iapetos) is one of the many major gods in the ancient Greek pantheon. This isn't meant to imply that interbreeding hadn't occurred over time. Interbreeding was unavoidable for all of Noah's descendants as the years progressed and is evidenced by descriptions of demigods born by the procreation of gods and mortals in ancient mythical legends. Pure genealogy could not be maintained and should be understood when considering that only eight antediluvian survivors made the journey to the New Age.

The conflict between history and myth has stemmed from the religious presumptions maintaining Noah's undiluted progeny, the identical physical make-up of our human heritage and, most importantly, no significant break in time between our civilizations.

Obviously, the Greek populace had honored the powerful, benevolent and respectable god-like entities of their ancient history. The notion that the population of Greece, or any region for that matter, was spawned by pure gods who were later glorified by their

154

HIS-STORY AND MY-STORY

descendants doesn't make sense or allow for the many civilizations discovered and dated prior to 6000 BC.

> Meanwhile, the Indian branch of this Aryan family also traced themselves back to the same man. In the Indian account of the Flood, "Noah" is known as *Satyaurata*, who had three sons, the eldest of whom was named Jyapeti. The other two were called Sharma and C'harma (Shem and Ham?). To the first he allotted all the regions north of the Himalayas and to Sharma he gave the country to the south. But he cursed C'harma, because when the old monarch was accidentally inebriated with strong liquor made from fermented rice, C'harma had laughed at him.[28]

Here again is a nearly identical similarity to the ancient Hebrew Old Testament where Noah's grandson Canaan (son of Ham) is cursed because of his reactions to Noah's inebriation and nakedness. These coincidences provide substantial evidence that the patriarchs influenced all known societies of ancient times. They must have been antecedent to everything in our era.

Patriarchal descendants, who presided over specific regions, coexisted and mated with evolutionary humans in order to assist them with their progress over a long duration of time. It's clear in Custance's anthropologic research that Japheth's influence extended from Greece to parts of the Middle East and into the Indus Valley, where he and his sons were venerated by civilizations that already existed after a long duration of establishment by Ham's descendants and their influence.

> Centuries later, spreading at a more leisurely rate, Japheth settled slowly into the areas already opened up by Ham, in almost every case adopting the solutions, suited to local survival, which the predecessors had already worked out.[29]

ALPHA TO OMEGA

Noah and his family were gods to the undeveloped, uninformed, uneducated and archaic people in the new age, which began about 200,000 years ago and is evidenced by progressive human attributes in early Homo sapiens. Noah's intervention was carefully planned and implemented over thousands of years for the sake of the souls of their prior civilization. They were early gods of the ignorant who provided power to a developing primitive civilization in incremental steps, which is delineated by each of Noah's sons.

A piece of subtle evidence supporting the incremental steps of patriarchal influence can be found again in Mexico's ancient Olmec civilization. Evidence of human and animal sacrificial rituals are found in remaining altar-like structures at many of the Olmec sites. These types of customary rituals, which were deemed appropriate and described in early religious texts, have always seemed out of place in my assessment of the religious experience.

I had often pondered the meaning of such a barbaric ritual until a reasonable explanation had finally dawned on me. In retrospect, we may see it as barbaric, but it was a necessary practice in the progressive teachings, which advocate life as temporal, the soul as eternal and God above all. For creatures without even a clue or a concept of God, there had to be a way to teach the initial concept in an indelibly impressive manner. The initial understanding of God could not have been expressed in any other possible way to the archaic, uninformed savages of the ancient world.

In further analysis of Custance's work and the Old Testament, Noah's role throughout the long process of human development is rarely mentioned. Similarly, his wife or the wives and daughters of

156

HIS-STORY AND MY-STORY

his sons are rarely mentioned or accounted for in the Table of Nations. Could it be that these women were the goddesses of Greek and Egyptian folklore? We must assume it to be so within the context of this analysis. The Greek and Egyptian pantheons, although complex, are undoubtedly a direct correlation to the patriarchs and matriarchs who came from the antediluvian world and bore children thousands of years ago.

Noah bears remarkable resemblance to the similar gods of ancient Mesopotamia: Utnapishtim, Zisudra, Xisuthros and Atrahasis. Legendary folklore like this exist for one reason only—they are shattered tales that survived the eons of time because of their crucial significance to the origin and destiny of our species. There was one Great Flood and one Great Patriarch of the new age. Noah is the central figure and is revered in all of the myths of Mesopotamia, India, Greece, Central and South America.

> And his body was white as snow and red as the blooming of a rose, and the hair of his head and his long locks were white as wool, and his eyes beautiful. And when he opened his eyes, he lighted up the whole house like the sun, and the whole house was very bright. And thereupon he arose in the hands of the midwife, opened his mouth, and conversed with the Lord of righteousness.[30]

Is there evidence suggesting Noah's influence outside of the Egyptian center? We need only to briefly touch on the legendary gods of the ancient Aztec and Inca traditions to find remarkable similarities in their descriptions of a large white man with blue eyes and a silver beard—a teacher, benefactor, healer and God of peace with great powers.

157

ALPHA TO OMEGA

Viracocha, the ancient Incan god, and the Aztec's renowned Quetzalcoatl are the mythical and highly idolized gods of South and Central America. Based on mostly oral tradition, these appear to be the same god who aided in the development of both the Incan and Aztec high societies of the Western world. Most written evidence and many important artifacts of each culture were destroyed in the Spanish conquests of the 16th century, but much has been unearthed to undoubtedly prove that both advanced civilizations significantly revered their ancient mythical god.

As the myth explains, Quetzalcoatl was the God of the new sun of the Fifth Age followed by a catastrophic deluge that destroyed the Fourth Age. He was a bearded white man just like Viracocha. Viracocha's capital was Tiahuanaco, the famed ancient and mysterious megalithic city in the Andes. Quetzalcoatl's was Teotihuacan, the ancient city of Mexico known for its mysterious pyramids and referred to as the city of the gods.[31] Could these ancient legends be descriptions of Noah?

Tiahuanaco, an ancient ruined city of Bolivia, is believed to be a city raised by the inspiration of Viracocha and evidenced by statues depicting him much in the same manner with which he had been described in ancient texts. Situated 12,500 feet above sea level, the ancient city is comprised of giant boulders—some weighing in excess of hundred tons—transported tens of miles and used in the construction of the entire city and surrounding walls. Monoliths weighing up to 20 tons and carved to depict the gods of their times are scattered throughout the city and its outskirts.

158

HIS-STORY AND MY-STORY

Another spectacular construction within the city is known as the Kalasasaya, a 450 square foot enclosure interspersed with 12 foot high monoliths carved into human figures. According to an archeologist named Arthur Posnansky who studied the site for almost 50 years, Tiahuanaco is approximately 17,000 years old. He based this information solely and exclusively on the difference in the obliquity of the ecliptic between the period in which the Kalasasaya was built and that which it is today. Simply put, he demonstrated that the angle of tilt in the Earth's axis changes with predictable precision, between 22.1° and 24.5°. He was able to date the Kalasasaya because the cycle gradually alters the position of sunrise and sunset over periods of time and that the alignments of the Kalasasaya suggest a tilt, which corresponds to approximately 15,000 BC.[32]

Teotihuacan is quite as mystifying and remains an enigma because of alignments and positioning of three pyramids at the center of the city. They bear a resemblance to the Egyptian necropolis in that they were constructed on separate levels with one of the pyramids being offset from the others. Most impressive, however, is that Teotihuacan might have been originally designed as a precise scale-model of the solar system. An American engineer named Hugh Harleston, noticed correlations to structures throughout the city with inner and outer planets of the solar system, when using the center line of the Temple of Quetzalcoatl—a monument in the center of the city—as the position of the sun. At the very least, these discoveries suggest advanced observational astronomy at Teotihuacan long before the discovery of the outer planets of our solar system.[33]

ALPHA TO OMEGA

Egypt's famed tales of ancient gods bear clues to similarities that beg us to wonder if, in fact, history has ineffectively translated the oral traditions preceding ancient texts.

> Ra was ancient Egypt's God of heaven and earth who reigned for a thousand years and was said to have arrived by a Celestial Barque (a massive ship) called the *'Ben Ben'* (meaning 'Pyramidion Bird') from the "Planet of Millions of Years." [34]

Is this a coincidental legend or time's translation of the truth describing antediluvian gods ruling over a new age, separated from theirs by millions of years? Osiris, the fifth god in succession to Ra, is remembered much like Viracocha and Quetzalcoatl—a benefactor of mankind, a bringer of enlightenment and a great civilizing leader.[35]

An interesting contrast to those of Adam's time is notably important. In Adam's age, Absolute Knowledge is the complete provision for the knowledge of God, supreme intellect and omnipotence. In our era, we've demonstrated that power was first, knowledge or intellect was later introduced thousands of years later, which was followed by attempts to bring about a God consciousness in early humans centuries later.

> With this very brief explanation of how we are using the terms, we can go one step further and observe that while Semitic people have tended to lay the emphasis on the search for righteousness, the Japhetic or Indo-European peoples have laid the emphasis on the search for understanding, and the Hamitic people have searched for power.[36]

HIS-STORY AND MY-STORY

In a brief evaluation of the legendary Greek and Egyptian pantheons, a colossal amount of time predated the emergence of epic events and calamities. Marriages of incest, clashes between gods, goddesses, demigods and Pharaohs, are much later depicted in the embellished renditions of a legendary history, to which we will never be certain. Even the Bible specifically denotes the marriages of incest, infidelity and the commonality of infertile women.

> Now these are the descendents of Terah. Terah was the father of Abram, Nahor and Haran; and Haran was the father of Lot. Haran died before his father Terah in the land of his birth (Haran), in Ur of the Chaldeans. And Abram and Nahor took wives; the name of Abram's wife was Sarai, and the name of Nahor's wife, Milcah, the daughter of Haran, the father of Milcah and Iscah. Now Sarai was barren; she had no child. (Genesis 11: 27-30)
>
> *(Nahor's wife was his niece. Author added parenthetical notation to illustrate a region had already been named for Haran before his death)*

It is conceivable that conflicts and power struggles developed between gods and societies after hundreds of centuries. Perhaps the eon-long process was extremely difficult to learn from a stubborn student's perspective and very frustrating to an advanced teacher. From the early Hamitic tribes of Neanderthal man through 15,000 BC is a very long time.

Noah and his three sons and wives arriving from an antediluvian world doesn't imply each generation of descendants was equally dedicated to the cause or that conflicts didn't arise after thousands of years. It doesn't imply that frustration was uncharacteristic of

ALPHA TO OMEGA

gods long removed from the pure genealogy of their distant ancestors. It is rather easy to imagine how, over time and generations, the effort to enlighten the darkened souls of a new race was an enormous task, which slowly played its part in the erosion of Noah's seeds and the long but eventual homogenization of the species.

Reasons for disputes can easily be presupposed by positing each of Noah's sons to represent separate enduring epochs of learning in postdiluvial development. We showed the emergence of Japheth long after Ham's worldly contribution. Could Shem's spiritual contribution have seriously threatened the ancient power arrangement?

Curiously, a discovery in La Venta, Mexico by Matthew Stirling in the 1940's may provide clues illustrating conflicts among the gods. La Venta was an ancient Olmec site where Stirling unearthed a stele 14 feet high, 7 feet wide and almost 3 feet thick.[37] The carvings on it showed an encounter between two tall white men, which for some reason must have been of immense importance to the Olmecs, evidenced by the grandeur of the stele itself and the unearthed construction of the remarkable stockade of columns built to contain it. [38]

The record of the encounter itself provides clues to possible conflicts between gods, which were witnessed by the ancient Olmec. Why would the Olmec include these depictions with the other important carvings of their lost civilization? Why else would two large white men be in ancient Mexico's Negroid civilization long before white people knew the land existed?

In Peru, aerial explorations of the arid plateaus and tablelands surrounding the Palpa Valley reveal a remarkable network of lines

HIS-STORY AND MY-STORY

and trapezoids interspersed with giant animal figures. These giant figures, known as the Nazca Lines, carved into 200 square miles of plateaus are a nearly impossible accomplishment for any society of prehistory. They weren't popularized until modern-day flight aided in their discovery and worldwide recognition. More than 70 carved drawings depict animals, birds, fish and human figures, some measuring 660 feet across.

Pyramids and megalithic structures are found all over the ancient Western world. In fact, there are ten times as many pyramids found in Mesoamerica than in Egypt.[39] Although not as sophisticated as the Great Pyramid of Egypt, some are quite large. The most notable is in Cholula, Mexico not far from Teotihuacan. The base area of Cholula's pyramid is 45 acres and stands at a height of 210 feet.

Is it possible that descendants of ancient gods and their followers were earnestly trying to re-create the magnificent time-energy device of ancient Egypt? If so, what were their motives? Is it possible that the Nazca lines were desperate attempts by Noah's descendants to summon the Angels for rescue from their labors? Did 200,000 years of effort prove to be futile and frustrating to the gods of the ignorant?

Unless we peruse thousands of legends for similarities that we can somehow connect, the real truth to these mysteries lies in whether or not we are willing to accept theorems that run counter to what we have been schooled to believe. We must realize that traditional historical assumptions are based on the same limited evidence with which these have been derived. Prehistory is a big mystery.

ALPHA TO OMEGA

Solving the mysteries of history can ultimately define our world and our place in it. While our new assumptions may add credence to the many ancient myths and legends later ostracized by early religious and historical authority, they present new factors and questions for examination.

Chapter 5

FIGURE OF SPEECH

The Truth is always revealing itself.

Bliss of an Infant

An analogous glance at the birth of ancient Egypt can assist in discovering additional clues to their majestic wonders. History, as we know it, has been founded where we might find more hints to our mysterious past and the road to our future.

The Great Pyramid was constructed as a perfect model of a magnificent civilization only one step removed from Supremacy. The Ark provided an unusual and remarkable power, but offered no provisions for knowledge. Power can be shared, while knowledge needs to be acquired. In our age, power precipitates knowledge and is fully exemplified by the ancient Egyptians in the midst of the Great Patriarchs, Matriarchs and the Great Pyramid.

We can put it into clearer perspective with an analogy of our human condition. When we discussed the crucial reason for

ALPHA TO OMEGA

Noah's empowerment, we demonstrated the three specific entities of human beings—ego, soul and Spirit—and their relation to each other in bringing the illumination of spirit to the soul.

Born into this world, we are devoid of knowledge, ego, consciousness and sub-consciousness. We are born with a body and a mind, but the mind is empty. Without knowledge, awareness or experiences, our ego and soul do not yet exist. If we can agree that Spirit does exist, then we must agree that we are bound only to pure Spirit at birth and therefore have limitless power potential.

I will venture to infer that all infants could cure any congenital birth defects if they were consciously aware of their ailments. Infants are born without knowledge and self-awareness, which means that ego hasn't developed and therefore awareness of the power potential is missing. Ignorance smothers the potential power of Spirit, which is a distinct contrast to those who were afforded Absolute Knowledge and Absolute Power simultaneously.

Although children possess unison to Spirit at infancy, they remain humble during the earliest years, because self-awareness is undeveloped and prevents them from knowing the power they possess. We can easily observe a child's remarkable acute perceptive abilities. They learn more than just the rudiments of a language (sometimes two languages) in two years. Science has proven we learn more during the first two years of life than we do during anytime afterwards.

A Supreme Being is completely aware in all aspects and can choose whether or not to abandon the use of power for temporal

FIGURE OF SPEECH

individual concerns. A child doesn't consciously relinquish the use of power but is humble while using it unknowingly.

> Truly I say unto you, unless you turn and become as little children, ye shall not enter into the kingdom of heaven. Whoever humbles himself like this child, he is the greatest in the kingdom of heaven. (Matthew 18: 3-4)

The Ark was the catalyst to life's rejuvenation on the planet and it greatly enhanced the power potential of those within its proximity for several millennia. Hunger, thirst, pain, disease, and even death, were largely reduced by the Tree of Life at the center of Egypt's early society.

The original Egyptians are analogous to an unknowing infant, whose power is indefinable and unrecognizable without knowledge and awareness. The birth of the new age is typified by the blindness of the ancient Egyptians and their power potential—much like a child—which contrasts to the birth of the previous age typified by perfect vision and absolute power.

Without awareness there is no soul and without knowledge, there is no comprehension. Much like the beauty of an unthinking rose, the Egyptians were the most beautiful humans on the face of the earth. And, much like an infant, they were innocent and unaware of their existence, beauty and potential power.

Could they have been the first to mate with the sons and daughters of Noah's offspring over 200,000 years ago? We cannot presume constant incest among Noah's family and in the context of this theory, it is highly likely for Noah to have expected the evolutionary humans in the Ark's proximity to be the finest and most suitable for

ALPHA TO OMEGA

mating with their children. Is this an explanation for biblical verses describing sons of gods mating with the daughters of men?

While the savage evolutionary humans throughout other parts of the world were experiencing their trials and tribulations, Egypt basked in a world of its own, oblivious to everything. The physical arrangements were fascinating but simple. Their source and center was the Tree of Life and the arrangement would continue for as long as the Egyptians remained innocent. What is innocence? Simply put, innocence is humble action in accordance with the knowledge we acquire—just like a child.

Despite Adam's transgression, his soul was brightly illuminated by the knowledge of God. His power was immense (as were all of those from the previous civilization), but his innocence was gone. In the light of absolute knowledge, innocence disappears after the first conscious mistake; the approach to the Cherubim guarding the Tree of Life was impossible (except for Noah and his family who remained innocent).

How could it have been possible for primordial humans to withstand the presence of the Cherubim in ancient Egypt? Subtly revealed here is the nature of God. In the time of Adam and Eve, Absolute Knowledge preceded everything. In the new age, complete ignorance is the origin and can be observed as pure innocence, which is forgiven through mercy.

This explains why the earliest Egyptians were not affected by the Cherubim—the capstone and Beacon to the Tree of Life. It also provides clues to why the Ark of the Covenant bears the description of a "mercy seat" between its Cherubim.

FIGURE OF SPEECH

The cherubim spread out their wings above, overshadowing the mercy seat with their wings, with their faces one to another; toward the mercy seat were the faces of the cherubim. (Exodus 37:9)

Early Egypt is categorized by their amazing power and complete innocence, but their power source was the Tree of Life. Unlike the preceding age of omniscience, there has always been a yearning for knowledge to explain the undefined in our new era. Over the millennia, the ancient Egyptians became more aware of their surroundings and physical nature. Their curiosity grew and, like a child, they began to become inquisitive.

The Egyptians and their mysteries can be explained by a very slow awakening to remarkable capabilities because of the Ark. Try to envisage the Egyptian society as the birth and awakening of a powerful child over 200,000 years or more. Imagine an unlimited power not recognized by the mind but somewhat reduced by the mind's awareness—a distinctly opposing arrangement to the previous age and an amazing similarity to an infant bound to pure Spirit at birth.

A gradual loss of truth and power is natural in the sensual awakening to a world of incomplete knowledge and it is evidenced by the incomplete and presumed realities exposed by our contemporary limited concepts. As children, our growing awareness is molded by the continual bombardment of sensory information and subconscious recognition of behaviors among those in our environment.

Presumed realities, which our growing ego imposes upon us, prevent us from recognizing or connecting to our true nature. As

ALPHA TO OMEGA

our poorly defined reality grows with our self-awareness, the Light and Truth of Spirit recognized at infancy becomes an increasingly obscure and deeply embedded memory in our subconscious soul. It's that precise memory that serves as the center of our wisdom.

Only the sixth sense of wisdom can expose what the other five have hidden.

Imagine the circumstances of the only unblemished evolutionary creatures on earth. They mated with the gods, coexisted with them and remained, innocent and powerful like a child for thousands of years. All of the myths of the Greek, Roman and Egyptian gods were tales of events occurring thousands of years after the very earliest Egyptian "infants".

I suspect at some point the very ancient Egyptians had become aware of their remarkable abilities and unique relationship with the gods. We awaken to a much limited world today and are not exposed to the same power as ancient Egypt. The gradual loss of power in ancient Egypt began with an enormous amount to begin with.

In the years that followed, the Egyptians would be implored to question and explain their unique arrangement. Just like a child becomes a teenager so too did the Egyptian society.

We have been led to believe that we have evolved into the civilized and intelligent humans of today because of our own ingenuity. The story of Noah is not a fable but rather an ineffectively translated truth, which helps to explain the mysteries and myths of our ancient world. Without the gods of the ignorant, our process of

170

FIGURE OF SPEECH

development would be much slower and more painstaking. Noah wanted expediency for the redemption of the Atlantean's souls.

Ball of Confusion

At approximately 15,000 BC, the Western world and Egypt's surrounding regions had become advanced civilizations reflecting the superior technology of the Hamites and the intellectual prowess of the Japhethites. Remarkable accomplishments far surpassing those of our present day were ordinary. One of the most apparent advancements was the ability to transport, carve, cut and dress extremely heavy boulders with ease and exquisite precision.

Advanced aqueducts for irrigation, skilled hillside agriculture and remnants of fantastic monuments are succinct evidence of advanced civilizations in Mexico and Egypt, which appear to have been formed almost overnight. Ironically, they seem to have disappeared almost as quickly and without explanation, leaving many to posit a cataclysm to have destroyed the advanced civilizations or that aliens had swiftly departed leaving us to fend for ourselves.

Did an extraordinary event cause an almost instant reduction in the abilities of the ancient and advanced humans? What evidence do we have that might support this idea?

The Tower of Babel has long been thought to be the origin of separate languages throughout the world. Notably, in Genesis, chapter 10, the generations of all the sons of Noah and their immediate families are outlined. Each description specifically denotes

171

ALPHA TO OMEGA

each was with his own language by their families in their nations after the flood.

> These are the sons of Japheth in their lands, each with his own language, by their families, in their nations. (Gen 10:5)

> These are the sons of Ham, by their families, their languages, their lands and their nations. (Gen 10: 20)

> These are the sons of Shem, by their families, their languages, their lands and their nations. (Gen 10: 31)

Anthropologists have used the above delineations as guidelines in determining the earliest heritages and their backgrounds. The table of nations is built upon the descriptions in those chapters and provides important clues to early mankind's development and regional influence.

In the first verse of Genesis, chapter 11, is an immediate start to the well-known story:

> Now the whole earth had one language and few words. And as men migrated from the East, they found a plain in the land of Shinar and settled there. And they said to one another, 'Come, let us make bricks and burn them thoroughly.' And they had brick for stone and bitumen for mortar. Then they said, 'Come, let us build ourselves a city, and a tower with its top in the heavens, and let us make a name for ourselves lest we be scattered abroad upon the face of the whole earth.' And the Lord came down to see the city and the tower, which the sons of men had built. And the Lord said, 'Behold, they are one people and they have all one language; and this is only the beginning of what they will do; and nothing that they propose to do will now be impossible for them. Come, let us go down and there confuse their language, that they may

FIGURE OF SPEECH

not understand one another's speech.' So the Lord scattered them abroad from there over the face of all the earth and they left off building the city. Therefore, its name was called Babel, because there the Lord confused the language of all the earth; and from there the Lord scattered them abroad over the face of the earth. (Genesis, 11: 1-9)

It has always puzzled me that Shem's descendants are described *again* in the very next verse—this time with the years of genealogy included. It's an indication that Shem's introduction to humanity coincided with dramatic events leading to confusion, disarray and power struggles—one of which may have been depicted on the stele unearthed in Mexico.

Before I get into a more detailed explanation of this possibility, languages had already been indigenous among different regions of the world by the time Shem made his way onto the scene. According to the recorded genealogy of Shem and his descendants, he was 290 years older than Abram. If we further agree with the historical presumption dating the exodus at about 1450 BC, then we can see Shem's influence arriving at approximately 2675 BC (we've established 937 years from Abram to the Exodus based on biblical chronology). By that time, many languages had flourished worldwide and are evidenced in the discovery of ancient texts.

The notion that language had become diverse at a singular point in time was chastised even by biblical literalists, who believe it to be a myth fabricated long after the event it was supposed to explain. Their argument rests on ancient Sumerian texts depicting the tower of Babel story long before 2500 BC, which is when literalists believe the flood to have occurred.[1]

173

It is impossible to find corroborating evidence in any historical account that could provide us with clues to the exact chronology of prehistory. We can evaluate some evidence demonstrating Babel to have preceded the earliest known Sumerian texts by at least 4,000 years. Likewise, we can use different evidence and find Babel to have occurred about 3450 BC.

The most important consideration is the significance of the story and the confusing beliefs lingering today. In my opinion, the Babel story represents an unexpected and colossal world-changing event, which marks the fork in the road dividing myth and written history.

Notwithstanding, even theologians are divided over the chronology of events, specifically the Exodus, which is believed to be either 1440 BC or 1290 BC. Either date is based on assumptions derived from backdating specific events historically believed to have occurred at a particular time. Importantly, neither date was derived from the Pentateuch, but rather the later historical books of Old Testament history.

An authority proclaiming to be sole possessors of God's word maintained control of public opinion for a very long period of time. Importantly, control could not have been possible without authoritative interpretations deemed reliable by a suddenly confused and somewhat anarchistic society.

Still, a complete and sudden diversity in worldwide language is just as difficult to assume, based on current historical presumptions, as Custance explains:

FIGURE OF SPEECH

When, however, according to scientific theories the first human couple were set back in time, not merely thousands of years, but hundreds of thousands of years; and when the picture of population growth thereafter was of exceedingly small families of scarcely human creatures scattered in dreadful isolation over the globe, developing their own embryonic forms of speech in total independence of one another through eons of time, then it seemed meaningless to speak of mankind in any real sense as ever having shared a single form of language.[2]

This is not to imply that Custance believed in the scientific theories of prehistoric humans, but how applying these theories provide explicitly for several original languages throughout the world. Since we are presenting history to be far more extended than Custance exhibits, we can use his observation to support our theory, but it will need to be examined more closely.

In our analysis we posit each of Noah's sons to be individual gods separated by thousands of years rather than hundreds. If we begin with the notion that a marked separation of intelligence hindered communication between the Hamites and primitive man, then we can surmise the far superior gods to have utilized extraordinary methods of conveying messages, which may have helped to gain the awe and trust of the primitives.

The early savages of primitive history were hunters, survivors and killers. It's reasonable to suggest Ham's descendants (Neanderthals) were considered a threat to the survival of ancient Cro-Magnon. Undoubtedly, remarkable feats, which could easily be recognized by Homo sapiens, were demonstrated to diminish and eliminate the primary hurdle of fear.

This leads me to suspect the development of language to have been secondary to some sort of telepathic communication between evolving savages and enlightened gods. The slow process of mentoring and communication may have begun with teaching primitives how to make tools, but in actuality, the rudiments of metaphysics were the objective of their teachings.

Thousands of years must have been necessary to develop the somewhat effective use of these exceptional skills, which is evidenced by marked advancements unearthed in the much later archaeological discoveries. Archaeology remains bewildered by evidence suggesting human intellect and abilities to have increased by leaps and bounds in an unexplainably short period of time throughout the world. Evidence confirms highly advanced technologies were being used between 15,000 and 11,000 BC in South and Central America and in Egypt.

Curiously, our concepts concerning the methods of power utilization in ancient times are based upon our observations of its use today, which might be the clue to understanding the mystery of the tower of Babel.

From a metaphysical standpoint, absolute power can be construed as the mental control of energy and matter, which greatly reduces time in the physical manipulation of a three dimensional world. Today, we use our mind by first conceiving of methods and tools required to achieve an objective, and secondly, conceiving ways of developing tools, equipment and processes to perform tasks that would be impossible without them.

FIGURE OF SPEECH

This observation helps us to see how the mind is foremost in all levels of power, but the more limited levels require several procedures and more time in the manipulation of energy and matter in our physical world. In the absolute sense, a Supreme Being or demigod has the power to manipulate the physical world in any manner conceivable by the mind.

Today, we are limited in achieving only what is physically possible by incremental utilization of the collective advancements of our civilization, but everything remains a production of our collective mind through time.

In the days when Neolithic man was performing spectacular feats throughout the world, a concept of a lesser physical arrangement did not exist. The collective reality was based upon the observable arrangements, which were believed to be the norm. Early humans were given advanced power and capabilities, but the underlying knowledge was foreign to them. Compare it to teaching a child to use the telephone where methods can be taught but the underlying knowledge of the device is foreign to the child.

The emergence of Japheth's intellectual contribution markedly increased the capabilities of humans as evidenced in the discoveries of advanced civilizations. As man became more intellectual, an exponential increase in power becomes evident by approximately 15,000 BC.

Humans were becoming educated, which allowed them to utilize their power more efficiently. Unlike Atlantis, knowledge was limited, but power wasn't because methods had been shared by the gods. Keep in mind, the objective of Noah and his family was to

ALPHA TO OMEGA

speed up the process of human progress in the hopes of a return to Paradise.

Humans had reached the point in their evolution where a more thorough understanding of God was necessary for an eventual return to Paradise. It makes complete sense for advanced power to have been the priority in developing a new and primitive world. It follows that intellectual gains would be the next step in the education of an ignorant race of people. Noah's premeditated plan was to provide the new era with remarkable abilities to quicken the process of his mission. The final step to man's progress would be learning to relinquish power and temporal concerns for the sake of understanding God.

Religious tradition professes Babel to be an act of God as punishment for man's power and temporal concerns. But, if the new era is marked first by unexplainable power, followed by knowledge and intellect, then it is fair to assume that man had only a vague, if any, concept of God to begin with. The only "gods" they knew where the descendants of Noah's family, who certainly didn't demand worship.

The Babel incident was a precursor to mankind's eventual understanding of God, rather than the effect of mankind's deliberate choice to turn their backs on a God they had yet to understand or discover. Renouncing power was a hard lesson for Noah and his civilization, but marks the beginning of a confusing and ill-translated chain of events and circumstances for the new era.

I suppose that both the advanced form of telepathic communication and paraphysical power had been instantly extinguished. Communication had been severed because people had to rely on

FIGURE OF SPEECH

their unique and secondary verbal modes of communication, which had been regionally developed over the many centuries.

Only the sudden and harsh reduction in a seemingly normal physical arrangement could catalyze the unquenchable search for lost power, knowledge and the eventual truths of humankind's purpose. If Paradise is to be restored on Earth, then absolute knowledge must be acquired through self-discovery, which is impossible without curiosity.

The final stage of human development in the ignorant age was Shem's spiritual contribution to mankind—the esoteric teachings of concepts and ideals regarding the true God. All of this was introduced in a world embroiled in confusion, upheaval and human nature. Spiritual concepts were completely foreign at that time and curiosity was at its peak in the aftermath of such a world-changing event.

By the time the earliest Sumerian texts of 3000 BC were transcribed, a story about the tower of Babel was contained in the texts. Several later tales from varying sources tell the same story. The common theme in each of these portrayals is that man had magnificent capabilities interrupted by sudden confusion.

I believe the tower of Babel to be representative of the many fantastic remains of ziggurats, monuments and pyramids throughout the world demonstrating remarkable achievements and unprecedented capabilities, which came to a sudden halt and spurred mass confusion.

Angelic intervention is evidenced in the Babel story where God says, *'Come, let us go down and there confuse their language, that*

ALPHA TO OMEGA

they may not understand one another's speech' (Again, the plural God, which we believe to be Angels doing the work of God, is represented in scripture). Could Babel's story be describing the effects caused by the removal of the Ark's Cherubim? If we believe Noah's sons to have been separate contributions to humankind over a long period of time, then Shem's arrival eliminated further need for the time machine.

If ancient Egyptians possessed incredible power because of their proximity to the Great Pyramid, then we can surmise equal confusion and unrest were prevalent in Egypt upon removal of the Cherubim. The Egyptians had experienced more superb conditions than the rest of the world. Suddenly, their way of life changed dramatically, but they were obviously able to retain a greater degree of power, which had been lost to the rest of the world. Proof is found in the battle between the Jews and Egyptians—the first major conflict of human history, which we will discuss shortly.

Egyptians had co-mingled and mated with the gods, witnessed the time machine's usage and had a direct connection to the center of Noah's operations for many millennia. They were a special breed and all of the mysteries of Egypt can be explained by their proximity to earth's rejuvenation headquarters.

Historical accounts dug-up by Manetho clearly differentiate between divine and semi-divine rule. Semi-divine, in my opinion, is another word for the offspring of early Egyptians and Noah's children. The word *'divine'*, witnessed in the historical analyses, is evidence of the concepts early man had placed upon Noah and his

FIGURE OF SPEECH

immediate family, who were not divine, but demigods from a previous society.

> In all, Manetho said, gods ruled for 13,870 years. A dynasty of thirty demigods followed; they ruled a total of 3,650 years. All in all, Manetho wrote, divine and semi-divine rulers reigned a total of 17,520 years. Then, after a chaotic intermediate period that lasted 350 years, with no one reigning over the whole (i.e., both Lower and Upper) of Egypt, Mênes began the first human dynasty of Pharaohs, ruling over a unified Egypt.[3]

Manetho's description of a 350 year "chaotic period" prior to the first human dynasty of Pharaohs could possibly be the great confusion and unrest brought on by the Babel incident. History tells us with pretty much certainty that the First Dynasty ruled by King Mênes occurred with the unification of Lower and Upper Egypt at approximately 3100 BC, which places the Babel event around 3450 BC. This explains the mysterious archeological evidence of technological and societal decay in succeeding centuries of Egypt's Old Kingdom. It also provides a better time-line for explaining the Babel story appearing in ancient Sumerian texts.

Archeological evidence adds some credence and support to Manetho's discoveries.

> Various modern archaeological discoveries that corroborate Manetho's 'Pharaohnic' list and order of succession include a document known as the Turin Papyrus and an artifact called the Palermo Stone, so named after the museums in Italy in which they are kept. The corroborating finds also include a stone inscription known as the Abydos List, in which the 19th dynasty Pharaohs Seti I and his son Ramses II, who reigned a thousand

181

ALPHA TO OMEGA

years before Manetho's time, depict themselves (Fig. 11). Carved on the walls of the main temple in Abydos, a city in Upper Egypt, it lists the names of seventy-five of their predecessors, beginning with "Mêna." The Turin Papyrus corroborates Manetho's divine, semi divine and chaotic-interval lists, and (including subsequent Pharaohs) names a total of 330 rulers, just as Herodotus had been told.[4]

Very little is known about the First Dynasty of Mêna and the succeeding Second Dynasty, both of which precede the Old Kingdom. The Old Kingdom begins with the third dynasty of Djoser at approximately 2686 BC. The Old Kingdom, by itself, is a huge mystery to historians who cannot understand how the Old Kingdom happened. With each new discovery, more questions emerge that cannot be answered by the currently accepted historical presumptions.

I had mentioned earlier the possibility of dating Babel's upheaval about 4,000 years prior to earliest known Sumerian texts. If Shem was the final god to exit the Ark and we refer to Manetho's chronology as a guide, then the end of the final *'divine'* ruler's reign predated King Mênes by at least 4,000 years—or about 7,100 BC. Biblical accounts require us to consider Shem's longevity of 502 years 'after' the flood or exiting the Great Pyramid. Did he begin his contribution to humanity somewhere around 7,600 BC?

According to biblical history's chronology, Shem's arrival is estimated at about 2675 BC as mentioned previously. If the Babel story predated Sumerian writings, as presumed by biblical literalists and evidenced by records of Babel in their earliest writings, then we would be forced to assume Babel to have predated Shem's

182

FIGURE OF SPEECH

introduction by at least 325 years or about 3000 BC. It doesn't make sense for Babel to occur before Shem's arrival because the upheaval instigated the Israelite-Egyptian conflict.

If we rely on Manetho's chronology, the *'chaotic period'* begins at 3450 BC, and ends at 3100 BC, which means that Shem arrived on the scene at about 3450 BC. This would have coincided with the Egyptians awakening to their advanced power, and set the stage for the major biblical conflict that began with Shem's introduction at about 3450 BC.

Taking into account the origins of historical tradition and the ineffective methods for gathering information during the advent of writing, the earliest historical records are much more susceptible to fallacies and errors. In the context of this presentation, biblical history is viewed as an organization of various recorded depictions and chronologies in an effort to standardize and unify concepts of the world and man's place within it.

> Shem had many sons and daughters and outlived all but Eber, his great grandson. Eber lived for twenty-nine years, after the death of Shem. Careful analysis of the Bible accounts shows there were fourteen generations from Shem to Joseph, the son of Jacob. Shem did not die until Joseph was thirty. Five years after Shem's death, Joseph settled his father, Jacob, in Egypt, who had been given the name, Israel.[5]

Taking this analysis into account along with Manetho's discoveries, we can estimate Shem's death to have occurred around 2950 BC and Jacob's settlement in Egypt at approximately the same time. This means that the exodus really took place around 2500 BC

183

ALPHA TO OMEGA

(exodus is chronologically reported to have occurred 937 years after Shem's introduction to humanity). All of the earliest chronological accounts were not synthesized until at least 1000 years later based on the known age of the earliest Hebrew accounts.

Again we are faced with incomplete evidence, conflicting stories and disjointed history. It's easy to understand how the earliest authorities would go to great lengths at unifying a confused mass of ancient people. The most important consideration is realizing that all of the major events long predated historical records and were extremely crucial in understanding human origins.

A battle between Greek, Egyptian and Jewish historical interpretations exacerbated the ineffective translation of the earliest events of prehistory.

Old paradigms can no longer provide meaningful answers to a curious and informed society. Many are turning their backs on an ill-defined God while trying to explain life's mysteries with more understandable solutions. Countless others continue to rely on their faith and the professions of leading church authorities. But faith, like God, is a word that often conjures a stigmatic concept.

The First conflict of humanity is not only a message of faith, but an exposition of the unobserved metaphysical nature of our everyday lives. It really doesn't matter exactly when the events transpired in history's chronology.

FIGURE OF SPEECH

Metaphysics of Faith

As we have shown, Divine Will is the incessant manipulation of energy and matter until the eventual expression of Creator can be perfectly mirrored in physical form—Supreme Being. This notion unequivocally suggests an unobserved constant:

The Truth is always trying to be revealed in our physical world.

Subtly, Divine Intervention is constantly happening all around us, but we don't see it as clearly as it really is.

We've expressed and clarified the relationship between knowledge and power. In a world of technological sophistication, an enormous amount of undiscovered knowledge remains. From an individual standpoint, the amount of undiscovered knowledge is considerably larger compared to the cumulative knowledge of mankind. Faith is the belief in unproven things or undiscovered knowledge, which invokes Divine Intervention for clarification.

Faith can be described as a wholehearted belief or conviction in any ideal, notion, concept or assumption, which invokes the actions and decisions we make in our lives. We've shown clearly how actions and decisions of today shape the individual and collective destiny of tomorrow. When our deepest convictions inspire our actions and decisions we encounter experiences that qualify or refute our beliefs thereby providing us with a new piece of knowledge.

The metaphysical nature of our relation to cause and effect begins with our beliefs, which are reflected in events designed by

185

ALPHA TO OMEGA

Truth to qualify or refute them. Our experiences continually change our beliefs, which create more experiences. This cycle works unceasingly to establish our individual beliefs and principles. Faith in our personal beliefs and the order in which we prioritize them empowers our actions, which determine our experiences.

Scientific power is the result of knowledge, not our faith in it. Instead, conviction or faith in a particular hypothesis inspires the scientific process of discovery. The power of belief is the designer of individual experiences. The combined faith of mankind, in a broad spectrum of beliefs, is the creator of humanity's experiences throughout history and today. The Truth is always trying to reveal itself in our physical world.

Faith has the potential for absolute power individually and collectively, but our adherence to diverse and incomplete beliefs stifles it. Our inherited concepts and temporal concerns are preventing us from moving forward because we don't see what is really going on around us. Inherent ignorance smothers the Absolute Power of Faith. (Figure 5)

> He (Jesus) said to them, "Because of your little faith. For truly, I say to you, if you have faith like a grain of mustard seed, you will say to this mountain, 'Move from here to there', and it will move, and nothing will be impossible for you." (Matthew 17: 20)

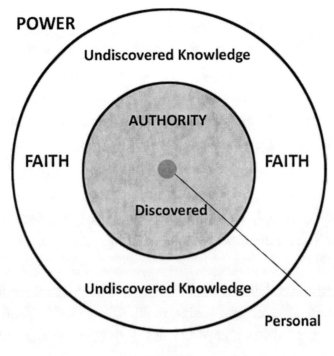

Figure 7

Faith in obscure concepts does not merit Absolute Power. We may know that God is real, but any power from faith is limited by vague notions and renders us powerless to the extent of personal beliefs and knowledge. The power of knowledge and the power of belief are equal. To move a mountain with the power of faith indicates believing in things much greater and knowing beyond any doubt.

> Now faith is the promise of things hoped for, the evidence of things not seen. For by it the men of old received divine approval. (Hebrews 11:1-2)

ALPHA TO OMEGA

The *"promise of things hoped for"* signifies a guarantee. The *"evidence of things not seen"* denotes knowing, without doubt or evidence. Believing in God doesn't warrant absolute power. We will get the desired results over time, but more experiences and time are required to clarify our concepts of God first. Return effects are limited by our slighted concepts of God and reality.

The evidence of unseen things is harbored in our soul, where the vague memory of Spirit—the embodiment of All Truth—resides. We can only discover it by a *prioritized yearning* for it and knowing beyond doubt we will find it through the sixth sense of our wisdom.

In order to totally relinquish the beliefs of our presumed realities to undiscovered knowledge requires unwavering faith in an eventual clarified vision of reality and the prioritized and dedicated actions. Resolute faith implies correctly prioritizing our concerns and knowing the end result will be inevitable.

Describing the concept is simple, but it remains a very difficult task. We have been born into a world of limitations. Many of our diversions are induced simply by the structure of our world. We need to work, eat, sleep and handle the responsibilities of living in a limited world. Our concerns are temporal by nature and our faith is incomplete and misplaced.

On a metaphysical level, all events are physical manifestations of faith, either exposing an uncorrected error of belief or qualifying a correct assessment in beliefs. On a collective scale, God is an integral part of myriad beliefs. Specific concepts may require

FIGURE OF SPEECH

adjustment, but opposing errors are diverse and not yet collective enough to be exposed by events necessary to correct them.

From an individual standpoint, most of us fall within certain categories of the collective mind and our individual experiences are the result of positive and negative variations of thought within the specific collective mindset. Eventually, God's Natural Intent to become expressed in consciousness will become manifested in physical events reflecting the errors of a collective consciousness. These events are most likely to be misconstrued by many individuals, but they will be the direct result of collective faith in flawed concepts and Truth's constant attempt to be revealed.

The physical manifestations of our world result from our incomplete knowledge and errant precepts. This is important because we cannot see the correlation to events and our ignorance. The major disasters of our physical world appear to be random events, but they are not.

This presentation began by seeing our world as a reflection of everything we do and everything we believe as a collective species. Our perceptual errors are being exposed in the physical world, which is nothing more than a manipulation of energy, space, matter and time through the collective consciousness. If we were collectively perfect, our physical world would be reflective of that harmony—Paradise.

Faith is nothing more than an invocation to action inspired by wholehearted belief, whether it is true or false. Unadulterated faith is the prioritized desire and method of bringing spiritual enlightenment to our darkened souls. We need only to look at the myster-

ALPHA TO OMEGA

ies of the ancient and first human conflict to verify these observations.

As was noted in the prior discourse, despite the confusion and loss of power to most of the world's inhabitants, the ancient Egyptians had retained power because of the advanced knowledge of which they had acquired. For thousands of years, they were at the center of the entire world's power delegation. They had remained innocent for a very long time. Manetho's description of semi-divine rulers suggests they later began to rule as demigods sometime in more recent eras of prehistory.

According to Old Testament Scripture, their abilities were considerably advanced and are exposed in the conflict with Aaron and Moses.

And the Lord said to Moses and Aaron, 'When Pharaoh says to you, "Prove yourselves by working a miracle," then you shall say to Aaron, "Take your rod and cast it down before Pharaoh, that it may become a serpent." So Moses and Aaron went to the Pharaoh and did as the Lord commanded; Aaron cast down his rod before Pharaoh and his servants, and it became a serpent. Then Pharaoh summoned the wise men and sorcerers; and they also, the magicians of Egypt, did the same by their secret arts. For every man cast down his rod and it became serpents. But Aaron's rod swallowed up their rods. Still Pharaoh's heart was hardened, and he would not listen to them; as the Lord had said. (Exodus 7: 8-13)

The significance of this story is not so much the power of the Egyptians, but the demonstration of greater power from faith bestowed on Shem's descendents. His arrival into the world signi-

190

FIGURE OF SPEECH

fies the relinquishment of power for a true God, which we denote as the initiation to the first conflict of humanity.

Confusion reigned, but the Egyptians did not want to surrender the remaining power they possessed. Egyptians believed they were godlike, which was a perceptual error much in need of correction for mankind to achieve true spiritual progress. Equal or greater power was necessary to challenge the Egyptians and it could only come from the power of faith—knowing it could be done.

The Egyptians were stunned by the observable accomplishments of a presumably inferior progeny. Notably, the Israelites did not have a complete understanding of God. This is why their faith was characterized as righteousness. The power they received through faith, led them to believe they were completely right.

> To what then shall we say about Abraham, our forefather according to the flesh? For if Abraham was justified by his works he has something to boast about, but not before God. For what does the Scripture say? "Abraham believed God, and it was reckoned to him as righteousness." Now, to one who works, his wages are not reckoned as a gift but as is due. And to one who does not work but trusts him who justifies the ungodly, his faith is reckoned to him as righteousness. (Romans 4: 1-5)

The Shemites (Semites) were the first to challenge the errant and long existing precepts of a great civilization. The Egyptian presumed reality of supremacy and power was an error needing correction, despite the limits of Jewish knowledge and power.

Plenty of evidence demonstrates the inherent ignorance of the Jews. Sarah committed adultery and Abraham was willing to sacrifice his son Isaac to prove their faith. Jacob had several wives

ALPHA TO OMEGA

and deceived his father in order to become the leader of the Hebrew faith. Moses murdered a man who was inflicting punishment on a fellow Jew. This is certainly not absolute knowledge or understanding in any way.

The faith of Moses and his followers is demonstrated by an invocation to act according to their beliefs. Their belief manifested in miraculous physical events, which exposed a major and primary conceptual error. It was imperative to alter the Egyptian belief.

The biblical plagues were manifestations of power, which significantly reduced Egyptian power and prodded their acceptance of the Israelites. Some have suggested the plagues were induced by circumstances brought on by the eruption of Thera, a huge caldera off the coast of Greece, which is known as Santorini today. Thera's eruption is known now to be far larger than the renowned Krakatoa eruption of 1883 and would have created exceedingly adverse conditions (Thera is believed to have erupted sometime around 1625 BC, which pushes the date of the exodus back almost 200 years).

Most important is realizing that any naturally occurring event does not exclude the power of faith as the impetus. In effect, timing is an integral part of Divine Intervention. Until the Israelite challenge, the power of opposing convictions did not exist. The precepts had been accepted by the majority because of the exposed capabilities of the superior Egyptians. Once the challenge was presented, Divine Intervention was inevitable to qualify the truth.

Moses' fear of the Egyptian power and might was most likely felt by every society in the Mideast. In the conversation with

FIGURE OF SPEECH

Moses, God (keep in mind that God works through Angels) continues to reveal the powers of Moses' faith to help him take the steps necessary to challenge the Egyptians. Chapters three and four of Exodus present Moses' fear and the power of his faith in conflict.

> Then Moses answered, "But, behold, they will not believe me or listen to my voice, for they will say, 'the Lord did not appear to you.'" The Lord said to him, "What is that in your hand?" He said, "A rod." And he said, "Cast it on the ground." So he cast it on the ground, and it became a serpent; and Moses fled from it. (Exodus 4: 1-3)

Inherent ignorance and fear prevailed. Moses' faith continued to manifest powers, despite his transgressions, because God's intervention (through Angels), removed all doubt in his mind. Moses may not have understood the reasons completely, but he knew for certain that his mission was to prove the ancient Egyptians were not gods and that the one true God had power over them. The power was in the truth of undiscovered knowledge, revealed in the miracles of Jewish faith.

The primary reason for each event was to change the stifling precepts of a powerful Egyptian civilization. The challenge to the ancient Egyptians and their false beliefs was a necessary accomplishment in the New Age. The Israelites were not exempt from the binds of original sin, but they preached a new concept, which the Egyptians vehemently opposed at the onset.

As Egyptian awareness had grown over centuries, their innocence had become eroded by the desire for power, which made it difficult to look beyond their physical realities. The newly imposed

193

ALPHA TO OMEGA

concepts were not clearly understood then, as is evidenced by Moses' confusion, but he was empowered by miraculous events to continue his mission to implant a new concept of God to an uninformed society. The infusion of a God concept depended upon the Israelites' faith to overcome the powerful Egyptians.

Today, our collective beliefs are diverse and obscure. Almost everyone has a different clouded view on the afterlife, God, Satan, heaven and hell. Are the diverse and fuzzy perspectives about to be exposed in unavoidable events naturally designed to reveal the errors in our precepts? How can we expect to see Truth with clarity if we do not want it more than anything else?

> Then Moses said to God, "If I come to the people of Israel and say to them, 'The God of your fathers has sent me to you,' and they asked me, 'What is his name?' What shall I say to them?" God said to Moses, 'I am who I am.' And he said, 'Say that to the people of Israel, I am has sent me to you.'" (Exodus 3: 13-14)

Doesn't, "I am has sent me to you" imply that God is within us? Moses was searching for something to verify his role in the course of important events, to which he would rather have had no part and is evidenced by his request to have another be sent in his place.

> But he (Moses) said, "Oh my Lord, send, I pray, some other person" (Exodus 4: 13).

The early Jews pioneered the power of faith in a limited world. Moses and his band of constituents overcame tremendous fear of the mighty Egyptians. They defeated Egyptian power and gained growing regional acceptance as holders of truth and power.

Bloody battles depicted in Old Testament Scripture are evidence of their efforts to successfully convince an uninformed and confused humanity, throughout the region, of God's veracity. The Crusade spread fear over the Mideast, which had begun to envisage God as an angry and vengeful deity. The Jewish church expanded as the power they possessed became stronger with each of the battles fought and won.

The Ark of the Covenant or the Ark of God is depicted as a powerful device and icon of the faithful. We mentioned it earlier and described it as a device similar to the apex of the Great Pyramid. It was either provided by the Angels and/or once rested atop the Great Pyramid. It was a vital instrument used in the fulfillment of their missions.

The Ark of God demonstrates the Jews' innocence because they could remain within its confines, despite their ignorance—just like the earliest Egyptians. It was used as weapon against the Egyptians and against those with intent to thwart their effort. It solidified the Hebrew quest to promote a God they couldn't thoroughly understand.

After the renowned battle with the Philistines, as mentioned in the first book of Samuel, the Ark was no longer mentioned. The Philistines had seized it and later returned it because its power destroyed some who attempted to use it for their own gain. As the years passed and the word spread about its mysterious power, it became a coveted instrument for gaining constituents, wealth and authority.

ALPHA TO OMEGA

Power from faith and the Ark became the earliest form of political and social influence in early recorded history. In later years, the Jews suffered losses that were most likely caused by the dilution of truth and desire for political and socio-economic power. The original confrontation, which signaled the beginning of God consciousness, eventually became an instrument for wealth, politics and power.

Power had remained in the hands of the possessors of secret knowledge and the lost Ark of the Covenant. Judaism had become a feared religion and power structure, whose influence gained the followers needed to guarantee its continued endurance. Throughout succeeding generations, the truth was reduced to dogma and ill-conceived concepts.

Over time, Jewish innocence was lost and they could no longer remain in the proximity of the Ark of God. The Israelite's ultimate weapon was as harmful to them as to their foes. For this reason, it disappeared in biblical scripture and remains hidden today.

While the Jews slowly became a major political and religious power of early history, Noah's mandate had failed. How could it be expected for anyone in the new age to possess enormous power and surrender it to the will of an unknown God?

Noah did everything he could by providing humanity with every possible chance to understand God. Instead we have become a predominantly faithful civilization in a limited world with diverse and faded concepts.

Do we truly believe in an eternal soul? In this evaluation we see it as the only reason for Noah's mission. The souls of the previous era, who remained confined in a limited dimensional prison, were frustrated and infuriated by the eventual turn of events. They had given up hope of ever being released from the chains that bind them.

What happens to our eternal souls when we die? Our souls are dark, due mostly to the nature of our new age. Our innocence has become diluted by failing to recognize and live by knowledge we have acquired. True enlightenment is an awakening to a clarified view of God and truth so it can be reflected in our soul and the world in which we live—the absolute will of God.

The limited world into which we are born runs on the overwhelming priority for power and temporal concerns. Our eventual destruction could easily come as a result of our diminishing innocence and our misplaced faith. By misplaced I'm referring to faith in presumptuous and shortsighted beliefs.

In order for the Atlantean's souls to be saved, Noah had hoped that man would achieve Paradise again. As for our souls, only upon death will the light of God reveal our darkness. If only one person in the New Age could overcome ignorance, win the battle with ego and achieve perfection, hope would be restored to those innocent souls of Atlantis, while offering salvation to each soul in the new age.

Part III:

BACK TO THE FUTURE

Chapter 6

WELCOME THE JUDGE

God is not emotion, but God is love. So what can we say about love? It is a perfect behavior of accepting, forgiving, understanding and letting go without judgment or emotion.

The Christ Principle

Most people believe Jesus Christ walked the earth 2000 or so years ago, but many believe Jesus to be no different than other great masters who preached abstinence, an internal search for truth and meditation helps us to become closer to God within us. Gautama Buddha and Sri Krishna are renowned masters of ancient history, who preached the same principles. Many of the Eastern religious advocates believe Jesus is no more than a dedicated man of virtue, who was just another of the world's great masters.

In the Eastern faiths, we see a prioritized desire for truth coupled with the abandonment of worldly concerns as the overriding principles of a true follower and we have shown identical principles as instrumental in our quest to discover God within us. Actions

ALPHA TO OMEGA

inspired by our faith in any belief will provide experiences, which will either refute or qualify them.

Believing Jesus was a Supreme Being immediately upon birth is an erroneous precept, which prevents us from seeing the nature of Jesus' life as an exemplification of Eastern religious principles. When we alter our perspective to view Jesus as a person who was subjected to the same original ignorance as each of us, we will recognize his eventual discovery of truth as a result of his faith in an undefined purpose throughout the years prior to his ministry. Jesus could not offer redemption to anyone without thoroughly defeating the Original Sin—the cause and effect of our dilemmas.

We have demonstrated our limited world, temporal concerns and other diversions as reasons for not prioritizing our search for God within us. Jesus could only overcome the inherent obstacles prevalent in all of mankind by completely prioritizing his search for truth. He had to embrace and transcend the human condition before he could discover his divinity. Simply put, Jesus had to defeat sin by overcoming the hurdles of modern-day ignorance and achieving Nirvana, or the state of Supreme Being, as taught by the ancient masters.

In chapter 2, we quoted written scripture explaining "Adam was a type of the one who was to come". The only way for Jesus to defeat Adam's mistake was to *become* like him—a Supreme Being—and make a proper choice. Many may find this difficult to accept or understand, but a closer examination will help to prove the claim.

> Then, as one man's trespass led to condemnation for all men, so one man's act of righteousness leads to acquittal and life for all

men. For, as by one man's disobedience many were made sinners, so by one man's obedience many will be made righteous. (Romans 5: 18-20)

The solitary component differentiating Jesus from any other person in our age was his earliest awareness, which began with a *belief* in his mother's testaments. As he grew older he knew he was completely different, because he believed he was born to a virgin by angelic intervention. Nothing more and nothing less, is to be construed by this.

He was not God incarnate anymore than each of us during our infancy nor was he any different in developing an ego than we are. Our developing awareness is what defines our reality. He did not have any special talents, powers or knowledge until the days of his final temptations, which we will demonstrate.

Try to imagine the conflicts Jesus faced during the years from boyhood throughout adolescence. Imagine having to cope with such an unusual belief and without understanding the meaning of his purpose. He had to be sure his mother was telling the truth and then he would have to decide in undeniable faith that it was so. He was no more or less human than any of us. However, the unique conflicts created by the conscious awareness of this normal boy would eventually unleash the hidden potentials that exist in every individual.

The significance of the virgin birth makes much more sense from this perspective. Remaining consistent in this presentation, angelic intervention occurs only in an attempt to promote self-discovery. Most Christians have been led to believe Jesus was a

ALPHA TO OMEGA

Supreme Being at birth, because he was born of a virgin by angelic intervention.

The error is exposed when we remember that Angels cannot provide any of us with absolute knowledge because self-discovery is the only way to absolute knowledge. Only by defeating ignorance completely can we find the true Spirit within—the Essence of All Truth, which defines the life of Jesus.

God works through his Angels and the appearance to Mary signifies an unexpected intervention. She was not expecting to bear a child and didn't have faith that such an event would happen. Some ancient alien theorists are beginning to suggest Jesus to have been an "alien" offspring, which is an irrelevant diversion because it makes no difference whether Mary was in-vitro fertilized or not.

The single most important notion is recognizing Jesus as a normal human born by extraordinary circumstances, which served as the impulsion to his unprecedented and insatiable quest to understand his purpose for being. Unrelated controversies regarding Mary's glorification or insemination are useless diversions. Jesus was propelled only by believing and dedicating his life to a unique and undefined purpose, which he easily recognized by the unusual circumstances of his birth.

An important fact many Christians either overlook or don't know is that Jesus had several brothers and sisters. It's mentioned in the Bible, yet it is never preached in the churches because it conflicts with the imbued precepts of Mary's virginity.

And when Jesus had finished these parables he went away from there and came into his own country. He talked to them in their synagogues so that they were astonished and said, "Where did this man get his wisdom and these mighty works? Is not this the carpenter's son? Is not his mother called Mary? And are not his brothers James and Joseph and Simon and Judas? And are not his sisters with us? Where then did this man get all this?" (Matthew 13: 53-56)

This is only mentioned to help us understand our faulty precepts and to help us realize how Jesus embarked on a journey and accepted his mission like no man before or after. By dedicating his entire life to find the meaning of his life's purpose, he empowered his faith to conquer ignorance and ego. His insatiable desire to find the Truth took precedence over everything in his life—unlike any of us. His entire life was built upon the belief and undeniable faith in his mother's words.

No Wasted Time

Many people forget that Jesus had a life before his ministry because most of the contemporary concepts of Jesus are based on our assumptions presented by church teachings. We continually mirror our human limits and fears upon our concept of God and upon Jesus the man with ingrained presumptions that prevent us from seeing another observable perspective. This observation is paramount in the final conflict.

Jesus developed an ego at an early age, just like all humans do. His parents must have constantly provided extra considerations for his safety, which strengthened his belief in his unique purpose. Miracles, or physical evidence of the Power of Absolute Knowledge

ALPHA TO OMEGA

through faith, are subject to universal rules and not until Jesus could understand them, would he be in possession of distinct power.

As time went on, Jesus began to see himself as someone with a profound reason for being, which gradually became more difficult to grasp as he aged. It's easier for a 12 year old to believe he is to be an important historical figure and much harder for an adult. As Jesus matured, he encountered a huge responsibility when trying to understand his special purpose.

Although he had always believed what he had been told, he surely began to understand the complexity of his situation and must have had recurring doubts about his mother's recollection of the events leading to his birth. It was obvious to Jesus there were no tangible differences between him and others his age because he was not a miracle worker or healer. Believing he was special and unique had to be extremely burdening and confusing. He was forced to serve an integral part in human understanding, yet he couldn't define or understand his role in all of it.

His knowledge of the world eventually enlarged enough for him to become empowered to diligently seek a clearer understanding of his life's purpose as the noticeable complexities of the world presented him with uncertainties. Teachings that once helped mold his early behaviors and beliefs must have begun to present ambiguities.

Realizing there were other philosophies and religious beliefs than Judaism, Jesus probably questioned the tenets and rituals of the Jewish belief system because we know that he became estranged

206

from his religion. Perhaps this was the start to understanding how he could teach a more universally accepted ideology. Would his parents accept his decision to include people of other religions in his life-work? Would his peers and members of the temple hierarchy accept it?

To believe in an undefined purpose required undeniable faith to venture into uncharted areas of discovery. His faith in future discoveries helped dedicate him to his purpose, but he had to choose between accepting it and traversing into the unknown, or denying it and succumbing to the mandates of societal norms. I can only imagine the great insecurity and fear Jesus had to overcome by his willingness to accept the burden of uncertainty and move forward.

Major conflicts and obstacles had to be hurdled, to orchestrate his life's design. Why do so many of us fail to see the human side of Jesus? Most Christians believe his life and search for meaning was easy, because most believe he was God from the day he was born. How can there be redemption without overcoming the weaknesses and inherent nature of human beings?

His actions were determined by faithfully accepting his unique and undefined challenge and allowing the judgments he would attract by questioning the strict laws of Judaism. Jesus was expected to be an advocate of Jewish faith because he and his parents were Jews but, he continued to pose questions because his questions were more important and had greater consequences.

In all probability, Jesus thoroughly studied Hinduism and Buddhism because he was renowned throughout the regions as a master, which requires strict meditation, dedication and abstinence. Throughout the New Testament of the Bible, Jesus is reported to have fasted for extended periods of time, which shows his dedication to practices espoused by religions other than Judaism. The teachings of Hinduism and Buddhism obviously helped serve Jesus' internal search for truth more efficiently than the comparatively limited requirements of Jewish tradition alone.

He made a choice to believe his purpose was universal because he recognized God as universal. His faith to unequivocally believe his mother's testimonies endured and led to new internal discoveries every day because he was completely dedicated to discovering the truth. Only by the prioritized curiosity to understand God, our world and place in it, can we discover the truth. Once again, *"Seek and you shall find"* were the words of Jesus who lived to typify and understand their meaning.

In time, Jesus became a master by eliminating earthly desires while his strict dedication and faith placed him among the very few masters who came before him. He had reached a state of consciousness revered by many, but all of his conflicts had not been resolved. His belief in a unique purpose demanded he go a step further than any master before him. Not one had ever questioned a seemingly perfect state of consciousness.

Ironically, Jesus' diligent study of Buddhism and Hinduism, which preached the suppression of ego through an ascetic lifestyle and meditation, were responsible for initiating his personal battles with ego. To reach higher levels of consciousness, we must suppress ego to allow the Spirit to shine through. He knew that his quest to

WELCOME THE JUDGE

understand the reasons for his existence was unprecedented. To him, there had to be much more than anyone before him.

Jesus had a struggle of the highest degree, because his belief was in a unique purpose. His ego solely defined his purpose—a presumed reality yet to be qualified or refuted by the actions of his faith and Divine Intervention.

Buddha and other masters were satisfied upon reaching higher levels of consciousness because their egos were dissolved. The constant battle between two opposing viewpoints typifies Jesus' conflicts. He realized his advanced spiritual gains were insufficient because he believed his purpose was to epitomize a perfect relationship between Creator and created. He had to take a step further than other advanced masters because his ego was still present to tell him he hadn't reached the objective of his belief.

The power of faith, which had been manifested to the Hebrews of earlier times, had not revealed its potentials in Jesus. He had not witnessed or taken part in anything miraculous, although his spiritual awareness was more advanced than any of the ancient Hebrews.

In contrast, the beliefs of the Hebrews had been qualified by the physical manifestations of power through faith to challenge an errant precept. Their beliefs were extremely shortsighted in comparison to Jesus, who had been denied any manifestations from his faith. The qualification of Jesus' faith through miraculous achievements could not be manifested physically until he could tangibly obtain the goal that his faith endowed.

ALPHA TO OMEGA

Interestingly, Jesus became aware that he was missing an integral element of truth. If God is All Truth, then sin is the failure to know all truth. Jesus accepted the plain and simple fact that he was still a sinner, regardless of his superior consciousness. Acknowledging his sinful nature would catapult him into a spiritual level unprecedented since Adam.

Take me to Higher Love

John the Baptist was an important person, whose role was to prepare the way for Jesus as the Savior of humanity. Most Christians are aware of his commitment to the spreading of a new concept of spiritual baptism. Like Jesus, extraordinary circumstances surrounded John's birth, which became part of his conscious awareness much like Jesus. John's father, Zechariah, was a high priest of Judaism, who was married to Elizabeth, a cousin of Mary, the mother of Jesus.

> "But they had no child, because Elizabeth was barren, and both were advanced in years." (Luke 1:7) "And there appeared to him an angel of the Lord . . . And Zechariah was troubled when he saw him, and fear fell upon him. But the angel said to him, 'Do not be afraid, Zechariah, for your prayer is heard, and your wife Elizabeth will bear you a son, and you shall call his name John. And you will have joy and gladness, and many will rejoice at his birth; for he will be great before the Lord, and he shall drink no wine nor strong drink, and he will be filled with the Holy Spirit, even from his mother's womb. And he will turn many of the sons of Israel to the Lord their God, and he will go before him in the spirit and power of Elijah, to turn the hearts of the fathers to the

WELCOME THE JUDGE

children, and the disobedient to the wisdom of the just, to make ready for the Lord a people prepared.'" (Luke 1:11-17)

Again, the peculiar circumstances of birth destined a normal man. Elizabeth was not a virgin but she was infertile and bore her husband Zechariah's son at an advance age, while pregnancy categorized her faith in an undefined purpose because of her infertility. Mary relayed to her cousin the story of her angelic experience and the circumstances revealed to her about Elizabeth.

> And behold, your kinswoman Elizabeth in her old age has also conceived a son; and this is the sixth month with her who was called barren. (Luke 1:36) In those days Mary arose and went with haste into the hill country to the city of Judah, and she entered the house of Zechariah and greeted Elizabeth. (Luke 1:39)

Mary's visit to her cousin and the recounting of her angelic visit, which had included information about Elizabeth's pregnancy, led them to believe their sons were going to change the direction of mankind's understanding of God. Surely, neither of them knew how it would come to pass. The burden rested upon the children, who would define their purpose by recognizing the unique circumstances of their birth.

As John grew up, he was undoubtedly informed about Jesus' unusual birth to his aunt. It wasn't hard for him to imagine the plight confronting Jesus, in the light of his own uniqueness. Instinctively he could imagine the nature of Jesus' task and the requirements necessary to fulfill it. John had the wisdom of a prophet because he could foresee the inevitable conflicts Jesus would face resulting from the circumstances of his birth.

ALPHA TO OMEGA

> ...And you, child, will be called the prophet of the Most High; for you will go before the Lord to prepare his ways, to give knowledge of salvation to his people in the forgiveness of their sins, through the tender mercy of our God, when the day shall dawn upon us from on high to give light to those who sit in darkness and in the shadow of death, to guide our feet into the way of peace. (Luke 1:76-79)

John's priorities were established by the nature of his birth and the knowledge of Jesus' circumstances. He dedicated his life, to the preaching of the new faith of repentance and baptism. This is important, because repentance signifies the admission of a sinful nature. This came at a time when Jews believed they had no sin, as God's chosen people.

> ...Bear fruits that befit repentance, and do not begin to say to yourselves, 'we have Abraham as our father'; for I tell you, God is able from these stones to raise up children to Abraham. Even now the axe is laid to the root of the trees; every tree therefore that does not bear good fruit is cut down and thrown into the fire. (Luke 2:8-9)

Everyone was considered a sinner, according to John's teachings, and many listeners took offense to this pronouncement. Never before had anyone heard or considered this approach to man's nature. He preached that admitting our sinful or ignorant nature humbles those who would believe to be exalted by religion. John was a visionary and could see the inherent ignorance as humanity's stumbling block. John's message proclaimed salvation could be obtained through ritual baptism by water upon admission of our sinful nature.

WELCOME THE JUDGE

John the Baptist spoke about the "sign of the times". He preached the truth did not rest upon anyone being Jewish or a descendant of the Hebrew faith. John's truth spurred a swelling resistance to the dominant and powerful Jewish church. New Testament Scripture depicts his beheading, which was barbaric enough to frighten many into refraining from similar actions. Judaism espouses all members to be God's only chosen people. Although the early truth had become diluted, the church power was formidable.

Jesus showed his love by accepting our ignorant nature.

> **God is not emotion, but God is love. So what can we say about love? It's a perfect behavior of accepting, forgiving, understanding and letting go without judgment or emotion.**

Many people believe there are different kinds of love; one for your friend, your brother or sister, your parents, husband or your wife. The truth is that love in its purest form is simply a behavior of acceptance without judgment. Varying emotions surrounding the beloved may lead us to think love is different, but love is the same all the time—an emotionless behavior of accepting, forgiving and letting go without judgment.

Jesus didn't pass judgment, seek revenge or ridicule his aggressors. Jesus realized his own ignorance during the years preceding his own baptism, but he came to understand that God's love embraces nonjudgmental behavior and the willingness to accept all religions and faiths and people. The closer we get to seeing All Truth, the easier it is to understand those that don't.

He made a conscious decision to be baptized, which confirmed he was a sinner and needed God's mercy. Jesus was admitting, in spite of his superb awareness, the confines of his continued ignorance. This is of extremely powerful significance. Would Buddha have done that? No, because Buddha was no longer concerned with ignorance after receiving clarity. Jesus was still unclear, because he had yet to fulfill ego's definition of his unique purpose.

Jesus was an enlightened master whose humility is ultimately expressed in his public baptism by water. Many people were awestruck to see an enlightened master admit sin and defy Jewish tradition in the practice of a new ritual. His leap of faith invoked Divine Intervention for the first miracle in Jesus' life. A Master's choice to admit sin—an enormous act of faith—became qualified as truth to everyone witnessing. Those who were present to witness Jesus' baptism heard the words, *"This is My Beloved Son of whom I am well pleased."* It was a miraculous sound heard by everyone and invoked by the faith and humility of a man, who had reached an unprecedented level of spiritual achievement in the New Age.

Precisely then, his life's journey was qualified to him, after his long and faithful adherence to an undefined purpose. Without his relentless pursuit of truth through faith in his belief and the final action consistent with that belief, the miracle would not have occurred to qualify it.

The final battles were no confronting Jesus. He had separated himself from other masters before him, but he still didn't know what it meant to be the Son of God. He may have said something to the effect "Okay, I'm the son of God, but what does that mean? What is my purpose and what am I supposed to do?" The first miracle of his life came with words confirming he was God's son, but created more confusion for him.

At that point, Jesus decided to challenge himself more than he had ever done before. He had fasted for long periods of time, restrained his ego and knew how to push his body into submission unlike anyone. He wanted to know his purpose and was willing to figure it out without any considerations for his well-being. He humbled himself again by walking into the desert on a final vision quest and believing he would define his mission and purpose by discovering the answers to his final questions.

His first temptation demonstrates how hard he pushed himself. He had gone without eating longer than ever before and had reached the threshold of his ability. Since he had no food, his internal conflict is presented in near death starvation and Satan's words of temptation:

> And the tempter came and said to him. "If you are indeed the Son of God, command these stones to be loaves of bread? (Matthew 4: 3)

This was Jesus' internal battle with his ego quickly becoming aware of his Divinity. In his hunger, he probably asked himself, "If I am God, why can't I turn these stones to bread?" He was wrestling with what it meant to be the Son of God. He had never realized power in the evidence of a personal miracle except for the sounds proclaiming him to be God's son after his baptism.

ALPHA TO OMEGA

Clearly, Jesus doubted his supremacy, because physical evidence of a miracle had not taken place. The temptation was a true challenge at such heightened awareness, but he immediately recalled a scripture:

> But he answered, "It is written, Man shall not live by bread alone, but by every word that proceeds from the mouth of God. (Matthew 4: 4)

Jesus didn't say, "Yes that's true but I'm still hungry." He immediately remembered why he walked into the desert. His faithful intent was to find the truth and he would not succumb to ego's temptation at any cost, even death. He totally and willingly accepted the word of All Truth as the necessary rebuttal to the question proposed by his ego.

He unequivocally knew any miraculous event could not come from the imposition of his will. The first temptation signifies Jesus' complete abandonment of personal will and temporal concerns within the highest state of consciousness. He would never question it again. He recognized his purpose required total alliance with God's will and complete faith for his future. Hence, without looking back, he moved forward in a remarkable step of faith while on the verge of deathly starvation.

Jesus' actions in faith had led to his baptism and the miraculous words from above. The complete self-denial revealed by Jesus' fervent action to move forward spawned the second miracle in his life. Instantly, Jesus had the power to turn stones to bread if he so wanted. Suddenly his hunger disappeared and power was bestowed upon Jesus through his faith and submission to Divine Will. He had

WELCOME THE JUDGE

become aware that he possessed the power to turn the stones to bread if he so desired. Unlike Adam, who was blinded by power, Jesus had become enlightened by it.

The second temptation demonstrates Jesus' sudden advanced awareness of power upon rejecting his first temptation and his increasing battle with a growing super ego.

> Then, the devil took him to the holy city, and set him on the pinnacle of the temple, and said to him, "If you are the son of God, throw yourself down; for it is written, he will give his Angels charge of you, and on their hands they will bear you up, lest you strike your foot against a stone." (Matthew 4: 5-6)

Jesus was quickly gaining an enormous amount of power as he was being thrust into a state of consciousness higher than anyone of this era. He was certain he could jump from the precipice and be saved by Divine Intervention.

With the discovery of his swiftly increasing power emerged his recognition of the effects of ego on human behavior and its influence on mankind's transgressions. It's almost impossible to separate Absolute Power from ego at such an extreme level of awareness, but Jesus tackled the second task with fortitude and strength.

> Jesus said to him, "Again it is written, 'You shall not tempt the Lord your God.'" (Matthew 4: 7)

At this precise moment, Jesus completely separates ego from Absolute Knowledge and Power. His unison to Divine Will remains unwavering, and he was suddenly a Supreme Being—just like Adam. At this point, the imposition of Jesus' individual will could create anything he so desired. He had been instantly conjoined to

ALPHA TO OMEGA

the omniscient and omnipotent Essence of God, which dwells deep within the confines of each and every one of us.

Jesus had become the complete reflection of God in physical form. He came into the world just like you and me, but became God's perfect endowment. The final temptation demonstrates his recognition of Absolute Power and a remarkable choice that would change the direction of every soul before and after him.

> Again, the devil took him to a very high mountain, and showed him all the kingdoms of the world and the glory of them; and he said to him, "all these I will give you, if you will fall down and worship me." Then Jesus said to him, "Be gone Satan, for it is written, 'You shall worship the Lord your God and only him shall you serve.'" (Matthew 4: 8-10)

It wasn't until this particular moment that Jesus recognized his true purpose and mission for the remaining days of his life. He could have returned from the mountain and provided everyone with Supreme power and a higher consciousness like his. Jesus could have created a world similar to Atlantis if he so willed. But, if Jesus were to create a world like Atlantis, he would be forced to exercise his personal will to make it happen.

Moreover, the inherent weakness of humanity would be exposed both by his willingness to do so and the inevitable failure of a new society with great power. Just like the Angels, who refrain from providing absolute knowledge and power, Jesus had to refrain as well, lest he halt everyone's progression to absolute knowledge through personal discovery just like him. His purpose, which he

WELCOME THE JUDGE

discovered at that moment, was to transcend Adam's mistake, by choosing *not* to succumb to his human will.

Jesus knew the only way to successfully complete the purpose of his life was the choice to prevent Supreme Power from ever blinding humanity again. His final choice was the alliance of Supreme Being Will with Divine Will and the abnegation of Absolute Power. The final conflict of Jesus exemplifies a Supreme Being making the right choice, which overcomes the mistake made by another Supreme Being. Jesus made all of this possible by his faith and acceptance in an undefined mission, which was eventually clarified by the actions consistent with his belief in his purpose.

The teachings of the three temptations exemplify the true Spirit of Jesus, God, and Absolute Knowledge in a perfect man. Jesus became the first Supreme Being since and is the only man in the new era to completely overcome sin and become thoroughly enlightened by the inborn Spirit.

Gnostic Wisdom

After Jesus had completely submitted to the will of God, he could foresee his future years. From that moment on, his actions or words were never inspired by a need to defend or explain himself. Absolute power and absolute humility define Jesus. He only spoke the truth and never again submitted to his ego. Because of this, many people would never completely understand him and he knew it. Every challenge he faced was overcome with absolute humility.

219

ALPHA TO OMEGA

He ignored derogatory remarks made by many of his accusers. He did not respond to anyone with comments influenced by his ego or use his omnipotence to prove his Divinity. He conducted his life as an example of perfection coupled with humility. His infamous words, *"Forgive them, Father, for they know not what they do",* is symbolic of an all-knowing and all-powerful God, who accepts and understands those who are unknowing.

Jesus never *performed* miracles. Instead, every manifestation resulted from the true faith of his followers. Faith and action reveals itself in the events that qualify or refute our concepts. Having faith in Jesus meant that God worked through Jesus in manifesting the truth of his Divinity.

Jesus did not impose his will to create miraculous events, which is precisely the definition of his purpose and his reason for self-denial. He often said, *"Your Faith has made you well . . ."* and, *"Be it done so according to your faith."* He knew that tales of miraculous events would bring attention towards him and eventually cause his persecution.

As stories of the miracles of Jesus' ministry spread through the district, crowds increased in size and new problems arose. Members of the church approached him and demanded him to either admit he was a fake or to prove that he was the Messiah. By the nature of his mission, he couldn't impose his will to prove anything to change the minds of those who did not believe or understand.

Confusion and conflicts arose, even among those who believed he was their savior or Messiah. Many scripture sources describe these types of situations, although there must have been hundreds

220

WELCOME THE JUDGE

that were not recorded. Jesus never submitted to his ego, which evidenced his total commitment and absolute faith in his purpose. His destination was the Will of God, and it would become the perfect sacrifice for the redemption from our inherent ignorance.

Absolute humility and the denial of self demonstrate this uncommon sacrifice, which typifies the true nature of God and love. Jesus knew he had to die in horrendous fashion and always said, *"Your will be done, not mine."* His agony in the garden before being arrested perfectly demonstrates his submission in light of his personal anguish and the ability to willfully alter his destiny.

Jesus' total enlightenment revealed his life-purpose to be one of sacrifice and death. He was forced to suffer the foresight of his destiny during the last three years of his life, which demonstrates untarnished humility, vision and purpose. He dedicated his life to find his purpose only to discover his bloody and barbaric sacrifice as the mandate of it.

This helps to provide a clearer understanding of the words of Jesus, *"My God, My God, why hast thou forsaken me"*. The absolute sacrifice is the pain and suffering of his death inflicted upon him by the same ones, whom his death would later redeem.

By taking the cross of everyone's self-will and temporal concerns, Jesus demonstrates the true purpose of life is to seek God, to love everyone and judge no one. His willingness to die for the sake of all who cannot see exemplifies the messages of his ministry. There is no room for ego in the total Spirit-consciousness of man. In love, there is no room for ego to say, "Look at what I have done for you."

ALPHA TO OMEGA

Characteristics of the first mistake became both our obstacle and the instrument for discovering All Truth. Doubt created curiosity in Adam, which led to the demise of Atlantis, but provides the avenue to truth in an uninformed generation. The Old Testament proclaims that the serpent will bite our heel and we will crush his head, which demonstrates how we can defeat ignorance by the same doubt and curiosity that caused the Big Mistake.

From this perspective, we observe truth as subjective, which remains to be discovered. Our doubts cause us to challenge presumed truth leading us to new questions, as we edge closer to arriving at every possible answer. The most important message is that Christ was the only man to thoroughly achieve this awareness, in our generation and subtly revealed is that nobody will ever be able to achieve it without first acknowledging it has already been done by Jesus. Our faith in his promise brings us internal peace and his Whole Spirit guides our thoughts and actions when we prioritize our curiosity for truth in our lives.

Does this mean that we can continue to do whatever we please, knowing that we will be forgiven at Judgment Day? The answers unfold in the simple commandments of Christ's teachings. *"...Do unto others as you would have them do unto you . . . Judge not lest you be judged . . . You shall love the Lord your God with all your heart, soul and mind . . . Love is the greatest of all these commandments . . ."* With knowledge comes responsibility to adhere to the golden rules with diligence.

These fundamental rules render the old rules of Judaism obsolete. The Old Testament is precisely old. It is to be used as a history

WELCOME THE JUDGE

book, to illustrate how people struggled to keep God in their lives, before Jesus' mission. We exhibited how the early Jews led the way through faith, which was vital in defeating the Egyptians, and their false precepts. Without the advances in human thought and ideologies, the message of Christ would never have taken place. Jesus' mission was to abolish rituals. He led the way to prioritizing our search for God and peaceful coexistence through acceptance.

The interpretation of Christ's teachings can foster acceptance and forgiveness, or judgment and ridicule. It is a double-edged sword. Judgment has defined the plight of humanity throughout the ages. It led the Pharisees to hold Jesus in contempt of their convictions, and led the Egyptians to reproach the Hebrews. It causes separate religions to judge each other while dividing nations and people.

Those who use Jesus' words to condemn others are creating evaluations, based on an assumption that they have total understanding of His teachings. The greatest sin of this generation is the failure to see our own faults. We are more inclined to believe in our own presumed realities. If we accept that we are all ignorant, as Christ acknowledged by his death, then it's impossible for us to judge anyone else or for them to place judgments on us. This is the epitome of Christ's message.

> And as he sat at the table in the house behold, many tax collectors and sinners came and sat down with Jesus and his disciples. And when the Pharisees saw this, they said to his disciples, "Why does your teacher eat with tax collectors and sinners?" But when he heard it, he said, "Those who are well have no need for a physician, but only those who are sick. Go and learn what this means,

ALPHA TO OMEGA

'I desire mercy, and not sacrifice.' For I came not to call the righteous, but sinners" (Matthew 9:10-13)

Sacrifice, on which the Hebrew faith had based its doctrines, was no longer a necessary ritual. It shows mercy as the characteristic of God, which we obtain by accepting of our faults and not in our presumed righteousness. If adhering to rituals of religious doctrine lead us to believe we are free from ignorance, we cannot obtain mercy because we have not admitted our blindness. Christ admitted his sinful nature, even as a master in the defined human sense.

The Pharisees believed heredity and religious association made their faith finite. It was very difficult for most of the Hebrews to accept Jesus, because of their religious roots. Although many converted, Jesus could not persuade the hard-liners of Judaism to change their concepts of God any more than the early Hebrews could persuade the Egyptians to change their beliefs.

Strict adherence to literalism and authority emerges from fear, because we are blinded by the realities defined by our senses. The spirit of truth as given to Abraham remains. It cannot be found in the tangibles of physical heredity or beliefs but only in the Spirit within each of us—one that Abraham surely recognized.

The Pharisees challenged Jesus and his apostles, because they were eating during a time of fasting.

And Jesus said to them, "Can the wedding guest morn, as long as the bridegroom is with them? The days will come, when the bridegroom is taken away from them, and then they will fast. And no one puts a piece of unshrunk cloth on an old garment, for the

WELCOME THE JUDGE

patch tears away from the garment and a worse tear is made. Neither is new wine put into old wineskins; if it is, the skins burst, and the wine is spilled, and the skins are destroyed; but new wine is put into fresh wineskins, and so both are preserved." (Matthew 9: 15-17)

In those days, fasting was an important ritual of Judaism. Since Jesus and his apostles were Jews, they left themselves open to criticism and ridicule. Jesus answered the criticism with an analogy revealing his teachings could no longer be held together by the old biblical laws. The use of Scripture as a tool for judgment is a common mistake of adherents to any religion.

The beliefs of the Pharisees would not permit Jesus' testimony to destroy their long-held beliefs. As the numbers of Jesus' followers increased, the conflict between the two ideologies surfaced and the heated battle between truth and belief began in the Roman Empire.

Only in wisdom through spirit can we understand the truth.

"But to what shall I compare this generation? It is like children sitting in the market places and calling to their playmates, 'We piped to you but you did not dance; we wailed and you did not come to mourn.' For John came neither eating or drinking, and they say, 'He has a demon'; the son of man came eating and drinking, and they say, 'Behold a glutton and a drunkard, a friend of tax collectors and sinners!' Yet wisdom is justified by her deeds." (Matthew 11:16-19)

The difference between wisdom and the prescriptions of presumed truths is exposed here. The Jews had been hoping for the coming of the Messiah and were unable to recognize Jesus because

ALPHA TO OMEGA

of their precepts. He was calling to them, but Jesus did not match their precepts of the Messiah. Once again, fear (instead of faith) spurred their actions.

Extreme hard-liners feared losing a presumed direct connection to God, which was espoused by their religious teachings. Their perspective is fortified by the literal interpretation of Scripture and by fear. The perceived need to retain ideals that support earthly concerns instead of everlasting truth is embedded in everyone because of our failure to understand our mission in life.

In Matthew 12:22-28, we are told that Jesus exorcised a man who was blind and dumb. Witnessing the miraculous cure, the Pharisees claimed that Jesus had cast out demons by Beelzebub, the prince of demons. Again, we see fear causing the reluctance to accept the truth. Fear opposes faith. Lacking faith and wisdom, the Pharisees believed Satan had given Jesus his power. Jesus' reproach explains that the prince of demons would not order the expulsion of demons.

Christ warned his apostles about the leaven of the Pharisees after the Pharisees asked him to show them a sign to prove he was the Messiah (Matthew 16:1-6). Jesus admonished his disciples to beware of the judgment, ridicule, and fear of the Pharisees. The leaven has promoted the "rise" in this type of behavior, which continues to blanket every aspect of humanity today. These examples illustrate the conflict created by ego's attempt at embracing something tangible—in this case the written word or doctrine—while failing to understand the intangible spirit of wisdom.

WELCOME THE JUDGE

> Then the disciples came and said, "Why do you speak to them in parables?" And he answered them, "To you it has been given to know the secrets of the kingdom of heaven, but to them it has not been given. For to him who has shall more be given, and he will have abundance; but from him who has not, even what he has will be taken away. This is why I speak to them in parables, because seeing they do not see, and hearing they do not hear, nor do they understand." (Matthew 13: 10-13)

Jesus acknowledges the apostles were privy to things most had not understood at that time. He challenges all of us to perceive truth with true wisdom.

Closer inspection of Scripture shows evidence of man's misunderstanding, even at the time of Moses. While the Hebrews believed that they were perfect through faith, Christ explained their iniquities.

> And the Pharisees came up to him and tested him by asking, "Is it lawful to divorce one's wife for any cause?" He answered, "Have you not read that he who made them from the beginning made them male and female, and said, 'For this reason a man shall leave his father and mother and be joined by his wife, and the two shall become one? So they are no longer two but one.' What therefore God has joined together, let no man put asunder." They said to him, "Why then did Moses command one to give a certificate of divorce, and to put her away?" He said to them, "For your hardness of heart Moses allowed you to divorce your wives, but from the beginning it was not so. And I say to you: whoever divorces his wife, except for unchastity, and marries again commits adultery; and he who marries a divorced woman commits adultery." (Matthew, 19: 3-9)

The most important lesson of the above scripture is not to expose a judgment by Jesus, but rather to demonstrate inherent ignorance or sin as commonplace in the new era. Jesus distinctly points to errant beliefs as the nature of inherent ignorance. He wasn't setting a rule (regarding marriage) for people to judge each other in his name, but instead was contrasting man's failures in their precepts. We cannot use Scripture to pass judgments on others, because judgment is not ours.

The apostle Peter found it difficult to let others know he was a believer in the divinity of Jesus. Peter refused to accept the fact that Jesus had to die, which means he was lacking in complete understanding of Jesus' purpose.

> "God, forbid, Lord. This shall never happen to you!" But he turned and said to him, "Get behind me Satan for you are not on the side of God, but of men." (Matthew 16:22-23)

Clearly, this signifies human nature's habit to hold firmly to the presumed reality of our limited awareness.

Jesus purposely did not provide everyone on earth with his state of consciousness. His decision prevented physical evidence of his power from being seen by mankind throughout the successive centuries. Although the truth was revealed in Jesus' resurrection, not everyone had witnessed it or believed it after hearing about it. Belief and truth remain divided. One faction consisted of those who had been firsthand witnesses, and their converted followers. The opposition consisted of those who remained influenced by the controlling religious and civilian authorities.

WELCOME THE JUDGE

Debates continue regarding the resurrection of Jesus today. For Christians, the resurrection is solid affirmation of Christ's unity to the Deity. For those who embrace the doctrines of non-Christian theosophies, it is a very difficult notion to accept. The denial of any substantial difference between Jesus Christ and other teachers is the foundation for this scrutiny. The debate will continue, as long as doubt and suspicion prevail.

In the matters concerning Jesus' resurrection, fundamental arguments set the advocates of his deity against those who see him as nothing more than a remarkable man. The personal and varying beliefs of an individual are unique. Any and all judgments must be withheld.

The widely held Christian belief is envisioning Christ's resurrection as a full body experience. Many hints within New Testament accounts imply this to be untrue. The failure of the apostles and others to recognize him after his resurrection are evidence there was more to it than what we have been taught to accept. His appearance to the apostles while locked in a room fearing persecution proves our concepts to be skewed. How many Christians know that Jesus had brothers and sisters? How many ever considered or believe he was born a sinner like all of us?

I believe in Christ's resurrection, but his body was not part of this event. A Supreme Being is observed as Spirit and Soul united and fully illuminated. Jesus defeated human ignorance, which allowed Spirit and Soul to unite fully in the aftermath of physical death. Spirit cannot perish but it is only visible in a perfectly illuminated soul.

ALPHA TO OMEGA

> And after six days Jesus took with him Peter and James and John his brother, and led them up a high mountain apart. And he was transfigured before them, and his face shone like the sun, and his garments became white as light. (Matthew 17: 1-2)

The remarkable manifestation, which remains one of several events that qualified the belief of the apostles, helps to explain the discrepancies found in the limited verses describing the resurrection.

The emergence of this idea has fueled heightened controversies in debates I have encountered with many Christians. Refusing to accept the concept of physical resurrection is challenging to those attesting that scriptures prove otherwise. The empty tomb, discovered by Mary Magdalene, is usually the largest argument. The presence of an angel at the entry of the tomb has always been the reason to accept the inference of physical resurrection. The fact remains that when Christ did appear to Mary, she did not recognize him either. If, in fact, his body did regain its life, then the ability to recognize him would have been quite easy for both her and the apostles.

> So is it with the resurrection of the dead. What is sown is perishable; what is raised is imperishable. It is sown in dishonor; it is raised in glory. It is sown in weakness; it is raised in power. It is sown a natural body; it is raised a spiritual body. If there is a natural body, there is also a spiritual body. Thus it is written, "The first man Adam became a living being"; the last Adam became a life-giving spirit. But it is not the spiritual that is first but the natural, and then the spiritual. (1 Corinthians 15: 42-46)

Paul clearly distinguishes the body as perishable and the spiritual body imperishable and concludes saying,

WELCOME THE JUDGE

"I tell you this brethren: flesh and blood shall not inherit the kingdom of God, nor does the perishable inherit the imperishable." (1 Corinthians 15:50)

Christ was a Supreme Being—a thoroughly enlightened soul. His is the first and only perfect Soul to escape the binds of death. His Whole Spirit is the gift that guarantees this same resurrection to those who believe in him—the guiding light to our complete enlightenment.

Our notions are dimmed by our incomplete knowledge. We are further stigmatized by the credibility we have given to sources we deem true. Closer examination provided proof that his resurrection was a Spiritual revealing and not a physical one. If this is true, then the remaining curiosity surrounds an explanation regarding the empty tomb. What happened to Jesus' body?

Few Scriptures describe Christ's Ascension, which has been described as His rising into the heavens on a cloud of glory. We have heard that his return will mimic his departure. When we choose to believe our resurrection will be spiritual, we will see how consistencies of the past will solve the riddles of the future.

The reason Jesus *chose* to die was to allow the progress of self-realization. To return before that happens would be redundant. He would not be able to accomplish any more than he could have when he was here, which would be to create a supernatural world for us. He will not return until the world's collective consciousness ascends through higher levels by the process of self-realization and other external forces.

ALPHA TO OMEGA

Events and circumstances can occur practically overnight for this to happen and we will demonstrate the possibility. Individual choices concerning what is true or what we believe to be so—just as demonstrated in every conflict so far—will be epitomized in the final conflict. Only after we've made our final choice can the return of Christ be seen as a judgment, in the absolute sense. The Book of Revelation describes this battle. Using these observations, we can explain it.

Chapter 7

RUNAWAY TRAIN

If Supreme Being is the reflection of God in physical form, then the beast is the collective reflection of man's ignorance in the form of an unyielding entity.

Roman Siege

An enormous amount of secular history centered on Christianity and its relatively quick acceptance throughout the Roman Empire exists. Many of us fail to realize Rome's influence on early Christianity and its contribution to both the incomplete translation of Christ's message and the instilled portrayal of his persona.

The uneasy coexistence between the Jews and pagans, which had formed the structural base for the Roman Empire after centuries of political and social agreements, became unglued as the popularity of Jesus' message grew. The chief priests and rulers from many towns were worried about losing their civilian and religious authority and they feared the new messages of Christ's teachings being spread across the region. They and their followers urged

ALPHA TO OMEGA

Pilate to crucify Jesus in hopes that crucifixion would promote fear among the growing advocates of a new ideology.

The Roman Empire, the Jews, and the pagans were suddenly faced with challenges to the status quo. The Jews remained steadfast in believing the promised Messiah was yet to come, Christ's followers continued to preach their message throughout the land and paganism had a stranglehold on the majority of people throughout the Roman Empire.

The pagans were a conglomerate of many beliefs and many gods embraced without judgment by all. Taking into account this evaluation of ancient history, it's not a wonder this was so. The pagans represent the majority of people in the Roman Empire who remained reliant on the oral traditions of ancient times, and without regard for the Jewish conquest of years gone by.

> (In the first century AD) The Roman marriage of the East and West was a more real thing, for behind it lay three centuries of growing intercourse and knowledge along Alexander's lines. In the sphere of religion we find it most clearly. There rises a resultant world-religion—a religion that embraces all the cults, all the creeds, and at last all the philosophies, in one great system. That religion held the world. It is true, there were exceptions. There was a small and objectionable race called Jews; there were possibly some Druids in Southern Britain; and here and there was a solitary atheist who represented no one but himself. These few exceptions were the freaks amongst mankind. Apart from them mankind was united in its general beliefs about the gods. The world had one religion.[1]

RUNAWAY TRAIN

As Jesus Christ's disciples traveled throughout the regions and the letters to the new Christian advocates were spread, belief in Jesus as the Savior of all people gained swift and mounting approval. Christ's teachings slowly eroded the long-held Jewish religious traditions and sparked major conflicts among them. Each faction passionately sought Rome's intercession and arbitration as the tensions between them increased. Rome realized the importance of preventing civil unrest because its major concerns were the uncontrollable population explosion and increased vulnerability to outside aggression. There was no room for civil division during this volatile time in the empire's history.

The Pharisees were the largest of three Jewish factions, which had been unofficially assigned to the legal interpretation of Jewish law in the Palestine region. In 37 AD, Judaism had reached the apogee of its power and prestige and the swelling upheaval after Jesus' crucifixion caused great concern to the Pharisees. Persecution of Jesus' followers, by both civilian and religious authorities, fomented anger and division. The Pharisees did not want to be blamed for Jesus' death for fear of losing their dominating influence in the region.[2]

The early advocates of Christianity had suffered greatly at the hands of officials due to popular opinion created by Jewish sentiment. The persecution of early Christians was the result of public opinion instilled by the early assessment agreed upon by Jews and Romans alike that the earliest Christians were outlaws and followers of a renegade, who they had crucified for being rebellious against authority. The early disputes between the Jews and Chris-

235

ALPHA TO OMEGA

tians created ample civil disorder to persuade popular opinion into believing it to be true.

The early followers of Christ were not welcome in Jerusalem. This preempted their flight to neighboring territories, while the converted Pharisee, Saul, (later named Paul) began his missionary journeys through Cyprus, Asia Minor, and Greece.

Christians, most of who were converted Jews at the outset, soon ceased to think of themselves as Jews. As time went on, throngs of pagans joined the ranks of the new religion, which coincided with other challenges to Judaism within the Roman Empire. Scrupulous Jewish belief led to the destruction of their temple in Jerusalem in 70 AD by the Romans. Roman rulers resented the power of the high priests of Judaism and their certitude that Jerusalem was their God-given territory.

Meanwhile, Rome was becoming concerned with the insurgence of Christians. After many years of peaceful coexistence among the pagans, Christianity became a perceived threat to Rome mostly due to Rome's increasing political vulnerabilities. Many historians believe the great fire of Rome in 64 was a plot by a paranoid Nero, who blamed the Christians. He feared the growing acceptance of the Christian faith and attempted to influence public opinion against them.

The Christians refused to worship any gods but Jesus and the Father and were propagandized as atheists to the predominantly pagan regions. Despite constant persecutions, the Christian movement was widespread. By 250 AD, advocates of the new religion lived in every part of the empire and in every class of society.[3]

RUNAWAY TRAIN

For over 200 years after the death of Jesus, the Roman Empire was embroiled in battles from all corners of its empire. The increasing mastery of travel by land and sea coincided with a large population growth. This presented new challenges to the Roman Empire. Everywhere, mutinies caused by insubordination in the military led to an unprecedented division of power. Rome's vulnerabilities in Persia and to the Barbarians, who wished to exploit the empire and seize control of its land and wealth, heightened the Empire's woes. Trying to curb the growing array of problems within the empire rendered the state economically and socially depressed.

During the same period, Christians throughout the region were killed, persecuted and dishonored by Roman rule. Political, military and social unrest was rampant throughout the region and Christian perseverance, in spite of persecution, was well-noted by the political leaders of Rome.

> Yet the dream has come true; that Church has triumphed. Where is the old religion? Christ has conquered, and all the gods have gone, utterly gone—they are memories now and nothing more. Why did they go? The Christian Church refused to compromise. A pagan could have seen no real reason why Jesus should not be a Demi-god like Heracles or Dionysus; no reason, either, why a man should not worship Jesus as well as these. One of the Roman Emperors, a little after 200 A.D., had in his private sanctuary four or five statues of gods, and one of them was Jesus. Why not? The Roman world had open arms for Jesus as well as any other god or Demi-god, if people would be sensible; but the Christian said, no. He would not allow Jesus to be put into that pantheon, nor would he worship the gods himself, not even the "genius" of the Emperor, his guardian spirit.[4]

237

ALPHA TO OMEGA

Constantine's conquest of Italy, in 312 A.D., is seen as the largest single political and social slingshot for Christianity's growth throughout history. He seized the riches of the pagan temples and the estates and treasures of the pagan wealthy. He gave vast sums to Christians for the rebuilding of their churches and authorized them to draw on government funds for repairs of damages from the former persecutions. His government allotted annual subsidies to the churches for distribution to the poor, which invoked a favorable image of caring, and aided in the growth of Christianity.

Constantine's government revised civil and criminal law in Christian interest. Divorce was made more difficult. Sodomy and illegitimacy were outlawed. Obstacles were put in the way of conversion to Judaism. The government favored Christians in every aspect and, unlike any religion before it, became an organized religion by the government and for the government. The state and church, although considered independent of one another, effectively governed the region by mandating subservience. The powers of the government protected the *presumably* higher authority of the ecclesiastic branch.[5]

None of this came without an effect on the true teachings of Jesus. Even then, interpretations of the teachings of Jesus varied. A group known as the Gnostics was very much concerned with Rome's dilution of Christ's teachings. The Romans persecuted and killed many of them and, by claiming they were heretics of minor Christian parties, Rome was able to seize their assets and estates. Since the government was now in charge of Christianity, the interpretations and the rules for worship were mandated by Roman rule. Soon, Christianity became known as an intolerant sect, not only prejudiced against those who idolized other gods, but biased against anyone who failed to worship in the prescribed ways dictated by the authorities.

Proof of Rome's firm imposition of Christian orthodoxy was confirmed in discoveries during a period from 1863 through 1945 in areas of Upper Egypt. Known as the Gnostic texts, these codices were hidden by several influential and early Christian Gnostics for fear of being destroyed by Roman rule. Much of the unapproved literature pertaining to Christ's life and death had been destroyed and the Gnostics were in fear of losing the remaining nuggets of truth. Isn't it a wonder how such a relatively few documents made it into the biblical canon? Is it possible that large volumes of undiscovered and important information are still missing?

The only canonized accounts of the work of Jesus, his immediate disciples and Paul, are four gospels (Matthew, Mark, Luke and John), written in the last quarter of the 1st century; the Acts of the Apostles; the letters of Paul, which date mainly from the fifties; a few letters by Peter and John; and the Apocalypse, which John also wrote. All of the events regarding Jesus' life, the role of the apostles, his arguments with the Pharisees and his teachings were matters of dispute from the start.

We can safely speculate that omissions factored heavily in getting mass appeal and Roman approval. The abolishment of Jewish rituals made Christianity a favorable alternative to Judaism, while concessions given to the overwhelming majority of pagans helped to gather massive approval.

ALPHA TO OMEGA

Constantine's beliefs were obviously overshadowed by personal wealth and power. By the 4th century, political and religious power had become homogenized. Bishops had been delegated throughout several regions to oversee the indoctrination and interpretation of publicized Christian documents. A concept of Jesus and his mission was popularized among the citizens for easy acceptance, which garnered dominating political and social clout.

Constantine, under political pressure brought on by feuds among Pagan, Jewish and Christian factions, summoned all the bishops of the church to a council at Nicaea in 325 AD to draft an official document espousing the faith of Christianity. About 300 bishops carefully drafted the Nicene Creed, which became the state's prescribed mandate for orthodox Christian belief. The document proclaimed, among many things, that Jesus and the Father were the same.

The foundation of Christianity had become established. Further developments led to the preeminence assumed by the Bishop of Rome, whom church leaders would later called the Pope. His favored status gave him the ability to create church policy and to develop the universal understandings of Christianity. Celibacy within the priesthood was not introduced, until sometime in the 4th century. The adoption of the presumed mystery of the Trinity was not completed, until late in the same century.

By the early 6th century, the government in Greece ordered all pagans to become Christians after concessions for pagan tradition, which are easily recognized in today's Catholic holidays.

Many believe that Jesus was born somewhere about 1 AD on December 25th, which is a pagan fabrication. We know that Herod the great ordered the killing of all children two years old and under during his reign because of rumors of Jesus birth. Joseph and Mary are known to have fled to Nazareth for this reason. Herod died in 4 BC, which means that Jesus had to have been born before then.

Scholars today have placed his actual date of birth sometime between August of 7 BC and April of 6 BC. Why do we celebrate his birthday on December 25th? According to old pagan tradition, the solar cycle begins with its rebirth on the 25th of December as the sun makes its way northward again.

Does anyone ever wonder why Easter is celebrated at different days in early spring each year? The first day of planting, according to Pagan tradition, was the first Sunday after the first full moon after the first day of spring, which is exactly when Easter is celebrated today. These were obvious endorsements later assigned to appease the sentiments of pagans, many who likely believed Jesus to be nothing more than another one of their mythical gods.

The power created by the church's wealth, favorable political influence, and rising popular opinion snowballed. Contributions began to exceed the tax revenues of the government.[6] The Catholic Church enlarged to become a wealthy and powerful entity, whose early growth ensured its survival through the tumult and fall of the Roman Empire and the clouded events of the Dark Ages.

Overall acceptance and unified belief within any empire are forces to be reckoned with. The Roman Empire relied on a unified ideology in the name of God no matter how much truth had been

ALPHA TO OMEGA

omitted or occluded. Maintaining influence in the governing process of their members depended upon the propagation of good and punishment for evil as dictated by an authority, whose primary goal was power and dominance.

From the single early church of followers, many divisions and branches of Christianity have grown. While the conversion of many to Christianity in all its forms has often been seen as a political attempt to obtain power, an overall willingness to embrace its tenets still exists. Jesus Christ defeated the inherent ignorance of all mankind, which is now widely understood and easily accepted.

Although many things may have been hidden, the constant search for truth is evidenced in the many derivatives of Christianity's analysis. Thus, no matter which particular avenue we evaluate, we can easily see wisdom work. The truth resides in our inborn spirit, which is intrinsic to the completely enlightened Whole Spirit of Jesus Christ.

We should pay close attention to the simplicity of Christ's message. The astonishing simple component in all of this is that our blindness is cured by the One who saw clearly. Nothing else is left to say. One person or group is not better than the other because each of our souls remain dark.

Let us not forget that Christ's death saved everyone—even those who do not believe.

Although this claim may bring about an enormous backlash from fundamentalists, it is the truth and claiming otherwise is cause for divisions among people and nations.

242

Any threat to the church's power has produced unbelievably vicious wars and great suffering, all in the name of Christianity. The early martyrs of Roman persecution were very conscious of the simplicity of Jesus' message. Mankind has taken the perfect and simple message distorted it to the point where many would kill in the name of Jesus, which is certainly not the message of Christ's ministry.

Although many conflicts over the veracity of Christian doctrine exist, faith in Jesus and the promise of his teachings have prevailed, despite what may have been lost or omitted. The church today resembles the prehistoric Egyptian society, the early Hebrew religious power, and the Roman Empire. The religious authorities mold our precepts, with the primary concern of retaining their influence and power. The search for truth is ongoing.

The judgmental characteristics of mankind can be seen as the product of the failure to know the truth and the belief that we have figured it out.

Today's confusions are earmarked by Christ's refusal to be exalted, which leaves us to search for the truths that lie within ourselves. Jesus pronounced this conflict when he said, *"...I have not come to bring peace, but a sword . . . ."* And so, the ongoing battle continues between the affirmation of truth and the limits imposed by our beliefs.

ALPHA TO OMEGA

Hereafter Forever

We agree that we are here to discover All Truth and that the collective beliefs of mankind are reflected in the world we see today. Our beliefs determine the actions that shape our individual and collective outcome. We see how our vague concepts prevent us from seeing the road and our journey, but it's important for us to understand how they contribute to the imbalance in our world and their effect on human progress.

A perfect example is in our beliefs about the afterlife. What happens to our darkened souls after death? Most of us don't give much attention to this question because everyone dies and it seems there is nothing to worry about. Complacency actually opposes our purpose, hinders our achievements and remains embedded in the collective consciousness.

It's this particular model of thinking causing us to place more emphasis on the temporal concerns of our individual lives and largely contributes to the collective consciousness shaping the world we see today. Is it possible that a rude awakening awaits us on the other side? Based on what we have discussed throughout the book so far, there is a way to explain it.

A soul cannot die, because it is born of both consciousness and eternal Spirit—the Essence of Life. When we are born into this physical world, we are linked to pure Spirit—a drop from the Essence of Life, which becomes embedded in the farthest reaches of our soul, while our ego awakens and poorly defines our realities.

The Essence of Life and its incessant will to become consciously expressed alter our life's experiences, which are necessary in the enlightenment process. The experiences result from the actions governed by our beliefs and are designed by the Truth to reveal the errors in our concepts. Individual and collective events can be seen as the metaphysics of cause and effect because Truth is always trying to reveal itself, as we have previously discussed.

Spirit cannot be destroyed and becomes an integral part of the soul, which is a unique entity endowed by awareness and experiences. Only through this personalization does soul exist and have the potential to become wholly enlightened through our awareness and experiences, which are molded by our priorities. If our priorities are not directed towards enlightenment, we will remain darkened. The unique entity endowed by individual expression of our personal experiences and awareness will continue to live for eternity, because eternal Spirit is the founder of our awareness and life at birth.

If we were to be exposed to the light of God in our physical realm, the overwhelming presence would expose our darkness and cause death. However, after physical death, we cross over and enter the spiritual realm where the exposed light of God reveals our darkened soul. This invokes an unquenchable and incessant longing for wholeness, but our exhumed imperfection traps us and prevents us from achieving it. The yearning becomes an unimaginable and deep burning desire that can last for eternity. The true Essence of our being can only be satisfied by Wholeness.

Christ defeated our transgressions and saves all from being eternally imprisoned by the mistakes of our ignorance and the unquenchable thirst to be complete in Spirit. His Whole Spirit was

ALPHA TO OMEGA

derived in the same vehicle as ours. We were condemned by one man and saved by another man. But this doesn't guarantee immediate relief from a temporary hell after death—an insatiable desire to become Whole. Imagine looking through a locked and unbreakable glass door at oases of water while dying of thirst.

Heaven and Hell are two widely used and misunderstood demonstratives. In a world where All Truth has not been fulfilled, heaven is unobtainable until we become completely illuminated by Spirit. Since neither of us has reached full potential in this era, no one gains heaven except through Jesus. He is the gatekeeper. Everyone ends up in the spiritual world crying out for salvation, which will only happen at a prescribed time.

> When he opened the fifth seal, I saw under the altar the souls of those who had been slain for the word of God and for the witness they had borne; they cried out with a loud voice, "O sovereign Lord, holy and true, how long before thou will judge and avenge our blood on those who dwell upon the earth?" Then they were each given a white robe and told to rest a little longer, until the number of their fellow servants and their brethren should be complete, who were to be killed as they themselves had been (Rev 6: 9-11).

We discussed mercy as the ability to be in the presence of the Cherubim as an unenlightened but innocent person. The white robes are indicative of a cover for our darkened souls, provided by the sacrifice of Christ. Thanks to Jesus, our ignorance will not cause our *eternal* suffering if we act according to the golden rules.

This is Universal Truth and every religion preaches the same ideal to prioritize God or Enlightenment, release our temporal

RUNAWAY TRAIN

concerns, accept others, and refrain from judgment. If we all do that, we can be guaranteed salvation, no matter what our religious beliefs, thanks to the sacrifice of Jesus.

> After these things I looked, and behold, a great multitude which no one could count, from every nation and all tribes and peoples and tongues, standing before the throne and before the Lamb, clothed in white robes, and palm branches were in their hands; and they cry out with a loud voice, saying, "Salvation to our God who sits on the throne, and to the Lamb." And all the angels were standing around the throne and around the elders and the four living creatures; and they fell on their faces before the throne and worshiped God, saying, "Amen, blessing and glory and wisdom and thanksgiving and honor and power and might, be to our God forever and ever. Amen."

> Then one of the elders answered, saying to me, "These who are clothed in the white robes, who are they, and where have they come from?" I said to him, "My lord, you know." And he said to me, "These are the ones who come out of the **great tribulation**, and they have washed their robes and made them white in the blood of the Lamb. "For this reason, they are before the throne of God; and they serve Him day and night in His temple; and He who sits on the throne will spread His tabernacle over them. "They will hunger no longer, nor thirst anymore; nor will the sun beat down on them, nor any heat; for the Lamb in the center of the throne will be their shepherd, and will guide them to springs of the water of life; and God will wipe every tear from their eyes." (Rev. 7:9-17)

We live in the latter days of the great tribulation, a two million year human expedition of suffering and confusion. This scripture describes a specific time when all innocent souls will be redeemed

ALPHA TO OMEGA

as the gates of Heaven will open for them. Contemporary Christian fundamentalists teach that the final seven years on earth is the period referred to as the great tribulation, but the idea is short-sighted.

Clearly, these are the souls of people from all over the world who have died and moved on into the spiritual dimension. The white robes, which cover a darkened soul, have been washed in the blood of the Lamb. All are innocent souls who lived according to the Golden Rules. No matter what their beliefs entailed before death, the washing of their robes signifies the new purity of their soul by the sacrifice of Jesus, which was recognized as universal truth upon their entrance into the spiritual realm.

From this perspective, we are innocent in spite of our soul's incomplete nature as long as we act accordingly. We were born into ignorance and have not reached higher levels of awareness, which helps to clarify the baptismal promise and ritual. It doesn't mean that we will not suffer an unquenchable longing for countless years while waiting for the right time and circumstances. After all, our complacency contributes in determining our priorities, which prevents us from seeking All Truth as our main objective in life.

The souls of Adam's era are still suffering until Paradise returns to earth. Many of them can never be redeemed when we take into account the knowledge and understanding that preceded their choices. Some are in an eternal hell of unimaginable non-fulfillment.

One of the most often overlooked facts about Jesus' death was his descension into hell before his Resurrection, as originally stated in the earliest Apostle's Creed. I envision this as Jesus visiting to release the chains of their mistakes from those of us in the new era. He was living proof that a man can achieve what had long been proprietary to the first generation alone. Essentially, Jesus separated the souls of this age from the souls of Atlantis. We are bound by different terms and conditions.

The prerequisite for reaching higher levels of spiritual being is to first achieve perfection or Paradise in the physical realm. The realized level in the physical realm weighs in the determination of our destiny after physical death. Our soul, after having been developed by the spiritual and physical expression of experiences here on earth, remains a living being after physical death. It is limited in illumination because of our limited physical world, which is a collective reflection of our limited ideas and beliefs.

Thanks to Jesus Christ, we don't have to suffer for eternity after physical death, but we cannot pass through heaven's gates until the doorway to truth's fulfillment on earth is opened. The specific time cannot happen until our earthly priorities change and our limited models of thought are replaced by a general acceptance of progressive thought aimed at humankind's enlightenment. Why do we bother believing in God if we don't take it seriously enough to consider our eternal life or to seek answers to the meaning of life and purpose?

If we can agree that our soul's illumination relies much upon the level of enlightenment we achieve here in the physical world, then our spiritual growth has stagnated. Our temporal concerns are cultivated by vague concepts believed to be unexplainable because

ALPHA TO OMEGA

our worldly concerns take priority over our yearning for the truth to define them.

If we closely examine the world around us, we can easily see how it mirrors our collective and shortsighted ideals. When the collective mindset prioritizes truth with as much fervor as our immediate concerns, its power will alter the world we live in. Only then can the doorway for truth on earth be opened and the gates to heaven for those who have gone before us.

Collective Reflection

Mankind's search for knowledge has led to progress and it will continue for as long as our species survives. Have we ever wondered why our progress is measured only in our technological achievements? We are captivated by the accoutrements, gadgets and toys of our sensual world, which keep us diverted from questioning our true purpose and destiny.

Authority is the key to understanding our world and its limits. Individual knowledge is miniscule when compared to the countless archives of authoritative knowledge. Thousands of scientific, religious and political authorities maintain their power by ensuring the succession of their teachings throughout the generations. Authoritative influence contributes not only to what we believe to be true but where we should focus our attention.

The power of authority is the power of knowledge divided.

Every authoritative entity is comprised of individuals like you and me. From the smallest to the largest, each of them works to satisfy the expectations of their advocates in order to ensure their longevity. Every group is largely embraced by individuals whose earthly desires take precedence over our yearning for Truth and spiritual progress. These intrinsic traits become mirrored in the entities enlarged by time and constituents.

For the most part, each governing entity reflects the standards and beliefs of its backers. Our fuzzy notions and shortsighted beliefs are magnified by the world we see around us. We consider it to be mere chance, but the world is representative of our confusion and complacent acceptance of the status quo, which is to primarily concern ourselves with things of this world. The myriad crises of the world today are born by our failure to define our purpose and believing we will find our peace when we die, which we've demonstrated to be otherwise.

The doctrines of organized religions are so enmeshed within the social and political foundations of our cultures that we have become comfortable. We are looking in the wrong direction and have collectively created the world we see around us.

The system in place today is the enlarged conglomerate of gigantic authorities. It has become an almost unstoppable power machine running on its own and fueled by our worldly concerns and the natural tendency of a system to provide its members with what is deemed appropriate and satisfactory.

If we are inherently ignorant, from an absolute point of view, then it is safe to say that the system is the sum total of our inherent

ALPHA TO OMEGA

collective ignorance. Why are we fooling ourselves? Many of the basic morals and political ethics are swiftly eroding, while millions in the world are suffering without food, education and medicine. Immediate satisfaction is becoming more important than ever before.

Our myopic concepts may often run counter to our internal hopes and dreams, but they are infused into our inescapable system by the aspirations of every individual on up to the most powerful controllers. The runaway train is at full speed and we are the fuel.

The system is an entity that cannot survive without members. Sadly, the ambitions of many are stifled and controlled by relatively few whose obvious concerns are power, wealth and other worldly tangibles. What we need to ask ourselves is whether or not the controllers of our system and its information are making the right decisions for us? Are we being denied information that would change our beliefs enough to alter our personal decisions? These are important questions that most of us consider as always having a favorable answer.

When we are denied information and truth, we are forced to rely on the integrity of those that hold our fate in their hands. More than likely, the powerful few harbor the same blurred concepts about our purpose and destiny as we do (and with much more zeal), which suggests that most of the important decisions would prioritize wealth and power above anything else. What are the consequences for those like you and me?

This isn't an attack on our system, but an attempt to demonstrate its long and solidified development. I'm not blaming the system for our problems because it is born and fueled by the shortsighted ideals of everyone. However, it has grown into such an enormous entity that it must sustain itself in order to ensure the sustainment of its members. If it were to crumble, the world would be cast into an age of darkness, anarchy and confusion and the powerful leaders would have nothing left to control.

The dominating countries of the world are measured by their ability to control their resources, influence world markets, expand their tax revenues, provide a thorough social and economic system for their citizens, and defend the system from aggressors. While this may sound simple, each system becomes a fine-tuned machine dependent upon many parts working in unison to keep it running. If a major breakdown occurs in any of the parts, the system could become vulnerable.

The largest financial and industrialized countries (United States, Great Britain, France, Germany, Italy, Japan and Canada) joined together to form the Group of seven known formerly as the G-7 in 1976. Russia has recently been added to the group, which meets regularly to discuss and enact policies to ensure the sustainment of economic systems and development (today, China, Brazil and India rank among the top 7 but are not included in the Group).

These powerful nations and their representatives are making decisions that affect the entire world. Most often, considerations for those countries with lesser wealth, widespread poverty, disease and social unrest are ignored. To coin a phrase, it's the nature of the *beast*.

Technology and information has increased exponentially over the last 25 years or so and its implications are staggering. Top secret discoveries in the fields of science and medicine exist without disclosure. Experiments, which began with Einstein, Tesla and other renowned scientists in the 1940's, are being conducted by contemporary scientists and have obviously grown to unbelievable proportions.

Research funded by large governments has likely produced unfathomable technologies. The development of modern marvels of weaponry, planes, tanks, laser systems and other well-advanced machinery has led to many secret devices, and computer based systems. There is no doubt that such research exists and we need only to look at the world around us to get an idea of what is possible.

In the field of medical science, cloning and genetic manipulation are commonplace. We are creating drugs to alter every aspect of our lives. Birth control, prevention of inherited diseases or birth defects, aging, and our physical appearance are just a few of many markets opened by research. Add the studies of the brain and its capacity to control how our body functions, and we have the ingredients for unprecedented consequences.

We are not privy to many of these discoveries because knowledge is power and authority is our filter to knowledge. The concealment of knowledge is a viable alternative to anarchy and loss of power. The practice is widely accepted and unchallenged because world leaders are presumed to have the same ideals as we do.

The world is not deliberately evil—at least not yet. It is just the way it is—an effect caused by our failure to understand our true purpose. The entire collective entity is saturated by limited ideals and beliefs that spawn improper and temporal decisions. We complain about the observable global crises confronting us yet we are collectively responsible for the seemingly unavoidable arrangement.

An example is the public outcry against nuclear power for generating electricity, especially after the 2011 Fukishima disaster in Japan. We think nothing of complaining when our power goes out and we cannot turn on the lights, operate our computers, or run our heat and air conditioning. The energy must come from somewhere, yet we exhibit our disdain with corporations and governments that have carefully weighed the need for energy with the risks associated with means to provide it. Accidents happen.

Are we willing to drastically reduce our use of energy? Are the gigantic energy corporations going to be willing to reduce their profits? The presumed satisfaction of society is determined by the easy availability of products, services, and technology. Corporate response to provide it is expected and unavoidable or so it seems.

There are a few subtle implications to this as well. Growing public awareness to the obvious systemic defects, inequality and the mounting global crises are equally well-noted by the controllers of the system. Generally, many of us have become instinctively aware that things cannot continue as they are and, more than likely, the most powerful people on earth are equally attentive and have seriously considered the future of humanity.

We can be certain that clandestine think-tanks have thoroughly discussed and assessed many possibilities for the future with more devotion than any individual. This begs us to ask what they have surmised and their plans for our future. If we agree that the system's continuance is dominated by the obsession with wealth and power, then its primary concern is to ensure its endurance.

Is it wrong for those of us with comparatively scant knowledge to question the motives of those who are privy to top-secret information and whose obvious priorities are wealth and power? Today's technology affords the system with an enormous amount of power over its citizens, which can be utilized whenever it is deemed necessary to favorably sway our sentiments. We have become individually powerless and, unless we jointly begin to question our purpose and spiritual destiny, we shall remain so.

In order to decipher the clues in the book of Revelation, we must recognize these fundamental concepts. By observing the system as a separate entity founded by centuries of procuring wealth through the ignorance of its members, we can see the nature of the beast with clarity.

> **If Supreme Being is the reflection of God in physical form, then the beast is the collective reflection of man's ignorance in the form of an unyielding entity.**

Ironically, the currently popularized ideas have us looking towards a New World Order or a leader from European Community as our future nemesis and antichrist. We are looking everywhere, except in front of us, which makes me wonder where the prevailing concepts originated and how they were able to gain such popular favor.

Ideas like these have been fortified by our reluctance to ardently search for answers and to think independently, which gives power to those who, not only think for us, but have become an integral part of the unyielding entity responsible for shaping our perceptions.

The Harbinger of Doom, Fear and Hope

Confusion has been our age-old hindrance, which is exacerbated by clinging to the vague concepts upholding our presumptions. We are convinced this is the way it must be and that we will be free when we die. We have come to accept the finite, while the truth constantly evades the answers to our questions. Why are we here? What happens when we die? Why are pain, suffering, war and disease still prevalent? Who or what is God?

We must earnestly seek answers to these questions and look for answers outside the dimensions of our defined reality. We believe we must die and suffer because we are human and that God is indefinable. Because truth is not our priority, we get a sense of security in knowing billions have come and gone before us, which continually nurtures our presumed realities.

Most of us live without concerns for impending death and the afterlife. We wait until we are faced with this reality before we even consider it. It's the reason for our complacency and our reluctance to search within ourselves for God and Truth.

We have envisioned God as an external component of ourselves rather than the Unifier of Truth and Essence within each of us. The

ALPHA TO OMEGA

answers are not beyond our reach, but our search is smothered by believing they are. Instead, we've allowed a portrayal of reality to inundate our senses without questioning the obvious horrors entangled within it.

Our directives will soon be changed by a course of events that will typify our inherent ignorance, incessant will to survive and undying struggle for truth without conflict. We will become united by a sudden responsibility to ask questions we have refused to consider. The aspirations of many are being suppressed by the authorities whose power is defined by wealth and military strength, but they are not dismissed in the collective consciousness.

The Book of Revelation is the story of man's return to Paradise following serious upheaval, terror, and deception. Revelation is the cryptic and final chapter of the Bible and humanity. The conclusion, like any story, must fulfill its premise and provide answers to connect the dots from beginning to a justifiable end.

Essentially, The Book of Revelation begins with the prophecy associated with the opening of the symbolic seals representing the course of events to follow Christ's death. None of this could have happened without the death and resurrection of Christ.

> I saw in the right hand of Him who sat on the throne a book written inside and on the back, sealed up with seven seals. And I saw a strong angel proclaiming with a loud voice, "Who is worthy to open the book and to break its seals?" And no one in heaven or on the earth or under the earth was able to open the book or to look into it. Then I began to weep greatly because no one was found worthy to open the book or to look into it; and one of the elders said to me, "Stop weeping; behold, the Lion that is from the

tribe of Judah, the Root of David, has overcome so as to open the book and its seven seals."

And I saw between the throne and the four living creatures and the elders a Lamb standing, as if slain, having seven horns and seven eyes, which are the seven Spirits of God, sent out into all the earth. And He came and took the book out of the right hand of Him who sat on the throne. When He had taken the book, the four living creatures and the twenty-four elders fell down before the Lamb, each one holding a harp and golden bowls full of incense, which are the prayers of the saints. And they sang a new song, saying, "Worthy are you to take the book and to break its seals; for you were slain, and purchased for God with your blood men from every tribe and tongue and people and nation. You have made them to be a kingdom and priests to our God; and they will reign upon the earth." (Rev. 5:1-10)

The weeping is caused by realizing no progress could have been made, until Jesus' sacrifice. We would have continued onward in our age of great tribulation and all of our souls would be forever locked in torment. Because of Christ's death, mercy is bestowed upon *everyone* in our era. His life and death epitomized mankind's struggle for truth. Only through the varying interpretations of Jesus' life and ministry can the conflicts emerge for the final ordination of truth.

Subsequent passages in Revelation portray the opening of the first four seals. Each is known as one the four horsemen of the apocalypse. The first is the white horse, the conqueror, which signifies the truths of Christ's testimony. The second is the red horse, known for taking peace from the earth, which represents the never ending battle between truth and belief. The third is the black

ALPHA TO OMEGA

horse, the balancer, which demonstrates the balance maintained between truth and our beliefs without serious upheaval. The fourth is the pale horse of death by sword, famine, pestilence and wild beasts of the earth, which typifies the inevitable suffering, war and disease caused by the inherent ignorance of our age.

We spoke of the fifth seal in a previous discourse about the hereafter. All of the souls who have died are waiting to enter the closed gates of heaven and were given white robes until the prescribed time and circumstance. They yearn for the awakening to truth in the physical realm so they can be redeemed by Christ to eternal peace and Wholeness.

We are at the dawn of the awakening to truth here on earth—a serious look at our life and reason for it. Imagine the collective yearning to know more than we have ever asked before. Just as a near brush with death inspired many toward an ardent quest for truth, likewise would humanity be cooperatively inclined by sudden calamity and destruction forged by a significant natural worldwide event. The omen to the end of days and catalyst to worldwide fear is depicted in the opening of the sixth seal.

And I saw when he opened the sixth seal, and there was a great earthquake; and the sun became black as sackcloth of hair, and the whole moon became as blood; and the stars of the heaven fell unto the earth, as a fig tree sheds her unripe figs when she is shaken of a great wind. And the heaven was removed as a scroll when it is rolled up; and every mountain and island were moved out of their places. And the kings of the earth, and the princes, and the chief captains, and the rich, and the strong, and every bondman and freeman, hid themselves in the caves and in the

260

rocks of the mountains; and they say to the mountains and to the rocks, "Fall on us, and hide us from the face of him that sits on the throne, and from the wrath of the Lamb: for the great day of their wrath is come; and who can stand before it?" (Rev. 6:12-17)

Imagine a monstrous earthquake coinciding with a global meteor shower. Imagine super-sized solar ejections of gamma rays, which affect the earth's magnetic poles causing unusual and unprecedented movements of the earth. Day and night a continual barrage of visible fiery meteors will crash to the earth like bombs going off randomly across the globe. Soon afterwards, the settling dust creates a filter for the light of the sun and the moon.

Would an event like this direct our attention to things we have not cared to carefully examine before? Would the unifying fear induce a new belief that our reality is not as secure as we might think? Would those who have known of this future event see it as an earmark to the dramatic final days? Although most people will be spared, many will die invoking an unprecedented fear in all of mankind; a fear that compels us to vainly beseech God as the urgent search for life's meaning begins.

Most important, the event doesn't have to be exactly as described in my interpretation. What is crucial, however, is that the harbinger or warning event invokes a worldwide fear in everyone, no matter who they are or what position they hold in this world. The event will be so dramatic that people from every nation will recognize its world-changing significance. Japan's tsunami of 2011 will pale in comparison to the spectacular event portrayed in Revelation's 2000 year-old story.

ALPHA TO OMEGA

This magnificent event is more than just coincidence or happenstance and for this reason it is predicted in Revelation. I've continually demonstrated all events as the effects of Divine Will's incessant process to be made manifest in our physical world—truth's inexorable nature to be clarified. The harbinger is the direct effect of the growing alliance between human aspiration and Truth's Will to be made manifest and by effects caused by the deliberate occlusion of truths that must be revealed.

Countless people have long-envisioned the world as chaotic and full of suffering and inequality. Silently they have loathed the seemingly unchangeable conditions of a world dominated by wealth, power and wantonness. The delicate balance between truth and our beliefs will be shaken by the overriding and silent longing for truth and justice. Finally, the doorway to the fulfillment of truth on earth is opened, as are the gates of heaven for the departed souls of our era. (The excerpt was quoted in the previous section when all those in white robes are redeemed)

The harbinger is followed by Revelation's depiction of the 144,000 servants of God.

After this I saw four angels standing at the four corners of the earth, holding back the four winds of the earth, so that no wind would blow on the earth or on the sea or on any tree. And I saw another angel ascending from the rising of the sun, having the seal of the living God; and he cried out with a loud voice to the four angels to whom it was granted to harm the earth and the sea, saying, "Do not harm the earth or the sea or the trees until we have sealed the bond-servants of our God on their foreheads." And I heard the number of those who were sealed, one hundred

262

and forty-four thousand sealed from every tribe of the sons of Israel: From the tribe of Judah, twelve thousand were sealed, from the tribe of Reuben twelve thousand, from the tribe of Gad twelve thousand, from the tribe of Asher twelve thousand, from the tribe of Naphtali twelve thousand, from the tribe of Manasseh twelve thousand, from the tribe of Simeon twelve thousand, from the tribe of Levi twelve thousand, from the tribe of Issachar twelve thousand, from the tribe of Zebulun twelve thousand, from the tribe of Joseph twelve thousand, from the tribe of Benjamin, twelve thousand were sealed. (Rev. 7:1-8)

Information about the 144,000 servants of God is minimal. They are chosen before depictions of, what appears to be, disastrous consequences of a major world war and redeemed as first fruits for God shortly afterwards.

The mission of these remarkable people should be easy to surmise, in light of the time of their arrival. I suspect them to be a bit more privy to utilizing the metaphysics of faith and find it fitting for each to be chosen from the tribes of Israel. I believe them to be modern-day prophets whose objective is to spread the truth about the harbinger and secrets of the future ahead.

Like anything that has happened on earth before, everyone will have different opinions and beliefs about the harbinger. Some will see it for what it is—a warning to change our ways, while most will figure it to be nothing more than a coincidence. Either way, our age-old habits to endure our suffering, while clinging to life and its apparent reality, will not be substantially altered. A short cooling-off period will take place as the general populace becomes largely convinced the event is an insignificant coincidence.

> When the Lamb opened the seventh seal, there was silence in
> heaven for about a half an hour (Rev. 8: 1)

Meanwhile, the most powerful religious and political leaders of the world will zealously debate the event presenting their various interpretations as mounting tensions will become typical in covert meetings. Individual fear can invoke irrational knee-jerk decisions and actions, but fear and tension among powerful leaders of the civilized world has the potential to cause exponentially larger damage by hastened decisions. Fear will become rooted by uncertainty in the assessment of opposing reactions as the controversy will infiltrate the religious, scientific, political and industrial factions of power at extreme levels.

The decisions confronting our leaders will rattle the seats of power. As the world's inhabitants begin to settle down, they will be oblivious to the intensity of conflict dividing the world's power factions. Decisions made by world leaders will catapult us into the final stages of our journey. Without compromise, World War III shall become a sudden reality.

Chapter 8

RISE AND FALL OF THE HEGEMON

Nothing that is hidden shall remain unseen.

War of Wars

Do we really believe the ancient biblical prophecy of Revelation to be an accurate prediction of future events? Some believe Revelation to be a description of battles during the Crusades or as an allegory to other historical events. Most people don't even care about it and many rely on religion to interpret it for them. Revelation was written for anyone who really wants to know the secrets to God and Truth.

Everything I have presented in this book has stemmed from my yearning to decipher Revelation, which has been the center of curiosity throughout my entire adult life. Surprisingly, my desire to understand the future has helped me to understand much more.

Revelation has thoroughly qualified my belief that an internal search for purpose and truth can yield the answers to things deemed unexplainable.

If you've been reading to this point, then most likely some of the presented concepts have struck a familiar chord with the very essence of your being. I didn't create these concepts because truth has always existed and needs only to be discovered or observed, which is why truth easily resonates with seekers of truth. I have found the book of Revelation to be a remarkable conduit.

As mentioned earlier, the events of Revelation are inevitable and, although I don't know when these events will occur, it is easy to see we are getting very close. Many of us don't want to believe or care to understand, but ignoring it is partially responsible for its inevitability.

If we remain blinded by the effects of our inherent nature and continue with a false sense of security in our presumed realities, then events will eventually happen to reveal the errors in our concepts. Why? I've stated it many times throughout the book: Truth is always trying to reveal itself in our physical world. The core of our being is always revealing itself.

The harbinger is an event that vibrates throughout the realms of our existence. Without it, we would be doomed in a seemingly unending torture in the spiritual world after death. If we understand the true battle for our souls, then Lucifer and his followers have held the advantage for the entire course of the new age—the Great Tribulation. Finally, everything changes after the harbinger.

RISE AND FALL OF THE HEGEMON

By awakening to our purpose and truth, we are invoking Divine Will's intercession. The final battle for our souls is not only the world war and its consequences, but the unbelievable events that follow. If Lucifer would have it his way, the harbinger would never happen and neither would the subsequent events predicted in Revelation. But Truth cannot be hidden or controlled forever because the core of our beings is the substance of All Truth. A collective internal longing to become whole, seek justice, equality and harmony with nature is the catalyst that finally tips the delicately balanced scales.

After the short cooling off period, the seven angel trumpets of the seventh seal begin.

> The first angel blew his trumpet, and there followed hail and fire, mingled with blood, and they were cast upon the earth; and a third part of the earth was burnt up, and the third part of the trees was burnt up, and all green grass was burnt up.

> The second angel blew his trumpet, and something like a great mountain burning with fire was cast into the sea; and a third part of the sea became blood; and a third of the creatures living in the sea died; and a third of the ships were destroyed.

> The third angel blew his trumpet, and there fell from heaven a great star, burning as a torch, and it fell upon the third part of the rivers, and upon the fountains of the waters; and the name of the star is called Wormwood; and a third part of the waters became wormwood; and many men died of the waters, because they were made bitter.

> The fourth angel blew his trumpet, and a third part of the sun was smitten, and a third part of the moon, and a third part of the

267

ALPHA TO OMEGA

stars, so that the third of their light was darkened, and a third of the day was kept from shining, likewise a third of the night. (Rev. 8:7-12)

The fifth trumpet is explained in the next section.

Then the sixth angel blew his trumpet, and I heard a voice from the four horns of the golden altar before God saying to the sixth angel who had the trumpet, "Release the four angels who are bound at the river Euphrates" And the four angels were loosed, that had been prepared for the hour and day and month and year, that they should kill a third of mankind. And the number of the armies of the horsemen was twice ten thousand times ten thousand; I heard the number of them. And thus I saw the horses in the vision, the riders wore breastplates the color of fire and of hyacinth and of sulfur, and the heads of the horses were like lions' heads and out of their mouths proceeds fire and smoke and sulfur. By these three plagues was the third part of men killed, by the fire and the smoke and the sulfur, which proceeds out of their mouths. (Rev. 9:15-18)

This is a detailed description of a future war written by someone who had no concepts of bombs, missiles, and modern weaponry of today. Added credence to the timeliness of Revelation's event is evidenced by the depiction of 200 million troops engaged in battle. How many countries can enlist such an enormous amount of troops? It wasn't possible until recently and neither has a third of the world's population ever been killed in a major war.

The inevitable battle will be a war of power factions for the power factions. This war will be different because those with the most power will try to dominate the military, and the industrialized complex of the entire world. Wealth, power and world dominance

RISE AND FALL OF THE HEGEMON

is the objective of the future war so it will have to be a most carefully planned and orchestrated war.

Let's be realistic in our assumptions as to what the largest countries have in place as responses for specific scenarios. Explicit and comprehensive documentations of procedures and protocols exist for responses to any events that may precipitate an all out war. Alliances among powerful nations are coordinated in their procedures, because every industrialized nation realizes the next war will determine the rulers of the entire world.

Considerations for the expectations of the world's remaining citizens will have already been addressed with careful planning for a unified ideal among post-war citizens. A world of anarchy, suffering and confusion must be held to a minimum. Top-secret technologies will be unleashed in the aftermath to provide our world with unprecedented capabilities and the restoration of hope and unity among all survivors.

This isn't a conspiracy theory, but a realistic approach to recognizing how world leaders are smart enough to realize the effects and conditions of a war they have continually averted. The harbinger is one of the scenarios that will create worldwide tensions and unavoidable conflict. The most prepared countries consist of those who have carefully considered every possible scenario and responsive option and who possess the superior technologies to win the battle.

World War III is not the battle of Armageddon, although many will believe it to be. It marks the beginning of the deliberate abuse

269

ALPHA TO OMEGA

of mankind's shortsighted beliefs for reasons not regarded as a possible scenario in the documents of procedures and protocols.

New Demigods, Old Mistake

Try to imagine the conditions of a world in the aftermath of nuclear war. Situations once typical of impoverished nations will be considered a luxury. People will be suffering and dying around the world. We can expect with a good degree of certainty that the United States will hardly be unscathed in an all out war. Rampant chaos will worsen all problems and, although the leaders had previously assessed these scenarios with diligence, the immediate consequences will be extremely difficult to contain.

Perseverance and the ability to rebound from almost any circumstance have characterized humanity throughout our new age. World War III is the final straw to mankind's complacency. We can expect no significant difference in the approach taken by the survivors of the future war, but we can expect much higher expectations for conditions of the future world by angry survivors of an unexplainable war.

People will demand clean water and energy, advanced and cleaner forms of transportation, drastic reforms to the socio-economic and political systems of government, peaceful coexistence and much more. Most people will be willing to take part in ensuring the development of these objectives because survivors of the future calamity will be very resolute. How long will it take to rebuild? What will it take to restore order and trust in the system?

270

RISE AND FALL OF THE HEGEMON

Questions like these have been topics of discussions among world leaders and covert groups for many years. Powerful people want to retain power and their objectives must be prudent enough to evaluate all options with diligence, including an event similar to our scenario. Clandestine meetings have served as the impetus to decades of secret technological developments that will eventually be unveiled to usher in the new world order.

Plans are already in place to ensure survival and order. Without doubt, our world will become much different than today and globally acceptable in a relatively short period of time, because secret technologies will markedly increase humanity's capabilities and efficiency. Later we will see this in more detail, but we need to understand the immediate nature of mankind after the war.

> And the rest of mankind, who were not killed with these plagues, repented not of the works of their hands, that they should not worship demons, and the idols of gold, and of silver, and of brass, and of stone, and of wood; which can neither see, nor hear, nor walk; and they repented not of their murders, nor of their sorceries, nor of their fornication, nor of their thefts. (Rev. 9:20-21)

Here is recognition of the unchanging perceptual constant, which emphasizes the priority placed upon long-standing habits and traditions. Scripture is pointing out that we will continue to believe our happiness lies in the false security of our earthly confines. We must remember the reason for the harbinger. Most people will not see it as an effect of Divine Will, but it is the earmark to the final battle between truth and our beliefs.

ALPHA TO OMEGA

Then I saw another mighty angel coming down from heaven, wrapped in a cloud, with a rainbow over his head, and his face was like the sun and his legs like pillars of fire. He had a little scroll open in his hand. And he set his right foot on the sea and his left foot on the land and called out with a loud voice like a lion roaring; and when he called out, the seven thunders sounded, I was about to write, but I heard a voice from heaven saying, "Seal up what the seven thunders have said and do not write it down." And the angel whom I saw standing on the sea and land lifted his right hand to heaven and swore by him who lives forever and ever, who created heaven and what is in it, and the sea and what is in it, that there should be no more delay, but that in the days of the trumpet call to be sounded by the seventh angel, the mystery of God, as he announced to his servants the prophets, should be fulfilled. (Rev. 10: 1-7)

This is an affirmation that nothing can prevent the events leading to the final fulfillment of truth because the doorway had been opened at the time of the harbinger. Do you want to know what the seven thunders said and why it wasn't written 2000 years ago?

NOTHING THAT IS HIDDEN SHALL REMAIN UNSEEN

The reason it wasn't written is because the truths had already been revealed to Christ's apostles. John understood the secrets to the metaphysical nature of life and Truth's will to be made manifest. By being asked to refrain from recording it signifies his awareness that it would be deciphered at a time when mankind understands the principles of Divine Will. The final trumpet signifies the final

RISE AND FALL OF THE HEGEMON

Revelation of Truth—the mystery of God—which means that nothing shall remain unseen.

Yet the time for Christ's judgment is not quite ripe as intimated in the very next verse.

> And the voice which I heard from heaven, I heard it again speaking with me, and saying, "Go, take the scroll which is open in the hand of the angel that stood upon the sea and upon the earth." And I went unto the angel, saying unto him that he should give me the little scroll. And he said to me, "Take it, and eat it up; it shall make your belly bitter, but in your mouth it shall be sweet as honey." And I took the little scroll out of the angel's hand, and ate it up; and it was in my mouth sweet as honey: and when I had eaten it, my belly was made bitter. And I was told, "You must prophesy again over many peoples and nations and tongues and kings." (Rev. 10:8-11)

What happens when we eat a piece of fruit that isn't ripe? It tastes sweet enough in our mouth, but it tends to upset our stomach. When the writer of this account realizes the bitterness in his stomach, he is told that he must continue with his prophesying and preaching. This signifies that the time is not right for Christ's return.

I have explained earlier why Christ cannot return until we have gone through the process of self-discovery to the point of achieving advanced levels of awareness and metaphysical power. He cannot provide them for us because everything must be revealed through self-discovery, which is why the various interpretations of Christ's mission on earth still divide humanity. Is it possible for mankind to achieve great levels of power in such a short period of time?

ALPHA TO OMEGA

The world will remain divided in beliefs, ideals, concepts of God and truth. Many will be anxiously awaiting Christ's return. The war will turn many away from God, but all of our vulnerabilities will be the same. I specifically left the fifth trumpet out of the earlier description because it wasn't a depiction of war, but of something much more important.

> The fifth angel blew his trumpet, and I saw a star (angel) fallen from heaven to earth and he was given a key to the shaft of the BOTTOMLESS PIT; he opened the shaft and from it rose smoke like smoke from a great furnace and the sun and the air were darkened with the smoke from the shaft. (Rev. 9: 1-2) (My caps and parentheses)

This marks the time when Lucifer is cast to earth, which is also depicted in the following passage.

> And there was war in heaven: Michael and his angels going forth to war with the dragon; and the dragon warred and his angels; and they prevailed not, neither was their place found any more in heaven. And the great dragon was cast down, the old serpent, he that is called the Devil and Satan, the deceiver of the whole world; he was cast down to the earth, and his angels were cast down with him. And I heard a great voice in heaven, saying, "Now is come the salvation, and the power, and the kingdom of our God, and the authority of his Christ: for the accuser of our brethren is cast down, who accuses them before our God day and night. And they overcame him because of the blood of the Lamb and because of the word of their testimony; and they loved not their life even unto death. Therefore rejoice O heavens, and ye that dwell in them. Woe for the earth and for the sea: because the devil is gone down unto you, having great wrath, knowing that his time is short." (Rev. 12:7-12)

RISE AND FALL OF THE HEGEMON

Angels will appear for the first time in thousands of years. Only this time, the angels will be part of the Lucifer rebellion. Everyone will be waiting for the return of Christ to the world and this will mark the return of Christ's body brought forth to the world by Lucifer. The vast majority of the world will believe that Christ has returned. New power and awareness will uplift our experiential and existential potentials to unimaginable levels. We will suddenly become demigods.

Our vulnerabilities will be exploited by Lucifer's deception, which shall be the greatest deception ever imagined or real. The outcome of this euphoria will unify everyone to an unimaginable degree. Drastically increased physical abilities will parallel the magnificent powers of the lost ancient worlds of the new era. The transformation of our physical world shall seem miraculous.

Everyone will be blissful and united in purpose and belief. Citizens of the world will perceive the new arrangement as perfect—Paradise. The sudden power and the enhancements provided by unfathomable technologies will make it difficult to imagine otherwise. Nearly every inhabitant of earth will be blinded by a power that magnifies and exploits our inherent nature, which will prevent us from questioning our presumed realities.

Unlike the mass confusion instigated by the sudden removal of power depicted in the Tower of Babel story, confusion and unrest instigated by World War III will be erased by the sudden increase of power and abilities. We need only to look at the beast described in the post-war passages of Revelation to verify this explanation.

ALPHA TO OMEGA

Scripture One

And I saw a beast coming up out of the sea, having ten horns, and seven heads, and on his horns ten diadems, and upon his heads names of blasphemy. And the beast which I saw was like unto a leopard, and his feet were as the feet of a bear, and his mouth as the mouth of a lion: and the dragon gave him his power, and his throne, and great authority. And I saw one of his heads seemed to have a mortal wound, but its mortal wound was healed; and the whole earth wondered after the beast; and they worshiped the dragon, because he gave his authority unto the beast; and they worshiped the beast, saying, "Who is like unto the beast? And who is able to war with him?"

And there was given to him a mouth speaking great things and blasphemies; and there was given to him authority to continue forty-two months; it opened its mouth to utter blasphemies against God, blaspheming his name and his dwelling, that is, those who dwell in heaven. Also it was allowed to make war on the saints and conquer them. And authority was given it over every tribe and people and tongue and nation, and all who dwell on earth will worship it, everyone whose name has not been written before the foundation of the world in the book of life of the Lamb that was slain. (Rev. 13:1–8)

Scripture Two (author caps and parenthetical remark)

Then I saw another beast, which rose out of the earth (bottomless pit); it had two horns like a lamb and spoke like a dragon. It exercises all the authority of the first beast in its presence and makes the earth and all its inhabitants worship the first beast, whose mortal wound was healed. It works great signs, even making fire come down from heaven to earth in the site of men; and by the signs which it is allowed to work in the presence of the beast, it deceives those who dwell on earth bidding them to make an

276

RISE AND FALL OF THE HEGEMON

IMAGE for the beast which was wounded by the sword and yet lived; and it was allowed to give breath to the image of the beast so that the IMAGE of the beast should even speak, and to cause those who do not worship the image of the beast to be slain.(Rev. 13:11)

Scripture Three (author caps)

But the angel said to me, "Why marvel? I will tell you the mystery of the woman (harlot), and of the beast with seven heads and ten horns that carries her. The beast that you saw WAS and IS NOT, and is to ascend from the BOTTOMLESS PIT and go to perdition; and the dwellers on earth whose names have not been written in the book of life from the foundation of the world, will marvel to behold the beast because it WAS, IS NOT, and IS TO COME. This calls for a mind with wisdom: the seven heads are seven hills on which the woman is seated; they are also seven kings, five of whom have fallen, one is, the other has not yet come and when he comes he must remain only for a little while. As for the beast that was and is not it is an eighth but it belongs to the seven and it goes to perdition. And the ten horns that you saw are ten kings who have not yet received royal power, but are to receive authority for one hour together with the beast. These are of one mind and give over their power and authority to the beast. (Rev. 17:7-13)

Scripture one and two can easily be explained because of scripture three. In the first paragraph of scripture one, we see the powers on earth mingling with Lucifer who is obviously headed by the one with a healed mortal wound. This can be understood to represent the bodily return of Christ, who is presumed by many to have physically risen from the dead. The second paragraph explains

277

ALPHA TO OMEGA

the blasphemous nature of the one who deceives everyone into believing he is the risen Christ.

In the second scripture, we can see more clearly the reason for deception. The beast has two horns like a lamb and speaks like a dragon representing the outward appearance of the lamb with the devil's authority and control. The signs and wonders it exhibits to the world reinforces the false belief that Jesus has returned. The image of the beast is the reflection of our beliefs in the bodily return of Christ, which are satisfied by the living person presumed to be Jesus Christ returned in physical form.

The third scripture completely explains the beast by illustrating the cooperation of worldly powers with Lucifer and the beast who WAS (Jesus Christ), IS NOT (Jesus Christ) and (Christ) IS TO COME, which is why the whole world follows him, because he is to come and the majority of the world considers it to be true. The beast is the perfect reflection of the concepts we have come to believe and accept. Lucifer was the angel at Jesus' tomb.

The bottomless pit is the demonstrative for hell. Clinging to the tangible and physical part of our existence is the inherent nature of our age. The beast qualifies our concepts to the highest degree. Hell or the bottomless pit is the end-all for those who are unable to release their shallow beliefs even after remarkable events spawned by Truth's will to be recognized, which we discuss next.

Jesus testified to these understandings in his descriptions of the signs of his second coming. Christ's resurrection was not a physical one and Jesus admonishes his disciples to clearly understand the truth.

RISE AND FALL OF THE HEGEMON

Then if any man says to you, 'Lo, here is the Christ!', or, 'There he is!' do not believe it. For false Christs and false prophets will arise, and show great signs and wonders; so as to lead astray, if possible, even the elect. Behold, I have told you beforehand. So, if they say to you, 'Behold, he is in the wilderness,' do not go out; if they say, 'Behold, he is in the inner chambers,' do not believe it. For as the lightning cometh forth from the east, and is seen even unto the west; so shall be the coming of the Son of man. **Wherever the body is, the vultures will be gathered together.** (Matthew 24:23–28)

Even as the first part of the beast already thrives, which we recognized as the invisible unyielding entity born of our ignorance, most of us are either unwilling to accept it or unable to recognize it. Our vague notions of God are matched with similar blurred impressions about the beast. Unfortunately, the beast feeds upon our ignorance and fuzzy concepts, while God remains undiscovered and undefined.

The hardest thing for us to imagine is an evil entity that would lead us to believe that truth has been revealed in its entirety. Our ignorance will seem to have completely disappeared in our newly found but blinding power. All members of the world will be united; there will be no division or conflict.

Lucifer is an angel with a different agenda as explained in chapter two. He has maintained a clear advantage for a very long time, but the harbinger and war forces him to play his hole card which is the significance of his being cast down to earth. Everyone living at the time will have been suddenly thrust into higher states of power and awareness. It would be impossible for anyone to avert decep-

ALPHA TO OMEGA

tion if not for the two people who will emerge to wreak havoc on a world deemed perfect. It's time for the final leg in the long human journey.

> For then there will be such great tribulation, such as has not been from the beginning of the world until now and never will be. And if those days had not been shortened, no human being would be saved; but for the sake of the elect those days will be shortened. (Matthew 24: 21-22)

Dual Torment

> And I will grant my two witnesses power to prophesy for one thousand two hundred and sixty days, clothed in sackcloth. These are the two *olive trees* and the *two lamp stands*, standing before the Lord of the earth. And if any man would harm them, fire proceeds out of their mouth and devours their enemies; if any man would harm them, thus he is doomed to be killed. They have the power to shut the heaven that it rain not during the days of their prophesying and they have power over the waters to turn them into blood, and to smite the earth with every plague, as often as they shall desire. (Rev. 11:3–6) (My italics)

Who are the two witnesses? Two clues are found in the italicized words in the above caption. How many readers know that olive trees live for a very long time? In fact, there are several in the world that have been examined and found to be well over 2000 years old. Is it possible for the two witnesses to have been on earth since the time of Christ?

A couple of biblical scriptures had always puzzled me until I discovered their significance. Jesus was explaining to his apostles

280

RISE AND FALL OF THE HEGEMON

that any man who would follow him must deny himself and take up his cross. Importantly, he said this right after Peter had exhibited a lack of faith in Christ's purpose by a comment to which Jesus rebuked him. He went on to explain that hanging onto our life will cause us to lose it. It appears his comments were directed at Peter after examining a couple of other scriptures.

> Truly, I say to you, there are some standing here who will not taste death before they see the Son of Man coming in his kingdom. (Matthew 16: 28)

In the book of John, we can read the testimony of Jesus' third appearance to his disciples after his death. After eating, Jesus questioned Peter three times regarding his love and devotion to Jesus. Each time Peter replied "yes", but was upset because he was asked a third time. We pick up this Scripture from there when Jesus spoke to Peter:

> "Truly, truly, I say to you when you were young, you girded yourself and walked where you would; but when you are old, you will stretch out your hands, and another will gird you and carry you where you do not wish to go." (This he said to show by what death he was to glorify God) and after this he said to him, "Follow Me."

> Peter turned and saw following them the disciple whom Jesus loved, who had lain close to his breast at the supper and had said, "Lord, who is it that is going to betray you?" When Peter saw him, he said to Jesus, "Lord, what about this man?" Jesus said to him, "if it is my will that he remain until I come, what is that to you? Follow me!"

ALPHA TO OMEGA

In the above Scripture, the allusions to Peter and another one of Jesus' disciples living until the end times is clear. The disciples had been given the keys and the secrets to the kingdom of heaven. Each of them was enlightened and privy to the spiritual knowledge that had been occluded by early Roman influence, thus the lamp stands.

The two olive trees and the two lamp stands are likely Peter, who had denied Jesus three times and another, possibly James or John. They have been on earth since the days of Christ and will finally be given the chance to follow in Christ's footsteps by testimony, death and resurrection. Only those who have the "keys to the kingdom" or the Truth about Jesus can serve as witness to All Truth.

As the earth's inhabitants revel in euphoria, the witnesses will emerge after centuries of crafty seclusion and anonymity. They will reproach the world and its inhabitants for failing to see the mistakes of ignorance and for believing in the beast. Their testimony to truth will directly conflict with the majority of mankind's beliefs. Their prophecy will continue throughout the forty-two months. Some will believe them, but most people will hate them.

The two witnesses will demonstrate remarkable physical abilities, but none greater than everyone else during that time. In order to prove their testimony they will cause plagues and suffering on earth to help convert those who remain blinded by power and presumed reality. Just like the Hebrews of prehistory, the witnesses will be forced to demonstrate the truth, because it is still beyond everyone's vision.

RISE AND FALL OF THE HEGEMON

They will proclaim the beast to be a false god by explaining how their efforts to cause suffering would not be possible over a true God. The presence of plagues is proof of the truth in their testimony. Nevertheless, the unwillingness to surrender the magnificence of a physical life and unprecedented power will not allow evidence of plagues to influence the majority of the world.

Christ's messengers will be frowned upon as evil tormentors sent by the devil to deceive the world. Many will believe them to be the "Antichrist," because their testimony conflicts with newfound ideals and the *image* of the beast. Christ's emissaries will attempt to expose the overwhelming ignorance and shortsightedness, but the words of their testimony will be unpreventable torment to the world and its inhabitants whose minds will be closed. The inherent nature of our age has prevented anyone from seeing All Truth (except for Jesus). Most will be blinded by Satan's exploitation of our ignorance and united in determination to reject the truthful testimony of the witnesses.

And when they have finished their testimony, the beast that ascends from the bottomless pit will make war upon them and conquer them and kill them, and their dead bodies will lie in the street of the great city which is allegorically called Sodom and Egypt, where their Lord was crucified. For three and a half days men from the peoples and tribes and tongues and nations gaze at their dead bodies and refuse to let them be placed in a tomb, and those who dwell on the earth will rejoice over them and make merry and exchange presents, because these two prophets had been a torment to those who dwell on earth. But after three and a half days a breath of life entered them, and they stood up on their feet, and great fear fell on those who saw them. Then they heard a

ALPHA TO OMEGA

voice from heaven saying, "Come up hither!" And in the sight of their foes they went up to heaven in a cloud. And at that hour there was a great earthquake, and a tenth of the city fell; seven thousand people were killed in the earthquake, and the rest were terrified and gave glory to the God of heaven. (Rev. 11: 7-13)

Omega

What more do we need to see? Our final challenge will be to search beyond the prevailing beliefs, despite our seeming invincible nature. The dilemma is intrinsic to every major conflict discussed throughout the book and is evidenced on a smaller scale today. In essence, the two witnesses will be the instigators to the final fulfillment of All Truth. Many will begin to question the overriding beliefs, which will erode the unified consciousness as suspicion and doubt escalates.

The initiation to the final conflict is earmarked by the death and resurrection of the witnesses and the evidence exposed regarding the nature of resurrection. Many will become inspired by wisdom to begin observing physical resurrection as a misconstrued belief, while others will remain reluctant to release the apparently pleasant physical reality, which is evidenced by the mass celebration of their death.

Some will truly believe Satan had been destroyed when the death of the two witnesses takes place even though they followed Christ completely. People will become divided between the physical use of power or its abandonment, even in the midst of extremely elevated levels of existential and experiential awareness—just like Jesus during his final temptation.

As the deception unfolds, we will be catapulted to higher levels of awareness and advanced metaphysical abilities that will parallel those of Mesoamerica, Egypt, Easter Island and many other mysterious places of prehistoric times of this era. We will be blinded by the light of Lucifer, who will exploit our vulnerabilities.

The final conflict will begin to erode the unified consciousness required for Satan's victory. An upstart in believing in something greater than the presumed reality is sparked by the death and resurrection of the witnesses. Curiosity, which will be reborn as throngs will begin to question the presumed wonders of society, is made possible only by the witnesses. The same doubt and suspicions, which have given Lucifer the advantage throughout the new age, will be instrumental in the search for the final truth that defeats him.

From our present vantage point, it is difficult to conceptualize the magnitude of extremes in the final years. But in the inevitable revelation of All Truth, we must take graduating steps upward one at a time. Our discoveries have always been ignited by the curiosities born of our ignorance and the speculations of our wisdom. With each new discovery a new awareness is born, which enlarges our imagination and search for something greater. As we inch closer to All Truth the possibilities grow larger. The return of Christ is symbolic of an elevated awareness enlarged by previous discoveries and the continued willingness to question our presumed realities.

ALPHA TO OMEGA

Lucifer will provide us with advanced knowledge and power, which Jesus could easily have done 2000 years ago. Although self-discovery is the requirement of the age, Lucifer's exploits will bring a search for truth to a screeching halt by the belief we have become totally enlightened. The underlying factor in the final deception is our unseen ignorance and the exploits of those who control the knowledge.

Ironically, our reluctance to search for more meaningful answers to our purpose, God and the afterlife, while relying on authority for answers, is what gives Lucifer the edge today. Although Lucifer's deception will be unimaginable in the end days, today's unyielding entity is infused with similar behavioral patterns that give birth to the final deception.

The final conflict will be the truest test of our nature and wisdom. Truth and belief will become an individual decision based on evaluation of all evidence. Only two choices will confront us, because everything else will have been revealed—just like in Adam's time. Everyone's final decision will be made from an unimaginable level of awareness. Everything will be revealed—a return to our past and future in the omniscient and omnipotent Paradise of Alpha and Omega.

Is resurrection Physical? Is it wrong to direct absolute power with human will? The battle between the opposing forces of human nature is perfectly exemplified. These are destined to be the last questions in the days of the final conflict as the ultimate battle of Adam's era resurfaces. The slow but inevitable revelation of All Truth will be discovered through our curiosity and wisdom. The

RISE AND FALL OF THE HEGEMON

requirements for an overwhelming unified consciousness in Truth upon Christ's return can only be as magnificent as foretold when the world is poised to ask questions when everything appears to have been answered.

As we have observed throughout this book, all events are caused by God's will to be made manifest in the experiences that show us our errors. The final seven bowls of wrath, which are depicted in Revelation, serve as the ultimate demonstration of this principle.

The seven bowls of wrath signify the huge imbalance between truth and belief on the highest scale and is observed by depictions of physical pain, suffering, and other aberrations uncharacteristic of a super human society. Just like the imbalance caused the cataclysm in the first generation, the final days will be the experiences of the physical manifestations of our ignorance.

Death of all things in the sea, rivers turning to blood, the scorching of the sun, and the defeat of the beast and his followers are all descriptions of monstrous disasters. It is irrelevant as to whether or not this is to be taken literally. The truth will prevail at the Day of Judgment.

> The sixth angel poured his bowl on the great river Euphrates, and its water dried up, to prepare the way for the kings of the east. And I saw, issuing from the mouth of the dragon, and the mouth of the false prophet, three foul spirits like frogs; for they are demonic spirits, performing signs, who go abroad to the kings of the whole world, to assemble them for battle on the great day of God the Almighty. (Lo, I am coming like a thief! Blessed is he who is awake, keeping his garments that he may not go naked and ex-

ALPHA TO OMEGA

posed!) And they assembled them at the place which is called in Hebrew Armageddon.

The seventh angel poured his bowl into the air, and a great voice came out saying, "It is done!" And there were flashes of lightning, loud noises, peals of thunder, and a great earthquake such has never been since men were on the earth, so great was that earthquake. (Rev. 16:12–18)

All of the secrets are revealed upon the seventh angel's trumpet. The thousand year kingdom of Supreme Beings will reign upon the earth.

Then I saw the thrones, and seated on them were those to whom judgment had been committed. Also I saw the souls of those who had been beheaded for their testimony to Jesus and for the word of God, and who had not worshiped the beast, or its image and had not received its mark on their foreheads or their hands. They came to life, and reigned with Christ a thousand years. The rest of the dead did not come to life until the thousand years were ended. This is the first resurrection. Blessed and holy is he who shares in this resurrection. Over such the second death has no power, but they shall be priests of God and of Christ, and they shall reign with him a thousand years. (Rev. 20:1–6)

The final fulfillment of truth is an awakening to the imperishable nature of our souls and the joy of being whole and illumined. We cannot arrive there without having been thrust into much higher levels of awareness beforehand. With each new height in achievement comes a yearning for something greater, which cannot be seen from the previous levels. But, discovery can only take place by questioning our presumed reality, and making a wise choice that

RISE AND FALL OF THE HEGEMON

transcends the boundaries of our current level of physical existence. We can only know God by looking beyond the realities of our limited awareness into the core of our being—the everlasting eternal Spirit of God and All Truth.

Epilogue

The most important assessment is the metaphysical nature of our journey, which can be seen as cause and effect, not only of past and future, but as truth's unyielding attempt to be made manifest through the experiences caused by our ignorance. Additionally and a little more subtly, the degrees of power and luminosity can be seen in spiritual beings, eternal souls and human ability, all of which are unobserved or acknowledged.

I've heard so many times from so many people, the adage, "Things happen for a reason." Unfortunately, the expression is always used in the context suggesting negative events of today occur so that more beneficial events will occur in the future. Careful observation reveals the notion to be a distortion of cause-and-effect, because current events actually occur to reveal the mistakes of our past and, only if we learn from them, will they help make our future events more pleasant.

Objectively, we can see the power of truth or divine will as the inexorable force of nature to become ultimately expressed in our world and consciousness, which implies that God is discoverable only when we look beyond our presumed realities. When we view our lives and events as happenstance rather than the incessant integration of these principles, then our failure to see will be continually expressed in the experiences and events designed to reveal the errors. As long as we continue to close our eyes to it, the cumulative effects will mount upon our world until we awaken by the lessons of experience.

We can look at our slow awakening as an increase in power over the centuries and can more easily imagine higher capabilities of the mind, while seeing the manipulation of our physical world as the actual utilization of the forces we deem unobservable. By acknowledging that God is discoverable, the Tree of Life is a physical possibility in higher levels of knowledge and power. There is an urgent need to change our concept of God.

Many of the New Age theorists believe in higher levels of consciousness and physical expression through an increased ability, but many espouse we will reach these levels by happenstance and/or our position in the galaxy as though it will be some magical occurrence. The magic is happening now as it always has been. And the only way to these higher levels of consciousness is through self-discovery in a prioritized yearning for truth above everything.

The single most important of these discoveries is recognizing one man's search and discovery of All Truth as the saving grace for both a world of people who will never prioritize their search with enough zeal to find it, and for the eternal souls who discover the true meaning of life only after death, when their incessant longing for wholeness is exposed by the light of the One who is.

In our ignorance and self deception, we grant power to those who would have us believe they have the cure for our troubles, as we wander aimlessly towards our certain death believing that our

EPILOGUE

physical world defines our entire reality. This idea is exemplified in the final days when our beliefs about ancient aliens will be exploited along with our indistinct notions about God and the purpose for our existence.

We are here at this point in time to recognize the true nature of our purpose for existence and the realities that exist beyond the end of time.

References

Introduction

1. Gregg Braden, *Deep Truth*, Hay House, Inc, NY, NY, 2011, Prologue
2. Graham Hancock, Robert Bauval, *The Message of the Sphinx: A Quest for the Hidden Legacy of Mankind*, Three Rivers Press, NY, NY, 1996 p. 249

Chapter One

1. (Translated by) Benjamin Jowett, *Dialogues of Plato--From Mobile Reference*, Sound, Tells, LLC 2003-2008 Kindle edition, location 28155.
2. *Fingerprints of the Gods*, Graham Hancock, Three Rivers Press, NY, NY, 1995, p. 199.
3. *Dialogues of Plato--From Mobile Reference*, Location 28247.
4. Ibid, location 2333.
5. *Columbia History of the World*, Harper and Row, NY, NY, 1972, p.18.
6. Ibid.
7. Ibid.
8. Ibid.
9. Ibid, p. 49.

ALPHA TO OMEGA

10. Ibid.
11. Mark Hamilton, Ph.D., Harvard University, *The Origin of the Hebrew Bible and its Components,* 1998, (pbs.org/wgbh/pages/frontline/shows/religion/first/scriptures.html).
12. Ibid.
13. *Columbia History of the World,* p.51.
14. Ibid, p.181.
15. Zecharia Sitchin (2011-01-14). *There Were Giants upon the Earth: Gods, Demigods, and Human Ancestry: The Evidence of Alien DNA* (Earth Chronicles), pp. 6-8, Bear & Company. Kindle Edition.
16. Ibid, p.22-23.
17. Ibid, p.27.
18. Ibid, pp.27-28.
19. Ibid, p.31.
20. *Fingerprints of the Gods,* p. 5.
21. *The Message of the Sphinx: A Quest for the Hidden Legacy of Mankind,* op. cit.
22. *Columbia History of the World,* p. 140.

Chapter Two

1. Behe, Michael J. (2001-04-04). *Darwin's Black Box,* p. 248, Simon & Schuster, Inc., Kindle Edition.
2. Berlinski, David (2009-08-26). *The Devil's Delusion: Atheism and its Scientific Pretensions.* Perseus Books Group. Kindle Edition, location 82.

REFERENCES

3. H. Wayne House. *Intelligent Design 101: Leading Experts Explain the Key Issues,* p. 28. Kindle Edition.

4. Ibid, p.145.

5. *Dialogues of Plato--From Mobile Reference,* Location 2327.

6. Divine Counselor, *The Urantia Book, The Universal Father,* Urantia Foundation, Chicago, IL,1955, p. 25.

7. *Darwin's Black Box,* p. 51.

8. Nick Herbert, *Quantum Reality: Beyond the New Physics,* Anchor Books, 1985, pp. 17-18

9. Ibid, pp. 211-231

10. Chuck Missler, Mark Eastman, *Alien Encounters: The Secret Behind the UFO Phenomenon,* Koinonia House, 1997, p. 132

11. Divine Counselor, *The Urantia Book, The Universal Father,* Urantia Foundation, Chicago, IL,1955, p. 22.

12. (Received by) Ceanne DeRohan, *Right Use of Will: Healing and Evolving the Emotional Body,* Four Winds Publications, Santa Fe, NM, 1986 pp. 96-97.

13. History Channel, *The Universe (Series), UFO: The Real Deal,* December, 2011

14. Rosemary Ellen Guiley Ph.D., *The Encyclopedia of Angels, Second Edition,* Facts on File, NY, NY, 2004, Locations 332-338, Kindle Edition.

15. Ibid, Locations 7295-97.

16. Melchizedek, *The Urantia Book, Ministering Spirits of the Local Universe,* Urantia Foundation, Chicago, IL, 1955, p. 419.

17. Divine Counselor, *The Urantia Book, Foreword,* Urantia Foundation, Chicago, IL,1955, p. 10.

ALPHA TO OMEGA

18. *The Encyclopedia of Angels, Second Edition*, Locations 480-482.

Chapter Three

1. *The Soul of St. Augustine*, http://www.articlecity.com/articles/religion/article_413.shtml, Nymph Kellerman, April, 2006, http://www.spiralstaircasebookshop.blogspot.com.
2. Tom Valentine, *The Great Pyramid: Man's Monument to Man*, Pinnacle Books, Los Angeles, CA, 1975 (seventh printing 1979), p.12.
3. Christopher Dunn (2011-08-23), *The Giza Power Plant: Technologies of Ancient Egypt* (Kindle Locations 1254-1255) Bear & Company. Kindle Edition.
4. Ibid, Locations 430-434.
5. *Fingerprints of the Gods*, p. 276.
6. *The Great Pyramid: Man's Monument to Man*, p.19.
7. *The Giza Power Plant: Technologies of Ancient Egypt*, Locations 1111-1114.
8. *Fingerprints of the Gods*, p.32.
9. *The Giza Power Plant: Technologies of Ancient Egypt*, Locations 1386-87.
10. *The Great Pyramid: Man's Monument to Man*, p. 60.
11. Ibid, pp. 63-64.
12. Ibid, p 97.
13. *The Giza Power Plant: Technologies of Ancient Egypt*, Locations 469-70.
14. Ibid, Locations 623-644.

REFERENCES

15. *Fingerprints of the Gods,* p.285.
16. *The Giza Power Plant: Technologies of Ancient Egypt,* Locations 1309-1314.
17. Augustine, *On Immortality of the Soul,*(revised from Latin translation of George Leckie, Appleton Century Co.,1938) A.D. 387, Chapter one, (http://puffin.creighton.edu)
18. *The Encyclopedia of Angels, Second Edition,* Location 450.

Chapter Four

1. Walter Cruttenden, Podcast: *The Cosmic Influence; In Search of Lost Civilization: An Interview with Graham Hancock,* April, 2006, (Paraphrase).
2. Ibid.
3. *Columbia History of the World,* p. 35.
4. Svante Paabo, et.al., *A Draft Sequence of the Neandertal Genome,* Science, May 7, 2010, Vol. 328 no. 5979 pp. 710-722 (http://www.sciencemag.org/ content/328/5979/710.full)
5. *Columbia History of the World,* p.44.
6. *Human Origins Project,* Smithsonian Institute, http://humanorigins.si.edu.
7. Graham Hancock, *Fingerprints of the Gods,* op.cit, Roger Lewin, *Human Evolution,* Blackwell Scientific Publications, Oxford, 1984, p.74.
8. *Columbia History of the World,* p.45.
9. *Dialogues of Plato--From Mobile Reference translated by Benjamin Jowett,* Locations 2212-14.

ALPHA TO OMEGA

10. (Translated by) R.H. Charles, *The Book of Enoch, Complete Edition*, IAP, Scotts Valley, CA, 2009, Introduction, p. 5.

11. Ibid.

12. Zecharia Sitchin (2011-01-14). *There Were Giants upon the Earth: Gods, Demigods, and Human Ancestry: The Evidence of Alien DNA* (Earth Chronicles) (p. 200). Bear & Company. Kindle Edition.

13. Michael S. Heiser, Ph.D. (Hebrew Bible and Ancient Semitic Languages, University of Wisconsin – Madison), *The Meaning of the Word Nephilim: Fact vs. Fantasy*, Dec. 2005, p. 4.

14. *The Book of Enoch, Complete Edition*, p.122.

15. *Fingerprints of the Gods*, p.42.

16. Arthur Custance Ph.D., *The Doorway Paper Series, Volume 1: Noah's Three Son's: Human History in Three Dimensions*, Part 2: Chapter 1, pp. 19-20, 1988, Doorway Publications, Hamilton, Ontario (CANADA) (2001 2nd Online edition)

17. Ibid.

18. Ibid, p. 14.

19. Ibid, p. 13.

20. Arthur Custance Ph.D., *The Doorway Paper Series, Volume 2: Genesis and Early Man*, Part 1, Chapter 3, pp. 1-2, 1988, Doorway Publications, Hamilton, Ontario (CANADA) (2001 2nd Online edition)

21. Arthur Custance Ph.D., *The Doorway Paper Series, Volume 1: Noah's Three Son's: Human History in Three Dimensions*, Part 1, Chapter 2, p. 3, 1988, Doorway Publications, Hamilton, Ontario (CANADA) (2001 2nd Online edition)

REFERENCES

22. Ibid, p. 2.

23. Ibid.

24. *Fingerprints of the Gods,* p. 121.

25. Ibid, p. 123

26. An interesting observation can be found by readers with a copy of Hancock's *Fingerprints of the Gods.* Notice the picture on the top of page 129 of a carving resembling a Mongoloid Olmec head. It was found in the same location as the Negroid carvings and adds credence to Custance's evidence suggesting Ham's descendants were both Negroid and Mongoloid.

27. *The Doorway Paper Series, Volume 1: Noah's Three Son's: Human History in Three Dimensions,* Part 2: Chapter 2, p. 2.

28. Ibid.

29. Ibid, Part 1, Chapter 2, p. 3.

30. *The Book of Enoch, Complete Edition,* p. 122.

31. *Fingerprints of the Gods,* p. 164.

32. Ibid, pp. 77-79

33. Ibid, pp. 166-7

34. *There Were Giants upon the Earth: Gods, Demigods, and Human Ancestry: The Evidence of Alien DNA,* p. 22.

35. *Fingerprints of the Gods,* p. 392.

36. *The Doorway Paper Series, Volume 1: Noah's Three Son's: Human History in Three Dimensions,* Part 1: Chapter 3, p. 2.

37. *Fingerprints of the Gods,* p. 133.

38. Ibid.

39. History Channel, *Ancient Aliens, Season 4: The Doomsday Prophecies,* February 17, 2012.

ALPHA TO OMEGA

Chapter Five

1. Arthur Custance, *The Doorway Paper Series*, Volume 6—*Time and Eternity and Other Biblical Studies, Part V: The Confusion of Languages*, Chapter 1, p. 2, 1988, Doorway Publications, Hamilton, Ontario (CANADA) (2001 2nd Online edition)
2. Ibid, p. 1.
3. *There Were Giants upon the Earth: Gods, Demigods, and Human Ancestry: The Evidence of Alien DNA*, p. 22.
4. Ibid, p. 23.
5. Matthew August Petti, *Heretical Wisdom: The Truths From Within*, pp. 156-7, Xlibris Publishing, Bloomington, IN, 2001

Chapter Seven

1. T. R. Glover, *The Jesus of History* (Kindle Locations 2108-2113) 1916, Released again by Project Gutenberg, 2004.
2. *Columbia History of the World*, p. 217.
3. Ibid, p. 221.
4. *The Jesus of History*, Locations 2267-2272.
5. *Columbia History of the World*, p. 230.
6. Ibid, p. 233.

About the Author

Matthew Petti was born in a small rural town in New Jersey in 1955. His life and career has been fashioned and directed by an extraordinary epiphany, which occurred only a year after finishing college in 1977. His perspectives and priorities were swiftly rearranged by a sense of urgency, insight and a deep yearning to make sense of an overwhelming experience, which he could not fully understand.

While working as a technician in the casino entertainment industry, he started a locksmith service company in 1981 and developed it into a very successful security hardware and burglar alarm business by the late 80's. Meanwhile, an unusual theory based upon his unforgettable experience emerged and became a hot topic in social and family gatherings.

A life-changing decision to walk away from his financial success, which was influenced by his memorable experience, altered his life's journey in the early 90's. Within two years, he resumed a free-lance career in the technical field, which placed him on the sets of movies and commercials, TV and live entertainment in the New York's tri-state region. It was especially fitting for Matthew to work in a profession that allowed him to see things from a unique perspective, as well as provide some free time to research his ideas.

His first book, *Heretical Wisdom*, was self-published in 2001 after devoting much of his free time and resources to learn some very valuable lessons. Now, a vision that began as insight is a timely and well-researched perspective guaranteed to invoke critical thinking by answering questions we may have never thought to ask.

For more information, including an intimate video of the author, please visit http://matthewpetti.com. Please submit all requests for speaking and public appearance information by fax: 888-776-9557 or email : cs@twosensepro.com.

You may obtain the complete audio CD version of this book for $97 by faxing or emailing the order form. Please be sure to include mailing and billing address along with complete credit card information including the security code. Offer good in US and Canada only. An email confirmation will be sent upon receipt of order by email or if email address is provided by customer in fax request. Credit card will not be charged until order ships.

ORDER FORM

Please rush me the complete set of audio CD's for ALPHA TO OMEGA – JOURNEY TO THE END OF TIME, by Matthew A. Petti. I authorize the credit card listed below to be charged $97 plus $14.95 shipping and handling.

Order before December 31, 2012 and get free shipping.

Billing Address (name as it appears on credit card)

Name_____

Address_____

Address_____

City_____State_____ Zip_____

Credit card type_____

Credit card number_____

Expiration Date_____ CSV Security code_____

Mailing Address

Name_____

Address_____

Address_____

City_____State_____ Zip_____

Fax to 888-776-9557 Offer good in US and CANADA only

Email order form to sales@twosensepro.com for email confirmation

CPSIA information can be obtained at www.ICGtesting.com
Printed in the USA
LVOW121838171012

303297LV00011B/22/P